BEYOND THE
BASSLINE

PREVIOUS PAGES Notting Hill Carnival 1979, with Asher G, photograph by David Hoffman.

This publication accompanies the British Library exhibition
Beyond the Bassline: 500 Years of Black British Music

26 April to 26 August 2024

Lead curator
Dr Aleema Gray

Consultant curator
Dr Mykaell Riley, Black Music Research Unit, University of Westminster

Additional curation
Jonathan Benaim, Karoline Engelhardt, Finlay McIntosh and Mia Roach Penn

Publisher's Note
The essays in this book have been commissioned from a variety of perspectives
and are informed by personal experience and opinions. Some contributions openly
address racism, discrimination and enslavement and some works contain strong
language. They have been commissioned to show the rich diversity of content and
voices throughout the long history of Black music in Britain. These voices, and the
views expressed, do not represent the opinions of the British Library.

'The Sea is History' by Derek Walcott from *The Poetry of Derek Walcott 1948–2013*
  (Permission courtesy of Faber)
'Carnival Days' by Benjamin Zephaniah from *Too Black, Too Strong*, 2001, courtesy
  Bloodaxe Books.
'Di Great Insohreckshan' by Linton Kwesi Johnson, courtesy LKJ Music Publishers.

Every effort has been made to trace copyright holders and to obtain their permission
for the use of copyright material. The publisher apologises for any errors or omissions
and would be pleased to be notified of any corrections to be incorporated in reprints
and future editions.

First published in 2024 by
The British Library
96 Euston Road
London NW1 2DB

Volume © The British Library Board 2024
Text © Individual contributors 2024
Images © The British Library Board and other named
  copyright holders 2024 (see page 288)

British Library Cataloguing-in-Publication Data
A catalogue record is available from the British Library

ISBN 978 0 7123 5489 9

Picture research by Maria Ranauro
Editorial by Roland Hall
Layout by Steve Russell
Front cover artwork by The Elephant Room
Printed in Czechia by PB Tisk

MIX
Paper | Supporting
responsible forestry
FSC
www.fsc.org   FSC® C004378

Edited by **PAUL BRADSHAW**

BEYOND THE BASSLINE

500 Years of Black British Music

BRITISH LIBRARY

Contents

The Frontlines

Cyberspace

Preface

PAUL BRADSHAW

Beyond the Bassline: 500 Years of Black British Music accompanies a British Library exhibition of the same name. Along with the exhibition curators – Aleema Gray and Mykaell Riley – I devised a structure to allow a narrative to unfold along a timeline which takes us from the court of Henry VIII to the 'Ends' of East and South London. The Black, the African presence in Britain goes back way beyond the Middle Ages and way, way back before the arrival of the HMT *Empire Windrush*. The thread that binds the journey within these pages is music, those who created it and its impact on the cultural fabric of Britain as we know it today.

As a journalist and editor/publisher of my own independent magazine, *Straight No Chaser: Interplanetary Sounds – Ancient to Future,* I have long been immersed in the rich, constantly evolving music of the African diaspora – a global community based on the enslavement of over ten million people from the diverse nations along the west coast of Africa. It would be fair to say that many forms of popular music today have roots in what reggae singer Gregory Isaacs called the 'Western slave market'.

The legacy of slavery and colonialism looms large over our islands and the momentum created by Black Lives Matter continues to thrust that legacy into the limelight, forcing a constant evaluation of our national history. As a result many Black artists – musicians, painters and authors – who have been previously overlooked or marginalised have enjoyed renewed interest through exhibitions like Tate Britain's *Life Between Islands* and the one that this book accompanies.

As commissioning editor, I was indeed fortunate to be able to tap into a board of activists and experts recruited to support and advise the curators of the exhibition at the Library. It also felt appropriate to get working musicians to contribute. I feel privileged to include pieces by Ade Egun Crispin Robinson; jazz pianist, composer and educator Julian Joseph; alto saxophonist and leader of the Mercury Prize-nominated Seed Ensemble Cassie Kinoshi; classical composer Julian Grant; poet/bandleader Anthony Joseph; and former Big Joanie drummer Chardine Taylor-Stone.

The Ocean is the focus of the first section of the book, which opens with 'The Sea is History', a profound poetic work by Nobel Prize winner for Literature Derek Walcott. It's a poem that sets the scenario and paves the way for the reflections of Dalia Al-Dujaili, a writer and activist whose work with refugees is intimately connected with the sea and with the migration – forced or otherwise – of people and culture. The past is always linked to the present.

The two world wars of the twentieth century involved thousands of recruits from the British Empire. This history, during the First World War, is wonderfully explored by filmmaker Jon Akomfrah in his three-screen installation *Mimesis: African*

Soldier. Following the death and destruction of the First World War, the hedonistic inter-war years saw the emergence, in the capital, of jazz age Black cabaret stars like Ken 'Snakehips' Johnson and Leslie 'Hutch' Hutchinson, who had fans among royalty and the upper classes. Meanwhile, a far from glamorous Soho hosted a vibrant underground club and jazz scene frequented by musicians and Pan-African activists from Africa and the Caribbean, including C. L. R. James and Jomo Kenyatta. For a deep dive into the music and history of this post-Second World War era, which produced independent labels such as Dennis Preston's Melodisc imprint, look no further than Honest Jon's' excellent *London Is the Place for Me* compilation albums.

As a team we are thrilled to have Ishmahil Blagrove, Jr, author of the mind-blowing, self-published *The Frontline: A Story of Struggle, Resistance and Black Identity in Notting Hill*, introduce the Frontline section of the book. Ishmahil appropriately penned his words while building a community centre in Santiago, Cuba. He illuminates the turbulent times of the post-*Windrush* era when Frontlines rose up in towns and across the nation as a form of open resistance and self-defence against the racist National Front, heavy-handed policing and institutionalised racism within schools, job centres and the national media.

From the 1950s right up to today, alongside the spiritual communion provided by the Black church, the African-Caribbean and African communities have had to find and promote their own safe spaces to socialise, to enjoy the music that they wanted to hear and dance to. The blues dances, the sound system sessions, clubs like 4 Aces or the Q Club are what the groundbreaking journalist Carl Gayle called the 'Black Underground', which played an important role in consolidating the presence of the community while introducing a Black music-based economy.

The Swinging Sixties offered a major shift in cultural awareness and in this book Richard Williams, a former editor of the *Melody Maker*, and Liverpudlian poet/writer Malik Al Nasir shed valuable light on an era that led to global success for bands like the Beatles and the Rolling Stones, who were inspired by the tail end of the blues boom and US rhythm & blues.

In 1964, 17-year-old Millie Small introduced the UK to ska with 'My Boy Lollipop'. She was the first Jamaican artist to dent the national charts with sales over half a million in the UK and seven million worldwide. By the mid-1970s, Jamaica's influence reached another level. Roots reggae – the message music of the Rastafari – had inspired UK bands like Cymande, Cimarons, Aswad, Misty in Roots, Steel Pulse, Black Slate, Black Roots, Matumbi and Linton Kwesi Johnson's Poet and the Roots. The arrival of the 'No Future' generation, in the guise of punk rock, gave rise to the activism/concerts of Rock

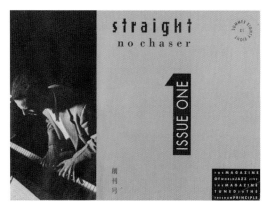

LEFT *Straight No Chaser* issue 1, 1988.
OPPOSITE The magazine celebrated issue number 100 in 2019.

Against Racism/Anti Nazi League. It proved to be a bright moment of Black and white unity and in the context of *Beyond the Bassline* has brought together former Big Joanie drummer Chardine Taylor-Stone and the Selecter's Pauline Black.

We've come a long way since the Southern Syncopated Orchestra arrived on these shores but jazz sits at the heart of British Black music history. From Joe Harriott and Ernest Ranglin to the Jazz Warriors and Tomorrow's Warriors, Britain boasts a relatively small but hugely influential pool of talented players, arrangers and composers. Their skills, which rely on a deep knowledge of the past, are set to project them into the future, to further what the legendary Art Ensemble of Chicago called Great Black Music.

There has never been one homogeneous music scene in the UK. There are regional variants, variants based on class, race and gender. Different scenes run in parallel and at times overlap. These scenes, such as rare groove, rave and grime, thrived by applying what the Black community had long done. By occupying alternative – sometimes illegal – spaces, they initiated a democratisation of club culture, primarily through the removal of racist door policies, so young Black and white punters, should they wish, could rave together.

Following that democratisation of club culture came the game-changing worldwide web. Radical advances in technology boosted the home-grown, electronic music scene, which grew via an underground network of clubs, pirate radio and the streaming platforms. In the Cyberspace section of the book we touch down on UK garage and Manchester street soul; travel from jungle to drill; and explore the Kingston–London–Accra–Lagos connection.

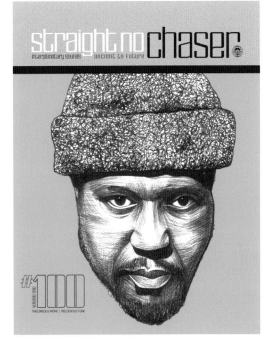

Beyond the Bassline offers an overview of Black British music and how, despite persistent marginalisation, it has evolved to permeate many aspects of contemporary music and culture in this country. While I can't even begin to list the names of those who haven't made it into the pages of this book, it's time to celebrate a creative continuum that has given us a twenty-first-century collective like SAULT. Centred around producer Dean Isaiah Clover AKA Inflow, SAULT delivered *(Untitled) Black Is* – the BLM album of lockdown – and the ultimate, immersive 2023 end-of-year concert which featured award-winning artists Cleo Sol, Little Simz and Michael Kiwanuka. SAULT's vision testifies to a new generation, hard at work shaping an economic and cultural identity while flexing across the spectrum of music, dance, theatre, film, visual arts, spoken and written word.

In the words of Malcolm X: '... Tomorrow belongs only to the people who prepare for it today.'[1]

Beyond the Bassline – Curatorial Reflections

DR ALEEMA GRAY

It's 2003. My dad has just picked me up from my djembe drumming class at Simba Project's supplementary summer school. Looking out the window of his Ford Galaxy, I nod to the pitchy signals of Conscious FM playing a medley of Ini Kamoze's 'England Be Nice' and Ms Dynamite's 'A Little Deeper'.

We make a stop at our local African cash and carry to pick up ingredients for mum's Saturday soup – yam, banana and pumpkin. Beyond the group of uncles debating outside the Western Union, I hear the start of a toasting session. Plugged into a vamp, one man is rapping in cockney rhyming slang, while another is singing in Swahili. Before too long, a crowd assembles. Pulsing on the street corner of Deptford High Street. We are transported.

These are the moments that come to mind when I think of Black British music. Raw. Innovative. Dynamic. Drawing on influences from across the globe yet blending and mixing it to our circumstances, it is an experience that cannot be studied. It can only be felt.

So, what would it mean to transform this feeling into an exhibition spanning 500 years of Black music in Britain? Where does one begin?

For a while, I sat with research pulled together by University of Westminster's Black Music Research Unit. I explored several thematic iterations; the success stories, untold histories and the seminal events that brought communities together. I thought critically about *the* story and the story that should be told. But the first question I had to come to terms with: why the British Library? As someone whose experience of the British Library had been marked by overcaffeinated study sessions in the reading room, the library represented a place to be quiet. Not a place to be loud. A place to think. Not a place to feel.

These preconceptions soon faded when I began exploring the Sound and Vision collections. Justifying UNESCO's classification of music as Intangible Cultural Heritage, the library's Sound and Vision collection represents one of the largest in the world, containing more than seven million recordings including music, spoken word, wildlife and environmental sounds dating back to the birth of recorded sound in the nineteenth century. Beyond sound, the collection boasts an array of printed music manuscripts, ephemera and photography, from British Jamaican bassist Coleridge Goode's diaries in the 1950s and Shirley Bassey's music score for 'Hey Big Spender' in 1973, to British rapper Shystie's 2004 debut album *Diamond in the Dirt* and fanzines documenting genres such as two-tone and ska.

Outside of the Sound and Vision collections, the library holds an extensive catalogue of material that paints a national picture of how Blackness has lived and moved in Britain. References of wedding gifts offered by King Henry VIII to John Blanke – the earliest musician of African descent on record in Britain – can be found in the medieval manuscripts collections, while handwritten poetry from Benjamin Zephaniah and Jean 'Binta' Breeze, and posters from African Caribbean supplementary schools can be found in the Contemporary Archives and Manuscripts collections.

OPPOSITE *Iwoyi*, directed by Tayo Rapoport and Rohan Ayinde in collaboration with Touching Bass.

The British Library collections are vast and endless. But for me as a curator, their true power was found when I looked at them not as they are, but how they *could* be. In other words, I considered what it would mean to situate these collections as part of contemporary Britain. What could they mean for the MCs on Deptford High Street engaged in a toasting session? Part of this approach explored collections held elsewhere – not just in terms of institutions, but private places where Black music continued to live. From Gary Cosby's double bass and Dennis Bovell's guitar to Adelaide Hall's travelling case, Pauline Black's iconic outfit and Jamal Edwards' camera recorder, the exhibition assembled a collection of material that exemplified how history is being made every day.

The more immersed I became in the collections, the more I was able to unlock a curatorial narrative that could take visitors on a musical journey through time and space. With multiple intersecting stories, the narrative of the exhibition soon became a conversation, one that brought together the people, places and moments that have formed part of the British soundtrack. The conversation is one that asks visitors to think about the specificity of the British space: not as something that is absent from history, but as what geographer Doreen Massey has referred to as a meeting up of histories.

Each section of the exhibition represents a space that forms part of a loose chronology of 500 years of Black music in Britain. We started in the Ocean as a way to confront the tensions associated with Black Britishness. For centuries the ocean acted not only as a mode of transportation, but also as a site of displacement. As one elder told me, 'my home is where my ancestors swim.' Rather than centring violence, the Ocean mobilises the silences to think about the traditions that had survived and been brought to Britain. From Nyabinghi drumming to African-American spirituals, we see the ocean as carrying the sounds of Black Britain and mapping a musical score of imagination, creativity and survival.

If the Ocean explores Britain as a site of contention and possibility, the second section looks at Britain as a site of optimism and performance. We explore various performance stages from the end of the nineteenth century, from classical arenas where Samuel Coleridge-Taylor and Amanda Aldridge performed to British broadcast platforms where trailblazing Black women such as Cleo Laine and Adelaide Hall found their spotlight.

But underneath the glamour and glitz, the second section also documents more underground spaces such as Soho, London, where West African palm wine and Scrabble met Caribbean rum and dominoes. These spaces represented pockets of migration to the British mother country and as such, became infamous for a kind of innovation, style and political appetite found in the work of Sir Frank Bowling, Amy Ashwood Garvey and Joe Harriott.

Despite the air of optimism, it was clear that surveying Black musical experiences in Britain must also confront the sentiments put forward in Linton Kwesi Johnson's poem 'Inglan is a Bitch'. The third section, Frontlines, looked at Black music as part of a community narrative, one that moved beyond London to spotlight how Black music was felt in cities such as Manchester, Birmingham, Leeds and Cardiff. From Claudia Jones' West Indian Carnival in St Pancras Town Hall to African Liberation Day celebrations in Birmingham and Manchester, the 1960s saw Black music developing as an educative force, one that inspired a generation who came of age in Britain.

If Frontlines was powered by community, the record shop explored the Black music economy. From the 1970s, record labels and shops exploded and Britain was at the heart of distribution and promotion of Black musicians. While the music had been dominated by the popularity of Jamaican music scene, a number of African artists got their break in England. Indeed, it was in Britain that South African Blue Notes musicians found refuge. It was a place where, as evidenced in the toasting session in Swahili and cockney, a way was paved, a new musical appetite and the founding of new musical genres from lovers' rock, two-tone and jungle.

The final section, Cyberspace, spotlighted the musicians, creatives and platforms that have come to embrace the term 'Black British' and brought the exhibition full circle. Although Cyberspace explored the relationship between music making, technological advancements and online communities, many of the themes captured solidified common threads throughout the exhibition: the cultural and political tensions between visibility and invisibility, the unapologetic aesthetic and style that Blackness has acquired in Britain, and the unceasing innovation despite all the odds.

Beyond the Bassline invoked a conversation that forced me to think critically about my responsibility as a curator and the library's position as a site of learning and engagement. Statements such as 'we do not see ourselves' have formed part of a legacy of contested discourses around the role of heritage institutions in a world of rapidly changing global politics and socio-economic inequalities.

And within this, I asked myself, what does knowledge and representation look like in the context of curatorial work and museum practices? As someone situated in both the

Black community and the institution, it was important for *Beyond the Bassline* to centre a story that could help, as opposed to hurt.

Part of my responsibility as a curator and public historian was to think about access, not as a noun, but as a verb. This demanded a kind of practice that was flexible, responsive and collaborative. Throughout the programme we worked with community artists and partners across the UK to interrupt each main section – from a dance group in Tiger Bay and Rastafari- and gospel-led organisations in London and Birmingham to young people in Leeds exploring activism and DIY sound systems. While such approaches challenged internal processes and ideas around preservation, ownership and care, they created access points where communities across the UK could participate in the production of knowledge.

The nature of participation wasn't just about our past and present, but our futures. What does a reparative Black British music future look like? Such questions formed the basis of Touching Bass' commissioned film. In response, Rohan Ayinde and Tayo Rapoport collaborated with the South London-based musical movement and put forward *Iwoyi: within the echo* (2024), a five-channel film and sound installation taking us on a non-linear journey into the Black radical imagination.

Beyond the Bassline is not an end point; it is the continuation of a conversation. One that moves below the bassline, in the cracks of British popular culture. It is a conversation that provokes. Excites. Reflects. Connects. One that materialises the experiences I felt driving through Deptford High Street. And ultimately, one that hopes to linger beyond the walls of the exhibition and the pages of this book.

A Personal Prelude to the First National Exhibition on Black British Music

MYKAELL RILEY

Embarking on the first national exhibition on Black British music at the British Library, my story intertwines with British music's rich, multifaceted tapestry. It's a journey that mirrors the evolution of Black British music genres that have shaped and been shaped by the cultural and social fabric of Britain.

When considering how to begin writing about my relationship with a national exhibition, a quote from James Baldwin, 'People are trapped in history, and history is trapped in them,' came to mind. Reflecting on these poignant words, I realise my journey to curating this exhibition is not just a chronicle of music-related events. It's an embodiment of history itself, a history that lives within me as I live within it. Each step in this journey has been a dialogue with the past, a conversation that speaks not only of the rhythms and melodies that defined generations but also of the struggles and triumphs they represent. His words resonate deeply in the context of Black British music and the tracing of its roots and evolution over half a millennium. It's up to us to remember our history, or it gets forgotten.

The significance of the connection between the British Library (BL) and the British Library Sound Archive for this exhibition cannot be overstated. In recognition of the fact that its collections have not been thoroughly investigated for material reflecting the Black British contribution to popular music, the library is actively addressing historical oversights and the resulting gaps in curatorial engagement. By uniting one of the world's largest collections of books with an equally extensive array of sound recordings, the exhibition transcends being a mere showcase of musical heritage; it represents a pivotal shift in cultural discourse. This collaboration is about embracing and celebrating the identity, struggle and triumph inherent in the impact of Black British music on Britain's cultural landscape. For the above reasons, as the national repository, the British Library had to be the venue to share this knowledge regionally and globally.

The music celebrated in this exhibition is more than a collection of sounds. It's a living history, echoing through the centuries, from the sixteenth-century musician John Blanke, a trumpeter in the court of Henry VIII remembered for petitioning for a pay increase in writing from the king and as one of the few recognisable Africans in Tudor Britain. The African and Caribbean classical and jazz musicians that followed, the joyous responses to Jamaican ska and reggae that gave us two-tone and lovers' rock. The raw energies of drum and bass, grime, drill and Afrobeats are UK ting. These by-products of the Black British experience are not just artefacts of a bygone era but chapters in an ongoing story. When initially conceiving of a national exhibition on Black British music, the first question was where to begin a story with many beginnings. Should it cover the nineteenth,

BELOW Duke & Chris Peckings, 2018 (detail), archival print & acrylic paint on canvas by Gerard Hanson..

twentieth and twenty-first centuries or look at the last seventy-five years – all were mooted. While all options had their merits, my years spent processing funding applications told me that a more powerful story was here to be told.

The decision to explore 500 years was complex but eventually boiled down to three factors. I first had to convince my institution, the University of Westminster, to take on the project. It would take all knowledge gleaned from decades of researching and developing funding applications and the resulting projects. I then had to academically reassure the BL that a timeline dating back to the Tudors was not only feasible but necessary. The aim was to challenge the very idea of Black British music and its relationship to British history – along with repositioning the arrival of the Windrush generation in post-war Britain and their subsequent contributions as a recent chapter in a larger, more complex story of British music. The association with the British Library started in 2012 with the then head of pop, Andy Linehan. His support until his retirement in 2022 was invaluable in forging and maintaining a connection with the BL. This relationship would underpin both the Bass Culture exhibition and the development of the national exhibition. While access to these spaces can prove elusive, once

inside the BL, the opportunities were palpable, and thus, the collaboration with the Black Music Research Unit (BMRU) came to be.

As preparations for this exhibition were coming to an end, and this volume was going to press, we learned the news of Andy Linehan's sudden passing. It is with deep sadness and regret to think that he will not see the embodiment of the idea we developed in those earliest of days.

Echoing the words of cultural historian Paul Gilroy, 'Black music has been a crucial vehicle for the social transformations that have shaped modern Britain.' My evolution from a member of the British roots reggae band Steel Pulse to a music curator embodies this transformative journey. But as with all journeys of this nature, little if anything was straightforward. The trek from songwriting and music production to developing the Reggae Philharmonic Orchestra (the RPO), Britain's first pop stings, or the setting up of the BMRU, which delivered the UK's largest exhibition on the impact of reggae, and in partnership with Live Nation, in 2018 successfully challenged the regressive London Metropolitan policing policy, form 696, as it was negatively impacting grime music artists, was a long haul. My journey was pretty much unique, but the challenges I faced were not.

On the back of these and the many other projects, one might say the pursuit of a national exhibition was predictable – it was not. It stemmed from an application drafted in 2012, soon after forming the BMRU, and I've since worked to realise this ambition. As Bob Marley stated, 'You never know how strong you are until being strong is the only choice you have.'

OPPOSITE Carol next to the photo by Chris Steele-Perkins, Wolverhampton Disco from 1978 (see page 219), showing her dancing. **RIGHT** After his time with Basement 5 – a 1970s post-punk reggae band featuring Dennis Morris and Don Letts – Leo Williams (E-Zee Kill) teamed up with Mick Jones from the Clash to create Big Audio Dynamite in 1984. This image of Leo, with his family, represents the diversity of Black British music.

In 2020, our AHRC-funded reggae exhibition, Bass Culture, was recognised by the Research Excellence Framework (REF) as world-leading. Our work is a tribute to the resilience and creativity of the artists and communities that have used this music as a form of expression and social change. But it's essential to add that at the BMRU, we not only research the history of Black British music, we also celebrate its transformative power in British culture.

The BL exhibition is an extension of this work. Furthermore, by engaging the British Library's archives in a critical conversation with community archives from various UK Black British regional groups, the project aims to increase the 'affective impact' in the broader community. It seeks to acknowledge the significance of their lived experiences and their resistance to cultural dominance, thereby fostering a stronger sense of inclusion within British cultural heritage.

The exhibition is crafted to provoke inquiry and provide new insights into the narrative of 'intimacy' in Black British music, and its power to challenge and redefine the mainstream British cultural, musical and political landscapes. It is an ode to the spirit of community and the radical force of alternative Black British music genres such as jungle, drum and bass, grime and Afrobeats. These movements, rooted in social, cultural and political resistance, engage in a conversation with the radical histories of Black British music that stretch back to the nineteenth and mid-twentieth centuries, as documented

in the archives. Moreover, the exhibition encourages reflection on how mass media have shaped or sidelined the networks of Black British cultural production and examines the significant roles of entities like the BBC, the commercial imperatives of music radio and the narratives spun by the British music press. Ultimately, the exhibition is expected to both electrify and provoke, but most importantly, to energise and inspire continued exploration into this essential facet of British cultural heritage.

Echoing the poignant words of Benjamin Zephaniah, 'Our stories are in our songs,' and Linton Kwesi Johnson's assertion that 'Music is an expression of our inner creativity,' this exhibition weaves together these multiple threads. James Baldwin's timeless observation, 'History is not the past; it is the present. We carry our history with us. We are our history,' serves as a guiding principle, reminding us that this exhibition is not just a retrospective but a living, breathing chronicle of Black British cultural identity and legacy.

A Personal Prelude... / Mykaell Riley

THE OCEAN

'The drum is the heartbeat, the first sound'

Ade Egun Crispin Robinson

Ogunda Tetura

The Sea is History

DEREK WALCOTT

Where are your monuments, your battles, martyrs?
Where is your tribal memory? Sirs,
in that grey vault. The sea. The sea
has locked them up. The sea is History.

First, there was the heaving oil,
heavy as chaos;
then, like a light at the end of a tunnel,

the lantern of a caravel,
and that was Genesis.
Then there were the packed cries,
the shit, the moaning:

Exodus.
Bone soldered by coral to bone,
mosaics
mantled by the benediction of the shark's shadow,

that was the Ark of the Covenant.
Then came from the plucked wires
of sunlight on the sea floor

the plangent harps of the Babylonian bondage,
as the white cowries clustered like manacles
on the drowned women,

and those were the ivory bracelets
of the Song of Solomon,
but the ocean kept turning blank pages

looking for History.
Then came the men with eyes heavy as anchors
who sank without tombs,

brigands who barbecued cattle,
leaving their charred ribs like palm leaves on the shore,
then the foaming, rabid maw

of the tidal wave swallowing Port Royal,
and that was Jonah,
but where is your Renaissance?

Sir, it is locked in them sea-sands
out there past the reef's moiling shelf,
where the men-o'-war floated down;

strop on these goggles, I'll guide you there myself.
It's all subtle and submarine,
through colonnades of coral,

past the gothic windows of sea-fans
to where the crusty grouper, onyx-eyed,
blinks, weighted by its jewels, like a bald queen;

and these groined caves with barnacles
pitted like stone
are our cathedrals,

and the furnace before the hurricanes:
Gomorrah. Bones ground by windmills
into marl and cornmeal,

and that was Lamentations—
that was just Lamentations,
it was not History;

then came, like scum on the river's drying lip,
the brown reeds of villages
mantling and congealing into towns,

and at evening, the midges' choirs,
and above them, the spires
lancing the side of God

as His son set, and that was the New Testament.

Then came the white sisters clapping
to the waves' progress,
and that was Emancipation—

jubilation, O jubilation—
vanishing swiftly
as the sea's lace dries in the sun,

but that was not History,
that was only faith,
and then each rock broke into its own nation;

then came the synod of flies,
then came the secretarial heron,
then came the bullfrog bellowing for a vote,

fireflies with bright ideas
and bats like jetting ambassadors
and the mantis, like khaki police,

and the furred caterpillars of judges
examining each case closely,
and then in the dark ears of ferns

and in the salt chuckle of rocks
with their sea pools, there was the sound
like a rumour without any echo

of History, really beginning.

Tides, Trade and Tribulation

DALIA AL-DUJAILI

For centuries it was the Atlantic Ocean that connected civilisations, religions, ethnic groups and cultures. The African diaspora in Britain today represents a mosaic of experiences and origins shaped by the Atlantic slave trade, the British Empire and post-war immigration. It reveals a complex history that underscores the significance of the ocean as both a barrier and a bridge.

The role of the ocean in shaping culture cannot be underestimated. It is only recently, a couple of generations ago, that migrations and movements have occurred less over oceans and seas and more over land. Connections over bodies of water have brought peoples of different civilisations, religions, ethnic groups and cultures into contact for centuries. As David Abulafia reminds us in *The Boundless Sea*, while overland migrations have been mediated by the cultures that lay along the land routes that people followed (think of the Silk Road), 'links across the sea could tie together very different worlds, as far apart as Portugal and Japan or Sweden and China'.[1]

Britishness is as much about foreignness as it is about nativeness. We know this much is true, for the very identity of Britain has for so long relied on its exportation of empire and importation of foreign cultures. Without centuries of migration, British culture would have evolved in an unrecognisably different way. In fact, it wouldn't have evolved at all.

In Steve McQueen's contemporary classic *Lovers Rock*, from his Small Axe film series, first- and second-generation West Indian immigrants

cosy into a home in Ladbroke Grove, lovingly held by the thumping heart of the reggae sound system that mirrors the fusion of their identities: the manifestation of the ancestral land's sounds and the making-new of a sound when communities migrate.

The history of Black British music is a testament to the profound impact of migration, both forced and voluntary, on the cultural landscape of Britain. It is a story of the resilience, creativity and an identity shaped by people who crossed oceans, leaving behind their ancestral homelands in search of opportunities, which lay over the horizon. It's a history that, in fact, began long before the *Empire Windrush* docked at Tilbury.

Genetic research in 2007 found that the DNA of British white people had traces of West African genetic material, and the DNA of Cheddar Man – a human male fossil found in Gough's Cave in Cheddar Gorge, Somerset, England which is dated to the mid-to-late ninth millennium BCE – reveals that the first Britons were very likely dark-skinned.

Black migration to Britain can be traced back to Roman times, when the legions of the Roman army contained soldiers recruited from the African continent. In *Black Salt: Seafarers of African Descent on British Ships*, Ray Costello notes that men from North and West Africa were brought 'on Viking longships to the British Isles' as early as the ninth century, and we have evidence of notable individuals of African heritage along the way, the most significant waves of migration occurring in the modern era, from the seventeenth century onwards.

ABOVE *Middle Passage* by Frank Bowling, 1970. Synthetic polymer paint, silkscreen ink, spray paint, wax crayon and graphite on canvas. The Menil Collection, Houston, Texas, USA, the original measures 310.5 x 310.5 cm.

The African diaspora in Britain today represents a mosaic of experiences and origins, shaped by the Atlantic slave trade, the British Empire and post-war immigration. This complex history underscores the significance of the ocean as both a barrier and a bridge for Black people migrating to Britain for various reasons.

The forced migration of African people to the Americas and the Caribbean during the seventeenth to nineteenth centuries left an indelible mark on the Black British experience. It was termed America's 'original sin', and we cannot forget that the brutal institution of slavery was fuelled by British colonialism and imperialism and their domination of the Atlantic. It is no coincidence that the patriotic anthem asks us to cry out, 'Rule Britannia, Britannia rule the waves'. Slavery saw the ocean serve as a harrowing passage of suffering and survival. The Atlantic Ocean, once a route for trade and exploration, became synonymous with the Middle Passage, the journey endured by millions of enslaved Africans.

To put the forced voyage into perspective, virtually every European country was involved in the slave trade. The Portuguese and the British were the most prolific. Approximately 12–15 million people were forcibly transported across the Atlantic Ocean, from West Africa to European colonies and plantations between 1500 and 1870. Some historians suggest the number of people transported may have been higher. It is estimated that British slave ships made around 10,000 voyages across the Atlantic, transporting approximately 3.4 million people, of whom only 2.6 million survived the journey.

Life on the plantations was brutal, dehumanising and physically gruelling. The produce of the slave labour – tobacco, cotton, sugar and indigo dye – ensured British port cities such as London, Liverpool and Bristol rapidly expanded due to the wealth generated. Would Britain have had an industrial revolution without the slave trade? Two hundred years have elapsed since slavery was abolished but the demands for reparations remain. In 2020 the Black Lives

Matter movement also demanded a re-evaluation of those who benefitted from the slave trade. While Black Lives Matter demonstrators toppled the statue of transatlantic slave trader Edward Colston and dumped 'him' in Bristol Harbour.

Stepping back in time, we know that the royal household of Henry VII and Henry VIII employed a respected trumpeter of African origin. His name is recorded as John Blanke (see page 42) and he arrived in England from Spain as part of Katherine of Aragon's entourage. While Blanke's presence remains something of a mystery, we do know that the transatlantic slave trade resulted in a wave of enslaved Africans arriving on the shores of the British Isles. By the end of the eighteenth century it was estimated that London's Black population was between 5,000 and 10,000. They brought with them not only their forced labour but also their rhythms, songs and deeply embedded spiritual beliefs.

The nineteenth century marked a pivotal point in the history of Black people in Britain, as the abolition of the slave trade in 1807 and the Slavery Abolition Act of 1833 led to the gradual dismantling of the institution that had forcibly transported Africans across the ocean. Emancipated Africans, referred to as 'freedmen', such as the celebrated street musician Billy Waters (see page 45), started to arrive in Britain, many seeking refuge from the vestiges of slavery in America and the Caribbean.

Olaudah Equiano, a former slave who became a prominent British abolitionist and author, provides a first-hand account of the horrors of the Middle Passage and the inhumanity of slavery in his autobiography, *The Interesting Narrative of the Life of Olaudah Equiano*, published in 1789. Equiano's work contributed to the abolitionist movement and laid the foundation for the emergence of a free Black community in Britain.

OPPOSITE Illustration depicting enslaved people rowing Dutch soldiers. The Vinkhuijzen collection, New York Public Library.
BELOW Enslaved people cutting sugar canes in their working dresses. From the book *Notes on the Present Condition of the Negroes in Jamaica* by Henry Thomas De La Beche, 1825.

From the African and Caribbean
colonies to the Indian subcontinent,
individuals embarked on transoceanic
voyages to the mother country.

The Atlantic Ocean acted as a powerful physical barrier that separated people from their homelands, but also provided a bridge that connected them to a different world of influences and experiences. The ocean served as a backdrop to an enslaved people's suffering, yet it also carried within it echoes of resistance and determination. From the chants of the enslaved on sugar plantations to the sea shanties of Black sailors who navigated the same treacherous waters (for example 'The Sailor Likes His Bottle O'' and 'Shallow Brown'), the ocean became a vessel of memory and hope.

Our world is a mixed one, as Édouard Glissant reminded us, and cultures are always melting into one another, impossible, and undesirable even, to contain in a vacuum. The fleet of British sailing ships recruited multi-ethnic crews from across the British colonies, casting a light on a tapestry of musical influences and how shanties developed at sea. For example, the songs of enslaved and free Africans labouring in the docks and ports in the southern states of America married harmoniously with the folk songs, fiddle, dance and march tunes, call-and-response work songs and 'minstrel' music already popular among sailors.

The height of the British Empire, during the nineteenth and early twentieth centuries, drew people from across the vast expanse of the Empire to the heart of the metropole. The ocean served as a conduit for the movement of people, ideas and cultures within the Empire. From the African and Caribbean colonies to the Indian subcontinent, individuals embarked on transoceanic voyages to the mother country,

bringing with them their languages, religions and traditions. The two world wars of the twentieth century were pivotal moments in Black British history. John Akomfah's *Mimesis: African Soldier*, a bold three-screen film installation, brilliantly illuminates the role of the Black soldiers and labourers from across the Empire who came to Britain to serve and support the war effort in the First World War. During both conflicts, the arrival of servicemen and women from the Caribbean, Africa and South Asia had a profound impact on Britain's demographic landscape.

The Windrush generation was a term coined to describe the post-Second World War wave of Caribbean immigrants to the UK, who arrived to help rebuild a battered and bruised Britain.

Moses, the protagonist of Sam Selvon's canonical novel *The Lonely Londoners*, boards 'a number 46 bus at the corner of Chepstow Road and Westbourne Grove to go to Waterloo to meet a 'fellar who was coming from Trinidad on the boat-train', a ritual he's maintained since he arrived himself from the West Indies during the Windrush generation. His name is an ironic nod to the magnitude of the ocean journey which brought him to Britain, whether by some divine intervention or by some colonial power.

The arrival of this first wave of people from the Caribbean was instrumental in shaping the trajectory of music in Britain. The coming together of the community of West African musicians – who had also arrived in London from the Empire between the war years – with a new generation of musicians from the Caribbean inevitably created something that was innovative and thrilling.

OPPOSITE The *Empire Windrush* arrived in Tilbury on the River Thames, 22 June 1948. Many of those on board experienced racism and a hostile environment: Britain was not the welcoming home they had been led to expect.

Ghanaian and Nigerian highlife fused with calypso, mento and jazz and gave voice to an optimistic generation of outsiders who were looking for a better life in the cold, urban landscapes of Britain's inner cities. By the mid-1960s the sound of ska and rocksteady had filtered out of the town hall dances, the underground clubs and blues dances to gently resonate within the working-class communities of London, Birmingham and Manchester alike. If you listened to Radio Caroline, an illegal pirate station situated on a boat in the North Sea, you could hear the sounds of young Jamaica alongside the music of hugely popular bands like the Beatles and the Rolling Stones, who were recycling the rhythm & blues and soul music of Black America.

While Black migrants have contributed immeasurably to Britain, racial discrimination, institutionalised racism and the struggle for civil rights have been recurring themes in the history of Black people in the country. From the race riots of the 1950s and 1980s to the advocacy of figures such as Darcus Howe and Claudia Jones, Black Britons have consistently resisted and fought against systemic inequalities through the many tongues of their musical languages. Linton Kwesi Johnson is just one of many examples. An acclaimed poet and dub reggae artist, he has consistently used his words and music to amplify the voices of those marginalised by society, and delivered a rallying cry for justice, equality and an end to police brutality.

The arrival of Rastafari in Britain in the 1970s, transmitted through reggae music, brought with it a militant Black consciousness that was rooted in the dark days of slavery, and offered a Garveyite vision of a fleet of Black Star Liners that would carry the people out of Babylon, back across the Atlantic Ocean and back to Africa. Young Rasta-oriented bands that shared stages with punk bands offered a natural, social and political awareness in the fight against the National Front through Rock Against Racism (see page 174). One young Black woman, Poly Styrene of X-Ray Spex, paved the way for others such as Pauline Black (see page 182) and Rhoda Dakar to follow. Their participation in punk and two-tone – genres often associated with a white, working-class, male demographic – is a reminder of the forgotten legacies of Black and minority ethnic artists to British music.

In the 1980s, Black British music continued to evolve, and its impact resonated on a global scale. Artists such as Soul II Soul and Sade achieved international acclaim, merging soul, RnB and jazz with electronic elements to create a distinctive sound. These artists represented a cosmopolitan, multicultural Britain and shattered stereotypes, demonstrating that Black British music was not confined to one genre or style.

The arrival of hip-hop in the UK in the late 1980s collided with a new generation of London reggae MCs such as Smiley Culture and Tippa Irie. Then the early 1990s marked another turning point in the history of Black British music, as rappers such as Rodney P and Roots Manuva embraced the genre's storytelling potential to depict life in inner-city London. The lyrics of these urban griots became a lens through which the whole world could see the challenges faced by Black British youth, from institutionalised racism to economic disparities. South Asian youth were inevitably drawn into the cultural affray through artists such as Apache Indian, Joi, Asian Dub Foundation and Talvin Singh's drum and bass session, *Anokha – Soundz of the Asian Underground*.

Emerging from the multicultural streets of East London in the early 2000s, grime represented a new generation of artists who utilised the digital age to create a sonic blueprint of today's youth and the zeitgeist. Artists like Dizzee Rascal, Wiley and Skepta brought grime to the forefront of the music scene, with its pulsating beats and raw, unfiltered lyrics resonating with young people who were facing austerity, housing crises, hardened policing and xenophobia across the UK.

In *Grime Kids*, DJ Target tells the story of a sound which 'began on East London housing estates, a sound influenced by everything from Jamaican dancehall and US hip hop to British underground music scenes like jungle and UK garage'. The ex-Roll Deep member grew up in Bow, 'the birthplace and epicentre of the early grime movement and, at the time, one of the poorest areas in the UK with the highest rate of youth unemployment'.[2]

In recent times, British youth of West African heritage have utilised Afrobeats to digitally traverse the Atlantic Ocean and unite London with Lagos and Accra – with the realisation that Europe is, in fact, not the centre of the world. Many in the diaspora now recognise the importance of connecting back to the homeland and in this technological age, it's never been easier for them to do so. African artists from the continent have exploded in the US and UK with an African diaspora desperate to reconnect with the sounds of their motherlands. The Nigerian sonics of Asake, Rema, Wizkid, Tems and Burna Boy, to name a few, have piqued the musical interest of the zeitgeist.

The ocean that once separated Black migrants from their homelands is now a metaphorical bridge connecting them to their ancestral roots. The concept of a Middle Passage is no longer synonymous with suffering but has evolved into a transcultural bridge, encompassing the fusion of diverse identities, narratives and histories. It is a testament to the enduring spirit of Black Britons who have journeyed across oceans in pursuit of better lives and social justice.

We live in a world that bolsters the lives of some on the condition of the oppression of others. The routes that those migrants, seeking asylum, safety and freedom, can take to this country are under the greatest threat we have seen in perhaps centuries of British immigration policies. One of the five priorities of the government in 2023 was to 'Stop the Boats', and exceedingly police the movements of vulnerable peoples, as seen in the Rwanda Bill, which was deemed illegal by court in late 2023, and the illegal refugee ban bill.[3] Maybe our history needs to be put in perspective. Britain is a nation that dispatched fleets of ships across the ocean, to the 'four corners of the world', to capture, kill, colonise and exploit people who were then designated to be children of the mother country and in the service of our king or queen. Should we be surprised that those in need should risk all, in small boats, to cross a treacherous stretch of sea to find a home in Great Britain?

Journey of the Drum: From Ayan to the Ends

ADE EGUN CRISPIN ROBINSON
OGUNDA TETURA

Oriki Ayan

Ayan Agalu
I greet you this morning
The one who gives us what it takes to extract
patronage, even from the miserly
Leading us into the 16 innermost secret places
of the market
The headlamp is the glory of the hunter
Blood is the glory of medicine
Not to be afraid of war is the glory of man
He makes one travel an unknown road
Ayan Agalu, go peacefully, keep cool

Ayan is the Yoruba deity of the *bàtá*, the spirit of the drum, the *orisha* of the transformational quality of sound. Historical records of *bàtá* drumming stretch back to the fourteenth century, to the ancient city-state of Oyo in what is now modern Nigeria. It forms part of the cluster of spiritual and artistic practices known collectively as Yoruba traditional religion or *Ìṣèṣe*. The enslavement and forced migration of roughly 12 million human beings via the Middle Passage carried Yoruba people (alongside dozens of other West and Central African ethnicities) across the Atlantic to Cuba, Brazil, Haiti, Trinidad, Jamaica, Grenada and other locations. In Cuba they became known as *Lukumí* and their practices blended with other African sacred world views to become the diasporic religious expression known as *Regla Ocha* or *Santería*. Cuba is the only place in the world outside of Yorubaland to retain a *bàtá* tradition.

Regla Ocha involves devotion to deities called *orisha*, spiritual beings that are petitioned for health, wealth, long life, children and practical help in daily life. *Àṣe* is a central concept that refers to a spiritual force that permeates the universe and all living things. Communication with *orisha* is achieved through harnessing *àṣe* via divination, spirit possession, by prayers and ritual offerings, animal sacrifice, music, song, dance and, of course, the drum.

In Jamaica, where my father is from, and across the Anglophone Caribbean, drumming was mostly prohibited, but that didn't stop the people. *Dis ya spirit kyaan quench*. Maroon communities maintained their own traditions, and Nine Night had its *Kumina* drums. We must also speak of *Obeah*, a creole ritual praxis drawing on ancestral powers found across the Caribbean, in Jamaica, Trinidad, Suriname and elsewhere. *Obeah* has resonance with the notion of *àṣe*, in the sense that practitioners are perceived to be using a pervasive, all-encompassing universal force. After *Kumina* came *Nyabinghi*, the Rastafari drumming that inspired Lee 'Scratch' Perry, Bob Marley and others to bring spirit to the forefront of the music. Reggae music, word sound power, a natural mystic.

In the UK we had no native drumming traditions – but we had sound system, bass culture and a fledgling Black consciousness. *JAH… Rastafari*. 'The drum is the heartbeat, the first sound,' the Rastas used to say.

ABOVE Errol Lloyd, *The Drummer*
(The Lion of Judah Roars in His Head),
oil on canvas, 1977, 86 x 71 cm.

When the mighty Jah Shaka, *ibae*, would play in Deptford, Finsbury Park, Southall, Northampton, Birmingham, Leicester, Leeds – *riddim sweet, riddim tuff, riddim harder dan steel iyah*... The music our heartbeat, carrying livity, vitality and sustenance, pumping the blood of life and culture through the people to carry us beyond. *Àşe.*

In Kodwo Eshun's seminal *More Brilliant Than the Sun*, he expresses it thus:

You can't catch the beat, the tails of sound as they turn the corner, disappear down a corridor... Where rhythm should be there is space, and vice versa... Every track ambushes you, confounds the process of pattern cognition by leaving the expected beat implied. By opening holes at the tightest moments of the groove, pulse falls through subtracted space, polyrhythm wrongfoots you, tugs and pushes at

expectation, yanks the floorboards from underneath you... The world turns into a giant drum with you at its centre. Beats ricochet off 360º, curving around the walls of the world.[1]

Just as this illustrates something of the experience of a shaka dance (or indeed, a drum and bass rave), he might as well have been describing the *bàtá*. In Cuba these drums form the centrepiece of religious celebration. In a *tambor* priests and religious people come together to sing, dance and praise *orisha*, using drums consecrated to *Aña* (Cuban spelling of Ayan) to summon *àşe*, summon spirit, call forth possession, healing, transformation. The three drums play simple parts that ingeniously combine to make complex rhythms seething with energy. Multiple meters are stated, implied, suggested, destabilising your awareness and pulling you into the music, into trance, into the sacred. The liminal space opens up and seduces you. Emotion, purpose, depth, serious intent and light-hearted joy – even mild confusion – all compete within for your attention. The *orishas* come. *Oban kuele lerio, oban kuele leri Aña*: Even the greatest of kings must bow before Ayan.

A verse of the sacred *Odu Ifa, Otura Ika*, contains the following line:

Olu Iwo, King of Modu Oba town, brought the calabash of wealth from Heaven to Earth. It scattered and spread everywhere.

Music is the wealth of the diaspora. This is the sound of the drum. Whether in Calabar or Havana, Lagos or Salvador da Bahia, Accra or

ABOVE Eighteenth-century drum made of wood, cedar root and deerskin. Made in Ghana, found in Virginia USA, now in the collection of the British Museum, London. Likely used by Adowa, Kete or Abofoe people, the drum would have been played with an open hand, not sticks.

Our forebears who made it across the Middle Passage could never have imagined the extent of the transformations and reach of this spirit.

Kingston, Dakar or New York, Kinshasa or Paris, Port of Spain or London, Bristol, Birmingham, Manchester – the drum connects us all. A living conversation spanning the Black Atlantic between *ara Aye* – the people of Earth – and *ara Orun* – the people of Heaven – the ancestors.

The flash of the spirit that uses rhythm as a means of transformation and connection is an African inheritance. Yea, indeed: *a Black sumting dis*.

The same spirit that calls forth *orisha* in Havana, that inspires Shaka to *leggo his siren wail*, led Faithless singer Maxi Jazz, *ibae*, to state where his place of worship is on 'God Is a DJ'. Our forebears who made it across the Middle Passage could never have imagined the extent of the transformations and reach of this spirit, this way of being in the world. *It scattered and spread everywhere.*

In the UK we took the sound system culture of our parents, the celebrations of the *bacchanalists*, the peacockery of *mas*, the inborn spirit of the drum, the first sound, and collided with Great Britain, with the city, with concrete, punk, rock, rebellion.

The aspiration of a global Black consciousness has had its movements and moments, its triumphs and failures, but the music has always been pan-African. We took that Caribbean sound system foundation and incorporated Black American soul, funk, disco and jazz. The technology changed and house and hip-hop ushered in the era of sampling. Dobie, London Posse, Soul II Soul opened the

gates. Goldie, Roni Size, Grooverider, A Guy Called Gerald were the sonic alchemists who converted that spirit into something truly new and unique, a Black British sound that changed people's understandings of what the music and technology were capable of. When US drummer Marque 'Inna-most' Gilmore first heard drum and bass he concluded 'the ancestors have landed in the estates of London', grabbed his sticks, packed his bags and came over to be a part of it.

The praise poem to Ayan above foreshadows all this, lists the qualities of this enduring spirit.

The one who gives us what it takes to extract patronage, even from the miserly

It bears repeating: music is the wealth of the diaspora. Who would deny that music and dance have been the pre-eminent forms of material and spiritual sustenance for Black people inna Babylon? Even racists dance to Black music.

Leading us into the 16 innermost secret places of the market

This is a reference to *Ifa*, the ancient Yoruba wisdom tradition whose sacred number is sixteen. It asserts the profundity and intelligence of drumming institutions, the guardianship of deep culture. It's also a reference to the power of music and the drum to enter all spaces, to dine with kings and to move with commoners, to exchange in the market hubbub of life.

*The headlamp is the glory of the hunter
Blood is the glory of medicine*

CUBA *Santería* Drummers, Jovellanos, Cuba, 1993.
Photograph by David Corio, who says the evening was
'an impromptu session after a bottle of Havana Club
was produced'.

These are references to traditional technologies and suggest that drumming, too, is a technology: a deep technology of the soul. Hunters used lamps and fire to either scare or dazzle their prey. Priests and healers use animal blood in sacrifice in order to make medicines and charms powerful. Modern aural wizards twist and warp and reshape sound in the urgent, endless search for the perfect beat. Fife and drum, New Orleans second line, Baby Dodds, Papa Jo Jones, Max Roach, Art Blakey, all evolved and developed the language of the drum kit. Guitarists T-Bone Walker and Muddy Waters began to change the sound, electrifying what had always been acoustic. Later, Herbie Hancock and George Clinton explored newly emerging synthesiser keyboards and brought the squelch to the funk. By the time we get to Lee 'Scratch' Perry, King

Tubby, Scientist and Jamaican dubwise, the technology is being pushed to its utter limits, the music going beyond anything anyone had heard before. Add drum machines, samplers, computers – and now a reckless, promiscuous, magpie culture that creates wholes out of fragments, order out of chaos, chaos out of order.

Not to be afraid of war is the glory of man

If Black music is anything it is courageous. A vehicle for resistance and a space for innovation. From Screaming Jay Hawkins howling 'I Put a Spell on You', through James Brown's 'Say It Loud – I'm Black and I'm Proud', Fela Kuti's 'Zombie', Johnny Osbourne's 'Thirteen Dead and Nothing Said', Aswad's 'Warrior Charge', Public Enemy's 'Rebel Without a Pause', KRS-One's 'Sound of da Police', Mad Professor's 'Kunta Kinte', to the fearless, techy explorations of the early junglists and drum and bass pioneers, the bruk

ABOVE *Santería* session, Matanzas, Cuba, 2011. Photograph by David Corio. **OPPOSITE** Workshop – youth with electronic drum machine/pads, *circa* 2010s. Photograph by Simon Wheatley.

beat scientists, eski magicians and dubstep sorcerers, boundaries have been consistently broken, lines habitually overstepped, old forms transcended, new
styles crafted, ancient futures rebirthed.

He makes one travel an unknown road

Who could have known where this spirit would lead? Only a few years before its release 'Brown Paper Bag' was inconceivable. Who could have foreseen Benga or Wylie? When Ayanbi and Atanda, two of the earliest African *bàtá* drummers in Cuba, progenitors of the Cuban *Aña* (Ayan) tradition, landed on those shores could they have dreamed the future? Did they know what was to come? Chano Pozo taking the spirit to Dizzy? Jazz, soul, gospel, rhythm & blues bursting out of America, reaching back to the Caribbean and touching mento, ska, calypso, all that would become reggae, bashment, soca? Music spiralling back and forth across the

ocean, the *Windrush* recapitulating the Middle Passage, a secondary, voluntary migration? Or even fellow Yoruba man Ambrose Campbell playing his drum in Piccadilly Circus on VE Day, leading a crowd of jubilant Brits? Could they have imagined sound system culture? Saxon? Sir Coxsone? Jah Shaka at the Moonshot Club, Arklow Road, New Cross, sirens wailing, bass bins shuddering, hi-hats skittering, *Rastaman dem jumping in joyful meditation?* Or everything ours that has come since – lovers rock, drum and bass, UK garage, dubstep, grime, Afrobeats and everything beyond?

The conversation continues. The road ahead is still unknown, the story still unfolding. The spirit is still with us.

Ayan Agalu, go peacefully, keep cool.

Àşe

John Blanke: The Black Trumpet

MICHAEL I. OHAJURU

By looking into the accounts of Henry VIII we get an insight into the life of an African trumpeter in the royal court, while speculating on the instrument and the music that would have been played outside of military occasions and in the more social settings with the shawm and sackbut ensembles.

John Blanke is celebrated today as the first person of African descent in British history for whom we have both an image and a record. We know him as a trumpeter to the courts of Henry VII and Henry VIII. His celebrated image is to be found at one of the most important events of the young Henry VIII's reign, the Westminster Tournament, a joust in February 1511 that was called to celebrate the birth of a son, born on New Year's Day that year, to Henry and his queen, the Spanish princess Katherine of Aragon. The joust is recorded on the Great Tournament Roll of Westminster, in the collection of the College of Arms. John Blanke appears in the accounts of John Heron, the Treasurer of the Chamber under Henry VII and Henry VIII, held at the National Archives, where there are several payments to a 'John Blanke, the black trumpet'. It was the historian Sydney Anglo who first made the connection between John Blanke's image and his record. In a footnote about a 1507 payment to a 'blacke trumpet' recorded in an article about the court festivals of Henry VII, Anglo noted:

I believe this John Blank [sic] was, in fact, a Negro. In the Great Roll of the Tournament at Westminster in February 1511, preserved at the College of Arms, a negro musician is twice depicted amongst the king's trumpets. This, I think, was John Blank, the 'blacke trumpet'.[1]

He was recorded as being paid 20 shillings a month, making his annual pay £12, which was about twice as much as an agricultural worker and three times an average servant. He was well paid when you also consider that in addition to his pay his board and lodging were paid for, and he received a clothing allowance.

A trumpeter at the court was a high-status position. John Blanke the Black trumpet's presence at the Westminster Tournament was part of the demonstration of the international reach, wealth and size of Henry's court. These were signals Henry VIII was giving to the major power bases of Europe at the time – the Pope, the Holy Roman Emperor, the kings of France and Spain – that England too could be as magnificent, if not more so, than they were. Black trumpeters played at many of the European courts, as recorded in Italy, France and Spain. John Blanke is believed by many historians to have come from Spain along with Katherine of Aragon in October 1501, when she came to marry Henry's brother Arthur. Black trumpeters were well known at Spanish courts. Black trumpeters' presence at European Renaissance courts can be traced back to the eleventh- and twelfth-century Islamic courts in Spain. The earliest recorded presence in a

ABOVE John Blanke in the Westminster Tournament Roll, 1511. This sixty-foot-long vellum scroll was painted by the heraldic artists of the College of Arms.

European court is in 1194, when the Holy Roman Emperor Henry VI entered Palermo to announce his presence as King of Sicily.

Music played a central role in Tudor court life, and no great hall could be built without a musicians' gallery. In the Tudor court, trumpets constituted the oldest ensemble, having been played together as a troupe well before the ascent of Henry VII. Trumpeters were at the heart of Tudor courtly life: they played at tournaments, funerals, coronations, banquets and weddings, taking part in all the great annual festivals such as Christmas and Easter, as well as announcing the arrival and departure of all important state visitors. Trumpeters also acted as heralds, taking messages abroad, enjoying diplomatic immunity that allowed them free passage through foreign and often enemy territory.

John Blanke played a natural trumpet even though the slide trumpet was well known. At the time most large trumpet groups at the European courts favoured the natural standard straight or double curved instruments, today known as cavalry trumpets. John Blanke's troupe is shown playing the double curved trumpet, which could only play notes of the harmonic series. The then-traditional way of playing the trumpet involved counterpoint over bass drones. Trumpets would have also been integrated into the less purely functional musical life of the court, playing in sackbut and shawm ensembles.

John Blanke seems to have been well regarded by Henry VII. We can deduce this from the headgear he is depicted as wearing on the Westminster Tournament Roll and his successful petition for a wage increase and the wedding gifts Henry gave him. He is the only one of the six trumpeters who wears headgear; the others are bareheaded. He wears a turban, which has religious and cultural significance. Although he was part of Henry VIII's Christian court, the turban indicates his Islamic cultural origins; he was allowed to display his cultural difference. This also indicates that he may well have come from Spain, as part of that country was under Islamic rule until 1492. Blanke petitioned the king for his pay to be doubled and backdated as his current wage was 'not sufficient to maintain and keep him to do your Grace like service as other your trumpets do'.[2] Henry approved and signed the petition. John Blanke's last known entry in court records is in January 1512, which records the king's instructions for him to be given wedding presents.

Thanks to Tudor court records we can now put a name to the face we see playing the trumpet on the 1511 Westminster Tournament Roll. We know that in his time the Black trumpeter was known at courts not just in England but across Europe, his presence signifying the international nature and aspirations of Henry VIII's court.[3]

The Life, Times and Music of Billy Waters

TONY MONTAGUE

Celebrated street performer Billy Waters brought African-American music and dance to the Strand and the rowdy taverns of St Giles – one hundred years before the first ragtime, blues or jazz recordings.

On a busy street in Regency London a Black sailor with a wooden leg begins playing the fiddle, dancing to the tune and loudly singing out. As various carts and carriages rattle past, a crowd gathers, mesmerised by the performer's movements, his voice, his sound, the swaying feathers on his bicorn hat. They've never seen or heard anything quite like it.

Billy Waters brought African-American music and dance to Britain, and became a celebrated and legendary figure around one hundred years before the first ragtime, blues or jazz recordings. Yet to date little is known about his music or performance.

Born in New York, *circa* 1776, Waters joined the Royal Navy in 1811 as an able seaman and was soon promoted to gunner. After an accident at sea his left leg was amputated, and he went to live in London, settling in the impoverished parish of St Giles, where he started a family. But his disabled veteran's pension was insufficient to support a wife and daughter. Waters began busking on the streets of affluent West End neighbourhoods and gained a very desirable regular pitch outside the Adelphi Theatre on the Strand. Later he played in rowdy public houses in or near the St Giles Rookery where he lived – 'The Holy Land' – an overcrowded slum close to the British Museum.

Sadly no sheet music for Waters has been found, nor is there a full account of what he did. However, by examining and linking up the snippets of reference that we do have, by looking at the communities in which he lived and grew as an artist, and by listening to recordings of old style African-American fiddlers, we may get a good idea of what and how Billy Waters played, sang and danced.

One couplet of Billy Waters' signature song has survived, and exists in several variants. Printed beneath a lithographed image of him in the National Portrait Gallery's collections in London are the lines:

Kitty will you marry me? Kitty will you toy?
Kitty will you go to bed and get a little – ?
– Pick it up my boy.

And reference is made elsewhere to 'Mr Billy Waters, nicknamed "Kitty will you go to bed"'.

Charles Hindley, author of *The True History of Tom and Jerry* (1888), gives instead:

Polly will you marry me – Polly don't you cry,
Polly will you marry me – Polly don't you cry: –
Cry – cry – cry!

Waters sang with a high and penetrating voice to be heard above the clamour of street or pub, and his fiddling was rough and rhythmic.

In 1959 in north Mississippi, American folk song collectors Alan Lomax and Shirley Collins recorded 'Polly Will You Marry Me?', played by octogenarian Sid Hemphill, who added 'That's an o-o-old song.' And when Billy Waters appeared in court on a charge of vagrancy, the *New Times* reported the circumstances of his arrest: 'our hero caught the eye of a fair lady... standing near the parlour window; towards this spot he drew, and commenced various evolutions with his wooden pin, and singing out in a very winning strain Billy will you marry me, Billy will you try, etc.'[1]

How to account for these variants? Too divergent to be due to imperfect hearing, they suggest Billy Waters brought elements of playful improvisation to his music, along with an animated engagement with his audience. Polly could become Kitty, or morph cheekily into Billy. His physical agility and quick wit – nurtured in Black Manhattan – fascinated Londoners. In *The Ballad-Singer* (1840), English writer Douglas Jerrold wrote: 'O, William Waters... They who saw thee not, cannot conceive the amount of grace co-existent with a wooden leg – the comedy budding from timber... Who ever danced as he danced? Waters was a genius.'

As with many later blues, Waters' songs likely comprised free-floating couplets and verses rather than having a narrative structure. Verses might be altered, added or even spontaneously created for a particular person or audience. Waters sang with a high and penetrating voice in order to be heard above the clamour of street or pub, and his fiddling was rough and rhythmic – with scratchy, droning sounds, rich in overtones. He himself talked of earning 'an honest living by scraping of catgut'.[2]

Engravings and illustrations by brothers George and Robert Cruikshank and others suggest that Waters played in a carnivalesque spirit, with broad movements of knees, hips and bowing elbow. The off-beat, syncopated rhythms and grooves were propulsive for dancers. It's evident that long before coming to London Billy Waters was already playing fiddle and dancing, skills he would have learned in New York in the 1790s and 1800s. It was a period of rapid growth and change, when the majority of its Black population went from being enslaved to becoming 'free Blacks'. Historian Shane White writes of 'a veritable explosion of Black music and dance' in Manhattan at this time, as an increasing number of 'dance-cellars' were opened by – and chiefly for – African-Americans.[3] Good musicians were in demand, and the fiddle was by far the most popular instrument. Most of the dancing in these spaces was performative, by solo males.

The music played by Blacks like young Billy Waters remained on the margins of New York society – largely unreported, heard in dance-

OPPOSITE An engraving of Billy Walters, drawn in 1819, while the musician was still alive. From the book *Costumes of the Lower Orders of London* by Thomas Busby, 1820.

BILLY WATERS.

Pub.d Nov.r 1 1819, for T.L. Busby, by Mess.rs Baldwin & C.o Paternoster Row, & at the Artists Depository, 21. Charlotte S.t Fitzroy Squ.e

The notorious Black Billy "At Home" to a London Street Party.

Tom and Jerry "Masquerading it" among the Cadgers in the "Back Slums", in the Holy Land.

cellars, back-houses, oyster-houses, brothels, waterside taverns, marketplaces, at holiday celebrations like Independence Day and the Pinkster festival, and on boats and ships. In these same years Irish immigrants began arriving in greater numbers, settling mainly near New York's East River, where many free Blacks also lived. Waters' music – his style, tunes and songs – would have reflected a lively mix of influences from hearing players of both African and European descent.

Dance rhythms and steps correlate closely with the music. Waters certainly knew the hornpipe, which sailors performed for agility training. It stressed foot sounds and beats – made later perhaps with the tip of his wooden leg. Another solo dance was the athletic juba, related to the African and Haitian giouba, involving improvisation, shuffling, stomping, slapping and complex rhythmic patterns. Waters may have adapted and blended elements of music and dance from both hornpipe and juba.

The shuffle and double shuffle were typical African-American dance-steps, well suited to taverns with sand-strewn floors. In a low-life scene from the hugely successful theatrical production *Tom and Jerry* at the Adelphi – in which an actor played and defamed Billy Waters as a rogue – the characters Dusty Bob and African Sal do a double shuffle. The real Billy very likely also played for the dance and knew the air of 'Dusty Bob's Jig'.

Billy Waters, Soldier Suke, Ragged Dick, Little Jemmy.

Like Manhattan's Lower East Side, London's St Giles was home to a large Irish community, especially in the Rookery. Waters would already be familiar with Irish jigs and reels, and as a community-based musician he no doubt played at Irish weddings, baptisms, wakes and other occasions. In a gin-shop scene In the fictional book *Life in London* (1821) Billy plays the traditional Irish set-dance jig 'The Sprig of Shillelagh', possibly associated with him and used also as a Morris dance air.

While we will never know exactly how Billy Waters sounded, vintage recordings of two African-American musicians may provide an indication, and are freely accessible online.[4] Sid Hemphill (1876–1963) inherited music and musicianship from his father and grandfather, and when Lomax first recorded him in 1942 he played many tunes on fiddle; Joe Thompson (1918–2012) from North Carolina also drew deep on family history for his old-time stringband fiddling. With their droning, slurring, scraping, rasping, yet wonderfully fluent and uplifting pre-blues styles, we surely hear echoes of Billy Waters, making the catgut wail in a heaving, smoke-filled pub in St Giles. Pick it up my boy.

OPPOSITE ABOVE Billy Waters, here referred to as 'The notorious Black Billy', in a busy street scene. Coloured aquatint, 1822. OPPOSITE BELOW 'Tom and Jerry "Masquerading it" among the cadgers in the "Black Slums", in the Holy Land', drawn by George Cruikshank and published in Pierce Egan's book *Life in London*, 1821. Waters can be seen in the background. ABOVE An image of Billy Waters playing fiddle from *The True History of Tom and Jerry* by Charles Hindley.

George Bridgetower: An Untold Story

JULIAN JOSEPH

A reflection on the reimagining of George Bridgetower, his life, his music... Beethoven... into a jazz opera for the modern-day audience.

The story of Bridgetower came to me at a point in my career when I began thinking about the potential for storytelling in jazz, and was looking for ways of developing a new sensitivity and skill set that would draw on the conventions of classical opera. It was the historian and novelist Mike Philips who suggested the Black violin prodigy who captivated and clashed with Beethoven, studied at Cambridge University, lived, worked and set up his family in Britain, and travelled extensively as a respected and accomplished musician, composer and educator until his death in 1860. Bridgetower's story was untold, and offered rich textures of historical significance, cultural dialogue and artistic challenges, presenting an intricate tableau upon which Mike could write his libretto and I could build a piece.

The opera is set against the monumental 1807 Act for the Abolition of the Slave Trade. Serving to frame a very British narrative, it shines a light on the long reality of a multicultural Britain that resonates to this day. More than this, by focusing on the life of a truly unique individual, the opera shows how talent can have a transformative power in a world rife with social inequalities.

For the orchestration I used a ten-piece ensemble rooted in jazz, mixing traditional jazz elements – piano, bass and drums with wind and brass instruments – to create a soundscape rich in tonal contrasts that would be fluid in its transitions, able to support the shape and character of the drama. In the score, Bridgetower was depicted by the violin that made him famous. It has a particular ability to express the nuances called for in jazz while embodying its classical heritage, and gave the characterisation of Bridgetower its own uniquely dramatic, musical dimension. The opera uses a tonal palette packed with wide-ranging influences from the jazz canon to create an ambitious dramatic universe, which also incorporates the sounds that were part of the musical landscape of the time. The opening declarative chorus uses four-part harmony derived from the chorales of J. S. Bach, while brass-led fanfares, harmonies and melodic decorations and turns typical of the music of Haydn, Mozart and, of course, the maestro of the era, Beethoven, figure across the scoring. These and many other elements were used to generate a kind of radiance, a transcendent quality of expression that would also reflect the very nature of Bridgetower's era.

Once I'd spoken to our director Helen Eastman the collaboration took on another dimension. It was Helen who suggested that a countertenor play the part of the Prince Regent (soon to be George IV), to highlight the foppishness of his

ABOVE Portrait of George Augustus Polgreen Bridgetower, 'violinist', graphite with watercolour, *circa* 1795–1800.

character and make the music all the more focused on communicating the darker and more sinister inferences of his characterisation. Bridgetower's transition into adulthood was also brilliantly conceived by Helen. The child violinist is isolated on stage under a single spotlight, and as he finishes his cadenza he transforms into the fully grown George Augustus Polgreen Bridgetower. Cleveland Watkiss, who I immediately envisaged as the lead for this opera, emerges and sings a song drawn from the upbeat sound of a traditional big band, laced with a hint of Charles Mingus raucousness. This gave Cleveland a chance to improvise and the band an opportunity to show its jazz pedigree.

Beethoven, of course, figures large in the story. For Bridgetower's visit to Vienna it was important for me to bring a certain authenticity to his encounter, so I forged an impression of

Beethoven using the character of his harmonic sound. The scene is played out as a duet, with myself on piano and Christian Garrick on violin, to dramatise the exchange between Beethoven and Bridgetower, with the classical and jazz idioms working together, each reflecting and reconfiguring the music's distinctive styles.

Before Bridgetower leaves for Europe he meets a woman called Mary Prince, a part sung by soprano Abigail Kelly. Mary had gone to Parliament to raise the plight of the many victims of the transatlantic slave trade. It was a scene that called for the use of the blues, which I set up with a harmonic motion inspired by the music of the jazz fusion band Weather Report. The dynamic between Bridgetower and Mary, although serious at times, is also playful,

I'm both telling the story of a forgotten virtuoso and commenting on the ever-present themes of racial identity, cultural legacy and artistic exploration.

characterised by a repetitive groove akin to a recitative found in Baroque opera, but which also opened the scoring up to improvisation by Steve Williamson on soprano saxophone.

Bridgetower's meeting with Beethoven is juxtaposed with Mary being snatched by dark forces. Helen suggested switching between the two scenes to draw empathy away from Bridgetower and establish a stark contrast with the brutality of what Mary is going through in his absence. The piano and violin duet switching to the band echoes this, and features in the ensemble an eerie melody in 3/4 time sung by Mary, which, as the scene builds, intersperses in the band's accompaniment elements of avant-garde abandon akin to the colours reminiscent of Charles Mingus's music.

The sense of movement, drive, urgency and change of mood when Bridgetower pleads with the Prince Regent (played by countertenor Jonathan Peter Kenny) to help secure Mary's return calls on the influence of a range of jazz writers and arrangers, particularly Mingus, Quincy Jones and Herbie Hancock. Many of the influences I hear come after the fact – I've not sought to deliberately combine them but more to give them a platform from which to emerge, and to give me an evolving palette of colours, techniques and inspirations from which to draw.

As the piece comes to a conclusion, Bridgetower and his father, who had been incarcerated in Newgate Prison, reunite.

The aria is an emotional and uplifting duet for Bridgetower's flexible voice and the rich bass baritone of his father, played by Franz Hepburn. In the final scene Bridgetower confronts his surrogate mother, Mrs Fitzherbert, played by mezzo-soprano Buddug Verona James. This was a scene that allows the characterisation of Bridgetower to find perspective and shows how he has gained the courage to take charge of his future on his own terms.

It's essential to recognise that *Bridgetower – A Fable of 1807* isn't just a historical recounting; it's a dialogue between past and present. Through a jazz-inflected musical vocabulary, I'm both telling the story of a forgotten virtuoso and commenting on the ever-present themes of racial identity, cultural legacy and artistic exploration. Bridgetower, in his time, was a boundary-pushing artist, and through this opera, I'm trying to do more than just pay homage to a historical figure; I'm hopefully continuing the dialogue Bridgetower began – questioning norms, breaking down barriers and forever pushing the envelope of what music can convey.

My decision to present George Bridgetower's life through the medium of jazz opera is not merely a retelling of a historical anecdote. It's an artistic statement, a challenge to conventions, and above all a testament to the enduring and ever-evolving spirit of music and storytelling.

OPPOSITE ABOVE LEFT Franz Hepburn as Bridgetower Senior and Jamal Hope as Bridgetower Jr in Julian Joseph's *Bridgetower – A Fable of 1807*. OPPOSITE ABOVE RIGHT Verona James as Mrs Fitzherbert, Cleveland Watkiss as Bridgetower and Jonathan Peter Kenny as the Prince Regent. OPPOSITE BELOW Julian Joseph as Ludwig van Beethoven and Cleveland Watkiss as Bridgetower.

The Ocean / George Bridgetower: An Untold Story

Empowerment and Recognition

CASSIE KINOSHI

The discovery of Samuel Coleridge-Taylor, a composer with African ancestry who was incredibly adept in his command of the orchestral 'ship', was life-changing for Ivors Academy Award-winning composer, arranger and alto saxophonist Cassie Kinoshi.

I've always thought of the art of composition as being akin to learning how to masterfully command and steer a ship – that ship being the orchestra or ensemble, the notes that the composer has choicely drawn together to express the inner workings of their mind, with others being the sails that the conductor and musicians then fill with wind. Thus the music of the composer serves to take the audience and the performing musicians on an abstract journey through sound.

As an artist who has grown up with little to no representation of Black composers working within the forms of European classical music, my discovery of Samuel Coleridge-Taylor as a composer who was incredibly adept in his command of the orchestral 'ship' was a life-changing and hugely momentous occasion. During my time studying composition at the conservatoire we studied many of the known white European, American and Russian compositional greats over the centuries, but there was a noticeable lack of representation of composers of colour, both historic and modern, on the curriculum.

Being able to see oneself in role models provides validation and comfort simply through knowing that someone else has lived a similar experience to yours, and in the context of music, sought to express themselves in similar ways to you. I dived deeply into Coleridge-Taylor's music and scoured the internet for more information on his life in London. At the time, the only recordings I could find online were very few. I became particularly enthralled with his *4 African Dances* for piano and solo violin and would repeatedly listen to them, connecting especially with the delicate simplicity and emotion portrayed in movement two. I was greatly excited by the fact that the title referenced a part of my own ancestry (Nigeria/Sierra Leone) and that I was also residing in South London, where this composer was born, grew up, walked the streets and lived his life while producing beautiful pieces of music such as this. Studying his works and learning about how authentic he remained in celebrating his African heritage through music and outspokenness in confronting the systems that sought to restrict him empowered me both as a composer and as a Black British individual.

Samuel Coleridge-Taylor's body of work proves him to be one of the nineteenth-century British composers who deserve respect and recognition for expert command of the orchestra and various other ensembles both large and small. Due to the work of innovators such as Chi-chi Nwanoku (Chineke! Orchestra) and many others, his works are now receiving the recognition and applause that they have always rightfully merited: recognition as a formidable composer whose works have always deserved to be immortalised in both recordings and the concert hall.

ABOVE Samuel Coleridge-Taylor, 1900. He died of pneumonia after collapsing on Croydon train station, in 1912, at the age of 37. King George V granted his widow an annual pension following his death.

Suite from the
HIAWATHA
Ballet Music

1. THE WOOING.   3.(a) BIRD SCENE.
2. THE MARRIAGE   (b) CONJURORS' DANCE.
      FEAST.   4. THE DEPARTURE.
          5. REUNION.

Price 4/- NET.

By S. Coleridge-Taylor
OP. 82.

NEW YORK   HAWKES & SON   TORONTO
          LONDON

56

OPPOSITE Cover of the sheet music for one of Coleridge-Taylor's most famous works, *Hiawatha*. ABOVE Two mirrored lives; one world; and a common passion: images from *Recognition* – a contemporary play where a post-Black Lives Matter music student, Song, alienated by the white classical canon, discovers Coleridge-Taylor and his legacy. Co-created by Amanda Wilkin and Rachael Nanyonjo and with original music by Cassie Kinoshi.

Sancho's Dance Mix

JULIAN GRANT

Ignatius Sancho's music is understandably overshadowed by his collected letters, and indeed, the sweep of his extraordinary life story.

Charles Ignatius Sancho (*c.*1729–1780), born on a slave ship, came to London as an orphaned infant where he entered the house of three spinster sisters. By chance he met John, second Duke of Montagu, who, impressed by the boy's intelligence, saw to his education, and emancipated him from the uncaring sisters. When the duke died, he was taken on by the duke's widow. Upon her death, she left him an annuity, which he squandered on gambling. He became the new duke's butler in 1766, but when gout and obesity affected his mobility, he was set up in a grocery shop (in those days more a coffee house and meeting place) in 1774.

Having gained celebrity as the first British African to vote and whose music and letters – with passing references to the injustice of slavery – were published, he sat for a portrait by Thomas Gainsborough. In fact, Sancho wrote to Laurence Sterne as he was writing *Tristram Shandy*, to ask him to use his fame to promote the abolitionist cause. Sterne incorporated a passage within his book that had considerable influence on contemporary thinking. So did Sancho's posthumously published edition of collected letters, which long remained in print as a seminal text.

The music Sancho published during his lifetime consists of three books of dances and a book of songs. These are straightforward, populist melodies for domestic music-making, dancing or inclusion in theatrical entertainments. Fashionable minuets, reels, jigs and hornpipes abound, and they almost all abide by the regular eight-bar phrasing required.

My 2014 arrangement *Sancho's Dance Mix* came about from a request by Paul Boucher, music archivist at Boughton House, Northants, originally home to the Montagus and now the Buccleuchs. In their collection was an early published edition of Sancho's dances. As it happened there was to be a fundraising

LEFT Ignatius Sancho. Composer, actor and writer. The first known Black Briton to vote in a British election and the first African to be given an obituary in the British press. From *Letters of the late Ignatius Sancho*, Dublin, 1784.
OPPOSITE Buskaid Soweto String Ensemble at Broughton House, during a performance of *Sancho's Dance Mix* (Ignatius Sancho, arr. Julian Grant), 2014.

concert by the Buskaid Soweto String Ensemble, the senior orchestra of the community music school run by the visionary Rosemary Nalden. This orchestra has toured the world, having appeared at the London Proms; yet the school prides itself in taking all comers willing to make a true commitment to the rigorous musical program. It is nothing short of synchronous that Buskaid, an African orchestra, would be coming to the duke's ancestral home to play Sancho's tunes: a homecoming indeed.

From the collection *Minuets &c. &c. for the Violin, Mandolin, German-Flute and Harpsichord compos'd by an African,* I selected five of the thirteen minuets, the single air, a jig and two reels, and from them fashioned a fifteen-minute, three-movement suite for strings. The edition consists of two staves, a melody and a bass line, with the exception of the air, on three staves, and optional transposed horn parts for two of the minuets.

In arranging Sancho's music I wanted to be respectful, yet performance practice of that era would have embellished the rather skeletal aspect of the printed music. I took my cue from notable twentieth-century reworkings of eighteenth-century music, Stravinsky's *Pulcinella* and Respighi's three suites of ancient airs and dances, adding decoration, counterpoint and imitation plus a touch of contemporary spice.

The first movement, 'Many Minuets', weaves a quasi-symphonic argument out of five of the minuets. No. 7 in G major opens the work, and I wrote a spiky introduction using the first bar only, which leads to its statement, the first part of which is Sancho's original, played in homage to him on a solo violin and double bass. The one minor-key minuet, in G, is elegiac, rare in Sancho's music, and thus doubly precious – after it the opening minuet concludes the movement, chastened and subdued, as if the dance party has moved elsewhere.

The very beautiful 'Air' is the closest in the entire piece to a transcription of the original, though we had no 'German-Flute' as Sancho specifies. I made amends by alternating the colours of massed strings against solo viola, cello and bass.

Of the collection of jigs, reels and hornpipes that make up the rest of the book, I selected three: 'Marianne's Reel', a jaunty, folksy melody, 'Richmond Hill', a scurrying jig, and 'Who'd a thought it', a reel with the simplicity and catchiness of a nursery rhyme. As my title suggests – 'Who'd a thought it: Reeling on Richmond Hill with Marianne' – all three dances alternate in playful and surprising ways and combine for a riotous conclusion.

And a riotous conclusion it was too, when a coach pulled up and disgorged the entire Buskaid orchestra from Soweto into Boughton House, the family seat of the Montagus, Sancho's employers, and later the Buccleuchs. It was thrilling to witness an African orchestra playing Sancho's melodies for a well-turned-out crowd which included the tenth Duke and Duchess of Buccleuch, in the sumptuously decorated great hall, over two centuries after they were first heard. What would Sancho have made of it?

Tones Loud, Long and Deep

JULIAN JOSEPH

The Fisk Jubilee Singers made the spiritual the first true and major cultural contribution of Black Americans. In 1783, the eleven-strong choir arrived in Britain on a fundraising mission. They toured the country; thousands of working folk flocked to hear their songs; they sang for the poor and for Queen Victoria. They confronted racism and discrimination with courage, pride and dignity, and an unflinching belief in the power, relevance and reach of their music.

On 6 October 1871 a mixed, all-Black ensemble, the Fisk Jubilee Singers, set out on a tour of the United States, hoping to raise funds to help rescue their university from financial ruin. Fisk University had grown out of Fisk School, an institution established in Nashville, Tennessee just months after the end of the American Civil War in 1865, and only two years following the Emancipation Proclamation, to give educational opportunities to former slaves of all ages.

One of its original members, Ella Sheppard, had trained as a pianist, having to go 'in the back way' to her lessons. She later became a friend of the renowned campaigner and spokesman Booker T. Washington and the writer Frederick Douglass. The other eight members were Thomas Rutling, Maggie Porter, Benjamin M. Holmes (who was about to be sold in a slave market when he saw the proclamation that would free him), Greene Evans, Jennie Jackson, Eliza Walker, Isaac Dickerson and the youngest,

14-year-old Minnie Tate, whose 'sweet, clear voice' was often showcased in the popular hymn 'Flee as a Bird'.

The choir initially encountered resistance from white audiences who found it hard to accept a group of Black singers performing a repertoire of classical and popular songs – music that they believed to be exclusively theirs. In response, the Singers began to incorporate music that had rarely been heard outside the Black community – spirituals, slave songs and work songs – music that was an integral part of their daily lives, which had enabled them to maintain their dignity in the face of dire servitude and communicated a valuable shared sense of identity. The Singers were reluctant to present what to them was sacred music to hostile, alien ears, but the emotional power of these songs drew audiences in, spellbound by their unfamiliar yet compelling intensity and uplifting energy.

By introducing these songs, the Fisk Jubilee Singers were also preserving a musical culture that was at risk of being lost in the upheaval following Black emancipation. Suddenly this music had lost its relevance. Meanwhile, Black performers were all but non-existent. Just a handful of singers could be seen performing church music or opera, but they were still subject to racist bigotry and restrictive discrimination. In the meantime, white entertainers filtered their own interpretation of Black life through highly popular minstrel shows, in which they covered their faces with Black make-up, their lips starkly contrasted with white paint, to portray

OPPOSITE Press advertisement for an appearance of the Fisk University Jubilee Singers, 16 and 17 December 1897, at the Town Hall in Streatham, London.

FOURTH VISIT TO GREAT BRITAIN!!!

THE
Fisk University Jubilee Singers.

Originally Organized Oct. 6th, 1871, from the Students of Fisk University, Nashville, Tenn., U.S.A. Materially strengthened for the present tour.

F. J. LOUDIN,
Manager
and
Director.

R. Johnson & Sons Ltd., Manchester.

FOR DATE OF CONCERT SEE PAGE FOUR.

B. W. THOMAS.   F. J. LOUDIN.   H. D. ALEXANDER.   THOMAS RUTLING.
MAGGIE L. PORTER.   JENNIE JACKSON.
JULIA JACKSON   ELLA SHEPPARD.   GEORGIA GORDON.   AMERICA W. ROBINSON.

unflattering comical stereotypes to appreciative white audiences.

The Negro spiritual was at the core of the choir's repertoire. With their deeply moving melodies and lyrics that drew on hymns and psalms, the songs expressed the abiding power of religious devotion and the strength of the human spirit to overcome the terrible hardships of slavery. They weren't 'simply religious music', as Frederick Douglass described them. 'They were tones loud, long, and deep; they breathed the prayer and complaint of souls boiling over with the bitterest anguish. Every tone was a testimony against slavery, and a prayer to God for deliverance from chains.'[1] The spirituals were not songs of anger but of belief in humanity and faith in the triumph of good over evil. They were also used as a means of coded communication. Drums, which had been central to African culture, were outlawed by American plantation owners, for fear that they could be used by slaves to send messages inciting rebellion or escape. Instead, spirituals were used to organise secret meetings and announce news of the Underground Railroad. The song 'Great Camp Meeting', for example, signalled gatherings to the slaves without alerting their owners.

In 1862 the American musicologist and abolitionist Lucy McKim Garrison, who co-published the first comprehensive edition of slave songs in 1867, commented on how 'difficult' it was 'to express the entire character of these Negro ballads by mere musical notes and signs. The odd turns made in the throat; the curious rhythmic effect produced by single voices chiming in at different irregular intervals, seem almost as impossible to place on score, as the singing of birds.'[2] The complexity and proportion that exists in this music is indeed hard to pin down, especially when applying

Western classical language to decipher a musical vocabulary that exists outside of its lexicon. Yet in May 1893, the Czech composer Antonín Dvořák stated in the *New York Herald* that:

the future music of this country must be founded upon what are called the Negro melodies. These are the songs of America and your composers must turn to them. In the Negro melodies I discover all that is needed for a great and noble school of music. There is nothing in the whole range of composition that cannot be supplied with themes from this source.[3]

The Negro spiritual allowed the world to see African-Americans as cultured, bright and capable human beings with something of great value to contribute, and offered a suppressed sub-Saharan expressive tapestry an outlet through which it could blossom. The term spirituals encompassed work songs, plantation songs and religious songs: a kaleidoscope of folk music that chronicled the African-American experience, and which would become viscerally influential in the development of American musical identity throughout the entire twentieth century.

The Fisk Jubilee Singers quickly achieved great notoriety, singing to audiences across America that included President Grant and Mark Twain, who commented 'I do not know when anything has so moved me as did the plaintive melodies of the Jubilee Singers.'[4] In 1873 a now eleven-strong choir was invited to England by the seventh Earl of Shaftesbury, Anthony Ashley-Cooper. The new members were Georgia Gordon and Julia Jackson, while Edmund Watkins replaced Greene Evans. They gave their first concert on 6 May in London's Willis's Rooms, which were was very well attended according to contemporary reports, and made up of members

of Parliament, the clergy, the aristocracy and the press. These included the *Globe*, the *Echo*, the *Daily News*, the *Evening Standard* and the *Daily Telegraph*, which reported that the Singers' 'impressive musical performances [were] destined to take up a prominent position among the most remarkable attractions of the present season'.[5] The response of *The Times*, however, was more circumspect, reflective of the general opinion of the British upper classes concerning race, and in fact pretty much anything they considered foreign or uncultivated: 'We cannot say that the expectations raised by these praises have been disappointed. Though the music is the offspring of wholly untutored minds, and, therefore, may grate upon the disciplined ear, it possesses a peculiar charm.'[6] This 'peculiar charm' was nevertheless sufficient to prompt the Duke and Duchess of Argyll to invite them to make an exclusive appearance before Queen Victoria. The choir's performance included 'Steal Away to Jesus', a version of the Lord's Prayer, 'Go Down Moses' and 'Let My People Go'. The queen was apparently delighted and noted that 'they sing extremely well together' in her journal.[7] The Prime Minister, William Gladstone, also asked them to perform at Carlton House, and hosted a breakfast for them at No. 10 Downing Street. With such prestigious endorsements, invitations came flooding in from all over the country. People who would have otherwise never allowed a Black person to enter through their front doors were now treating the Singers as celebrities.

The Singers' British tour gave audiences their first real sense of the experiences of enslavement in America. Songs like 'Nobody Knows the Trouble I've Seen' and 'Steal Away' communicated the reality of the hardship and cruelty the slaves had endured, their longing for freedom and their deep spirituality. The Singers were received with rapturous enthusiasm – 6,000 people queued to see them at the Metropolitan

Tabernacle in London's Elephant and Castle – while 7,500 labourers came to hear them sing at an evangelist meeting in Glasgow. They sang in hospitals and prisons, and in the streets to the poor at charity breakfasts. In August 1873 they arrived in Hull, where William Wilberforce, the figurehead of the abolitionist movement, was born. The choir's presence was hugely symbolic, and they were treated like VIPs, given tours of the city and the docks, with large crowds turning out to hear them. In Scarborough they performed outdoors to 4,000 people, including a group of fishermen, in the pouring rain. They returned to Hull four months later, at which point their success was beginning to be reported by the American press. They gave a performance to 3,000 schoolchildren at Hull's Artillery Barracks and were invited to William Wilberforce's house, where they sang 'John Brown's Body Lies Mouldering in the Grave' and 'God Save the

Queen'. On their third return, in April 1874, they were presented with a portrait of Wilberforce to take with them back to Nashville. From Britain they went on to Germany and the Netherlands, and by the time they finished their first European tour they had raised $50,000, enough to keep the university afloat and to build Jubilee Hall, which the civil rights activist W. E. B. Du Bois described as 'ever made of the songs themselves, its bricks red with the blood and dust of toil'. In it hangs a life-size portrait of the Singers painted by the British artist Edmund Havel and commissioned by Queen Victoria. By 1878, when their international touring came to an end, the Singers had made the staggering sum of $150,000, ensuring the long life of Fisk University. In 1978, the university awarded posthumous honorary

BELOW Fisk Jubilee Singers in Trafalgar Square, London, 1925. The choir travelled frequently to the UK and other countries around the world. **OPPOSITE** American singer Henrietta Myers (1878–1968), director of the Fisk Jubilee Singers, engages in a rehearsal for a concert at the Royal Festival Hall, September 1952.

doctorates to all nine of the choir's original members. The choir also still exists, performing and touring, to this day.

Through their exemplary work, executed so effectively and brilliantly, the Fisk Jubilee Singers were foundational in the early days of the American civil rights movement, their performances galvanising the conversation about Black equality – the disenfranchised population of unaccepted citizens – and inspiring action. In 1903 Du Bois described the 'Negro folk song – the rhythmic cry of the slave', as 'the singular spiritual heritage of the nation and the greatest gift of the Negro people'.[7]

In 1909 the Singers recorded 'Swing Low, Sweet Chariot', now held in the Library of Congress.[9] The song they had championed was to become the refrain of the civil rights movement during the 1960s, with its lyrics, which had referenced the nineteenth-century Underground Railroad, finding a new resonance

and traction in the late twentieth-century fight for racial equality and freedom from segregation.

The Fisk Jubilee Singers made the spiritual the first true and major cultural contribution of Black Americans, proving that the people subjugated through slavery were not only able to overcome their suffering but could also bring vast and tangible riches to a burgeoning national culture. They confronted racism and discrimination with courage, pride and dignity, and an unflinching belief in the power, relevance and reach of their music. The achievements and endurance of the Fisk Jubilee Singers are testament to their unique place in Black American history, while their songs, which transcended racial and geographical boundaries, have become some of the most influential and vital elements of modern musical culture the world over.

The Southern Syncopated Orchestra: Powerful Echoes of Memory

JULIAN JOSEPH

In 1919, helmed by eminent composer, violinist and bandleader Will Marion Cook, the thirty-seven-piece Southern Syncopated Orchestra set off from New York City to tour Europe. The Orchestra was a transformative mosaic of African and West Indian heritage, encapsulating the wide-ranging sonic palette of Black musical America. They performed thousands of concerts, travelling the length and breadth of Britain. Nothing like it had ever been heard before.

The 1920s saw American music, particularly ragtime and jazz, surge in popularity. Jazz marked a revolutionary departure in popular music. Jazz and the influence of African-American culture initiated a metamorphosis that broke down the barriers of established musical conventions, driven by syncopated rhythms and improvisation. Jazz also welcomed a new breed of musicians, democratising performance by inviting in amateur and creatively curious individuals – who may or may not have had formal training – to try their hand. Those driven by passion, innate talent, curiosity and joy thrived.

Even before that decade had begun, Europe and the UK resonated with a new musical vibration: the Southern Syncopated Orchestra (SSO). Beyond a mere ensemble, the SSO symbolised a transformative shift in musical temperament, signalling the dawn of the jazz era. Its music wasn't restricted to one genre; it was a symphony of gospel, classical, opera, folk and jazz. This ensemble profoundly influenced the

UK's music scene, its echoes resonating right up to the present day, enriching its legendary status.

At the heart of the SSO stood the eminent composer, violinist and bandleader Will Marion Cook (1869–1944). A prominent figure in the world of music and African-American musical theatre, Cook hailed from an intellectually gifted family. Both his parents were Oberlin Conservatory graduates, and his father further distinguished himself as one of Washington DC's pioneering Black lawyers, graduating from Howard University School of Law in 1871. This environment of academic excellence paved the way for Cook's flourishing artistic pursuits. His childhood years with his grandparents in Tennessee immersed him in the traditional melodies and sounds of his community, priming his ears and heart for a promising musical future. His formal musical education began at Oberlin Conservatory, where he studied violin. From there he went on to attend the Berlin Hochschule für Musik and the National Conservatory of Music of America in New York, whose director at the time was the great Czech composer Antonín Dvořák.

That Cook received this level of training as a member of the Black community was unprecedented. Anyone with Black skin faced racial prejudice and had their careers and potential for financial mobility severely obstructed. Although Cook aspired to be a classical soloist, racial barriers forced him to redirect his passion towards musical theatre, a realm where he was to leave an indelible mark.

This move meant that Cook acquired the skills that broadened his art, and opened up opportunities to work with key creative figures such as poet Paul Laurence Dunbar, with whom he produced stage works such as *Clorindy: The Origin of the Cakewalk* (1898). He also collaborated extensively with the vaudeville comedians George Walker and Bert Williams, and brought his irrepressible ambition to musical theatre, staging groundbreaking, full-length all-Black productions on Broadway. Cook's musical sophistication meant that he could imbue the sounds of his own culture – the African-American traditional melodies that he had grown up listening to – with contemporary musical styles.

Cook founded the New York Syncopated Orchestra in 1918, bringing jazz and ragtime to national and then, in 1919, international audiences, when the Orchestra changed its name to the American Southern Syncopated Orchestra. Cook took astute advantage of the appetite for jazz and Black American music that was growing across Europe, providing economic opportunities for his musicians and promoting their artistry on an international scale. By virtue of its diverse membership the SSO was not just about its performances; it was a movement that elevated perceptions of African-American artistry, combating racial prejudice through melody and rhythm.

With his unparalleled talent, training and vision, Cook brought together West Indians and African-Americans who could seamlessly blend European repertoire into music packed with the power of their own identity and culture. Comprising forty-six members – twenty-seven

musicians (including the prodigious Sidney Bechet on clarinet) and nineteen singers (including British vocalist Evelyn Dove and soprano Hattie King Reavis) – the Orchestra was a mosaic of African and West Indian heritage, encapsulating the wide-ranging sonic palette of Black musical America. The Orchestra showcased the musical evolution of Black Americans, blending classical elements with ragtime, blues, slave songs and the emerging sounds of jazz. It was completely original. Nothing like it had ever been heard before.

Starting in 1919, the SSO embarked on a hugely successful three-year European tour, arriving in the wake of the trauma of the First World War. Managed by George Lattimore, the ensemble delivered an astonishing 300 consecutive performances at London's Philharmonic Hall at 97 Great Portland Street (next to what is now BBC Broadcasting House), subsequently performing 1,300 times across England, Scotland and France. The Orchestra was lauded for its unique sound and vibrancy.

Their artistry led to an iconic performance at the Royal Albert Hall and a coveted invitation to play at Buckingham Palace for the Prince of Wales (later King Edward VIII), their reach extending from royalty to every walk of life.

That the jazz colossus Sidney Bechet was associated with the SSO also speaks volumes for its calibre. Bechet's technique was flawless. His melodic invention was utterly beyond that of his peers, and his contribution to modern jazz is such that he occupies an exalted place alongside Louis Armstrong as one of its greatest pioneers. Bechet was playing with the SSO aged just 21, and was to find the soprano saxophone that would redefine his musical voice in a shop in London while on tour with the Orchestra. At what would have been the start of his career, joining an orchestra like the SSO was a rare opportunity. Although the story of his time with the Orchestra is yet to be fully told, it must have been formative in creating the legend that he was to become, while his very involvement with the Orchestra gives us a valuable perspective from which to assess it and its significance as a jazz entity.

In 1921 tragedy struck. On 9 October the Orchestra was sailing to a performance in Dublin when their ship collided with two other vessels. The ensuing disaster led to the deaths of thirty-six people, nine of whom were cherished members of the Orchestra. Among them, the drummer Pete Robinson and vocalist Frank Bates from Barbados have been commemorated with English Heritage blue plaques at their former London homes in Vauxhall and Southwark. The surviving members displayed commendable resilience by completing their Irish tour, but the catastrophic event was to contribute to the Orchestra's eventual disbandment. Sadly, although the all-white Original Dixieland Jazz Band was the first jazz-sounding band to be recorded, in 1917, the SSO never found its way to onto record. The Original Dixieland Jazz Band could certainly emulate the style of great Black musicians like Jelly Roll Morton and King Oliver, but they could not represent the authenticity of their music. It is a loss to the history of jazz that we cannot hear the artistry of the SSO, but their impact on and contribution to the music is nevertheless undeniable.

The Southern Syncopated Orchestra remains emblematic in the annals of music history.

Its legacy, though marred by tragedy, offers a testament to the power of art to transcend boundaries, inspire generations and resonate through time. In the wide landscape of music, its story is a testament to the indomitable spirit of creativity and the enduring magic of melody. It stands as an early and sophisticated demonstration of a vision that brought something to the world which transcended prejudice and discrimination with excellence, that showcased the uplifting experience of a combination of Black musical traditions featuring the most innovative new music of the time: jazz.

When looking back at the story of the SSO it's hard not to ask what if: what if the tragedy at sea hadn't happened? What if Will Marion Cook had recorded the SSO? What if he had been able to really make a mark in American Black musical theatre? Perhaps the one thing I derive from his efforts, his training, ambition, his battles as a Black man against racial prejudice and social injustice, is his drive to create and showcase the brilliance of his people against almost impossible odds. Cook was a mentor to the great Duke Ellington and it's easy to imagine how the force

of his spirit, his achievement and his intelligence inspired Ellington's magnificence, whose impact and influence continues to nourish and enrich life and music across the planet, to this day.

The Southern Syncopated Orchestra represents the realisation of a democratic idea to champion the best and the highest quality of musical talent drawn from a diverse community. It proves that even in a society with massive discrepancies in opportunity, divided by racial injustice and social disparity, the good and the great can rise to the top. All jazz musicians like me owe Frank Bates, Pete Robinson and the SSO a debt of gratitude for shining their great light into our culture so we can radiate the echo of their memory back out again into the international vibration of all great music and musicians. The spirit of hope, resilience and positivity is the transformative power of music – in this instance, jazz – that unites us all. This at its heart is the legacy of the Southern Syncopated Orchestra.

OPPOSITE The Southern Syncopated Orchestra, outside the Brighton Dome, 1921. BELOW Inside the Brighton Dome. It was the first time a group of African-American and African-Caribbean musicians would perform at the Dome. They stayed on the coast for a month and later played a royal command performance for the Prince of Wales in Buckingham Palace.

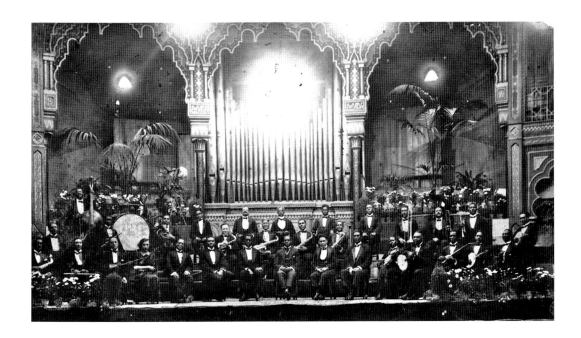

THE STAGE

'Jazz fans of the day learned to eat curried goat in the company of Caribbean musicians, and with Nigerians, it was fufu and hot pepper soup'

Val Wilmer

Ken 'Snakehips' Johnson: Snakehips Swing

STEPHEN BOURNE

Inspired by Cab Calloway, Guyanese dancer and swing bandleader Ken Johnson and his West Indian Dance Orchestra entertained London's wartime upper classes and fashionable elite in the Café de Paris, which tragically billed itself as the safest place to be during the Blitz.

In the late 1930s the British public witnessed the meteoric rise to fame of bandleader Ken Johnson, popularly known as 'Snakehips'. At first Ken and his West Indian Dance Orchestra were mainly known to the exclusive and fashionable elite of London who frequented sophisticated West End nightclubs. However, by the outbreak of war in 1939, audiences up and down the country were familiar with Ken and his Orchestra's swing music. They had successfully broken through to the mainstream of British entertainment with their BBC radio broadcasts. In the early years of the war the Orchestra, smartly dressed in white jackets, with the handsome, elegant Ken, six feet four inches tall, as their leader, provided a class act. In the world of music it was generally agreed that Ken was not a musician – a band member later recalled that he couldn't tell a B flat from a pig's foot![1] – but he had the gift of imparting his terrific enthusiasm for swing music to both jazz enthusiasts and the public. His nickname, 'Snakehips', has never been forgotten. After more than eighty years it is still mentioned in popular television shows, such as the BBC's *Strictly Come Dancing*.

Ken was born in Guyana but his middle-class parents sent him to England to be educated. They hoped he would work hard at his studies and train to become a doctor. However, in 1934, aged just 20, Ken visited Harlem in New York, where he saw the jazz giants Cab Calloway and Fletcher Henderson. This was a key element in Ken wanting to form his own swing band, even though his knowledge of music was extremely limited. Returning to Britain, in 1936, Ken's dream came true when the Jamaican trumpeter Leslie Thompson launched an exciting new swing band called the Emperors of Jazz. Thompson asked Ken to join them as a bandleader because he looked good and had charisma. Thompson later described Ken as a charming and vivacious young man: 'I took a liking to him. We had Ken out front – he was a tall, lean fellow, and he could dance. Ken didn't know any music but he could wiggle and waggle himself to the time of the music, and so keep onlookers amused and interested. Somehow he got his name put out there on the posters... he was such a nice boy, but he wanted money, and he got led off without being aware of the consequences.'[2]

In Britain the band was groundbreaking because it was the first to include Black musicians from Britain and the Caribbean. They included Leslie 'Jiver' Hutchinson (trumpet) from Jamaica, Carl Barriteau (clarinet, saxophone, piano) from Trinidad, and Joe Deniz (guitar) from Cardiff, Wales.

OPPOSITE Two images from *Picture Page*, featuring Ken 'Snakehips' Johnson, March 1938.

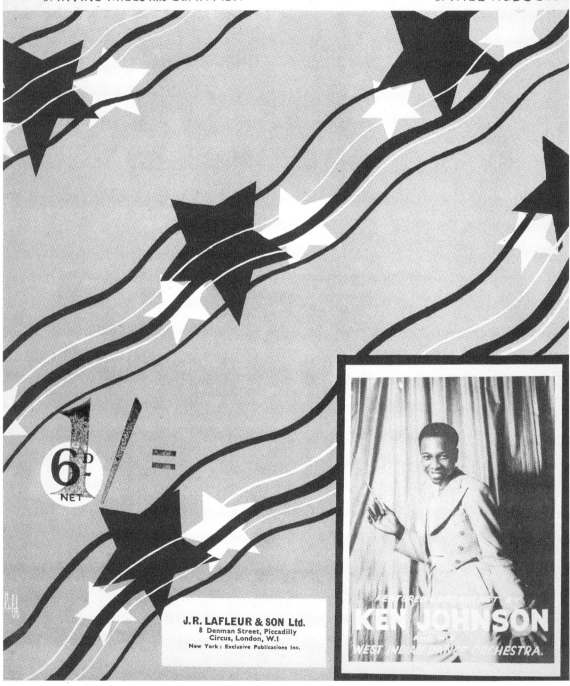

THERE'S SOMETHING ABOUT AN OLD LOVE

WORDS BY IRVING MILLS AND LUPIN FIEN

MUSIC BY WILL HUDSON

6ᵈ NET

1/- =

J.R. LAFLEUR & SON Ltd.
8 Denman Street, Piccadilly
Circus, London, W.1
New York : Exclusive Publications Inc.

FEATURED BROADCAST BY
KEN JOHNSON
AND HIS
WEST INDIAN DANCE ORCHESTRA.

Following Thompson's departure, Ken renamed the band Ken Johnson and his West Indian Dance Orchestra and he became the official 'front man'. Under his leadership, and with his extra-long baton, the band soon became the toast of London's West End. Ken's main achievement was to show that Britain could produce a Black bandleader as sensational as African-Americans such as Cab Calloway and Duke Ellington. The individual musical abilities of the band members combined to create a 'swing' sound that appealed across the board to jazz and swing enthusiasts as well as the general British public. In addition to live appearances, they reached a wide audience, with many radio appearances and superb recordings that included 'Snakehips Swing', 'Exactly Like You' and 'Tuxedo Junction'. They also enjoyed a long residency at the Café de Paris.

Everyone who met Ken commented on how kind and gentle he was. He always found something nice to say about everyone. Outside of music, he loved good food, wines and, above all, a cigar. Sailing was one of his favourite pastimes. Away from the bright lights, Ken was the lover of Gerald Hamilton. He was twenty years older than Ken and the younger man was amused by Gerald's Edwardian airs and malicious anecdotes. However, same-sex relationships for men were a criminal offence in Britain until the law was changed in 1967. This meant that gay couples like Ken and Gerald had to be very discreet or risk arrest and imprisonment.[3]

Ken had reached the peak of his popularity and the Café de Paris, situated underground, was advertised as London's safest nightclub. Saturday 8 March 1941 was one of the worst nights of the Blitz and an air raid was raging. Ken took to the stage at a quarter to ten, but five minutes later two high-explosive bombs crashed onto the dance floor, and one exploded in front of the bandstand. More than thirty people lost their lives, including young Ken. He was discovered without a mark on his body, his red carnation still in the buttonhole of his tailcoat.

Britain's first Black swing band was no more; its surviving members went their separate ways and joined other bands. In 1944 Leslie 'Jiver' Hutchinson formed his own band which included Joe Deniz. While he was alive, Ken Johnson's fame only lasted a few years, but he made a big impact on the British public, who mourned his tragic death. The fact that the name 'Snakehips' is still remembered is a testament to his legendary status in British show business.

Hutch: Not Just a Gigolo

AMAR PATEL

Too much is made of Leslie 'Hutch' Hutchinson's love life. What we should be talking about is how the trailblazing Grenadian cabaret star became the biggest entertainer in inter-war Britain.

It's 1932 and we are at the Malmaison club in London. Elegant diners engage in eager conversation. One by one their gaze turns to the suave gentleman with the tailcoat and Tinseltown smile, as he glides into his seat at the piano.

His diction is immaculate. There is a pomp and rapture in how he sings 'Close Your Eyes' – accenting certain words with vibrato while breathing romance and verve into others. His torso veers to the right, his eyes to the heavens.

His touch is precise. The left hand swoops across the keys with a showman's flourish. Then he launches into an agile solo and concludes with an impossibly high note. The well-heeled crowd applauds with genuine admiration. It's 1932 and this man is Black. Remarkable.

So much of what we hear about Leslie 'Hutch' Hutchinson revolves around scandal that the achievements are overshadowed. It reminds me of something Hanif Abdurraqib noted about Hutch's friend Josephine Baker in *A Little Devil in America*.[1] Like Baker, Hutch 'captivated and controlled' imaginations. It would be naïve to ignore the significance of race in this allure, an obsession with the 'exotic'. But what about ambition, talent, an ineffable something extra that makes the spell linger?

In Hutch's case, we should stop and consider what it took to reach the upper echelons of British society at the time, and to be holding court among smitten aristocracy, politicians and the Bright Young Things of the cabaret scene at a time of direct discrimination.

He would go on to make more than four hundred recordings and become the highest-paid entertainer in Europe for almost two decades. That takes more than sex appeal, social climbing or whatever else has been used as an anecdote for his existence. *Downton Abbey*'s Jack Ross he was not.

Long before arriving in England, Hutch had lived many lives. Born in 1900 in the Grenadian fishing port of Gouyave, he learned organ and piano at an early age. By 12 the prodigy could recite a piece of music after one listen. Two years later he won a scholarship to the capital, St George's. When he was 16, wealthy island residents sponsored Hutch to study medicine in the US but he spent more time in thrall to Harlem's nascent jazz scene. He learned the famous stride technique and was soon playing well enough to rival Fats Waller and Duke Ellington.

His father wasn't impressed and cut off his allowance. Hutch was penniless at one point and sleeping on a park bench, says biographer Charlotte Breese.[2] But you wouldn't have known it by looking at some of the fancy portraits that he sent back home. It was around this time that he married Ella Byrd and had Lesley, the first of several children by different mothers. He joined a Black band led by Henry 'Broadway' Jones. They often played for wealthy socialites such as the Vanderbilts, who introduced him to influential patrons.

In 1924, after a run-in with the Ku Klux Klan in Miami, Hutch fled to Paris, which was a haven at the time for Black performers like him and Baker, who arrived the following year. He began a residency at the Royal Box, a hip spot owned by Joe Zelli, and teamed up with cabaret personality Ada 'Bricktop' Smith.

Hutch became a protégé, close friend and lover of Cole Porter, recording cherished interpretations of standards including 'Let's Do It' and 'Begin the Beguine'. The Prince of Wales (later King Edward VIII) was a huge fan, along with Lady Edwina Mountbatten, who encouraged him to come to London where jazz, or 'syncopated music', was sweeping the nation.

Impresario C. B. Cochran had seen Hutch in Harlem and invited him to play in a lavish production of the Rodgers and Hart musical *One Damn Thing after Another*, which featured costumes by Coco Chanel. Confined to the orchestra pit, he craved the limelight and would take centre stage at Café de Paris in after-show cabaret performances.

Hutch was soon the talk of the town, playing exclusive parties at Chez Victor and building a national profile with the touring revue. He signed a recording contract with Parlophone, soon clocking up a succession of hit songs including 'High Hat', 'I'm a Gigolo' and 'Ain't Misbehavin'.

The spectre of prejudice remained despite his popularity. Here was a hysteria-inducing superstar who would arrive at nightclubs like Quaglino's with a white piano strapped to his chauffeur-driven car, only to be later directed to the servants' entrance of the Mayfair residences

where he entertained. Hutch turned his attention to the variety circuit, progressing from smaller theatres to three thousand-capacity venues such as the London Palladium. Up north, Glasgow's *Evening Times* hailed 'the cabaret idol of the exclusive set who has blossomed out as a variety star'.[3]

Breese says the further Hutch pushed out into the provinces the more discrimination he experienced. For many working-class audiences, he would have been the first Black performer they had seen on stage.[4] He adapted by expanding his repertoire beyond the sophistication of Porter and Noël Coward, and showcasing his musicianship.

Life in certain quarters of London was hedonistic and Hutch was in the thick of it. There were reputed affairs with actress Tallulah Bankhead and matinee idol Ivor Novello. His most notorious liaison, which opened some doors and closed others, was with Mountbatten.

It was through her that he ended up teaching Queen Victoria Eugenie of Spain's children to play piano and dance the Charleston.

Mountbatten and Hutch seemed unconcerned about what shocked who around Mayfair. But after *The People* newspaper alleged 'a scandal which has shaken society to the very depths'[5], the royal family tried to save face by forcing the Mountbattens to sue for libel. The case was settled in their favour in 1932 and Hutch paid the price. He took no further part in the Royal Variety Performance or Royal Command Performance. Lord Beaverbrook's papers tried to erase him (but the *Sunday Express* just couldn't forget Hutch in a 1935 fantasy variety programme). The BBC dropped him until 1937, when they broadcast *The Melody Man*, with Hutch starring as crooning waiter Paul Sanders. Perhaps the release of 'These Foolish Things' the previous year had reminded them, and everyone else, what they'd been missing.

He was among the first to offer to entertain troops as well as anxious crowds taking shelter in the Underground during the Blitz (with little recognition, like adopted Brits Adelaide Hall and Elisabeth Welch). The air raid siren would ring out and he would declare, 'Let's sing our answer to that,' as he began 'There'll Always Be an England'.

After a period in the wilderness of austere post-Second World War Britain, Hutch enjoyed a resurgence. 'The Famous British Radio and

LEFT Music sheet for one of Hutch's popular inter-war songs: 'That's My Desire'.
OPPOSITE Record label for 'These Foolish Things'.

Gramophone Star' lifted spirits at venues such as the Hackney Empire and Blackpool Palais de Danse. Hutch offered romance, escapism – life in the moment.

Back at a revived Quaglino's, he was the centre of attention once again in front of a new set that included Princess Margaret. Another famous guest, actor James Mason, funded a series of 78s for Hutch, which got him signed to Decca Records.

Hutch also appeared on TV and radio several times into the 1950s, a treasured elder statesman of showbiz, still important enough to be (lovingly) parodied by the likes of Kenneth Williams and Max Wall. But he struggled to command the same rapport with audiences as he did in his heyday, reduced to taking gigs in unsuitable venues. As the decade closed – variety halls morphing into bingo/bowling alleys and TV programmes challenging the intimacy of live performance – his star began to fade.

Hutch made a brief return to New York in 1958. It was as if he was trying to find his place all over again. He toured parts of the crumbling British Empire such as Kenya, India and Hong Kong, searching for his crowd. But music tastes had changed as bands like the Beatles began to set the tenor of the times.

By this point he was drinking heavily and gambling. The one-time millionaire had to sell his home of more than forty years in Hampstead (spot the blue plaque on Steeles Road). When Hutch succumbed to pneumonia in 1969, only forty-two people attended his funeral: a meagre farewell for someone Breese calls 'one of the towering figures

of British entertainment'. The biographer spent around ten years researching his life and speaking to thousands of people. In her eyes, 'He was distinctly a man of courage and one of experiment and he was determined to conquer, in a way that was very unusual for the time.'[6]

Drive aside, he had extraordinary magnetism, and the unmatched ability to win people over. 'Hutch's charm and talent for being what people wanted him to be caused many social barriers to melt,'[7] she adds. This freedom came at a cost to others.

Hutch was a flawed, self-absorbed figure whose indulgences left his children somewhere between curious and clueless about the man behind the celebrity. He rarely spoke about his wife Ella. The arrival of other West Indians in the UK in the 1950s dismayed him, apparently.

But as an artist, respect is due. In researching this story, I found almost no interviews with him. Perhaps it's all there in the music, the place where Hutch shone brightest. 'I always try to "live" the song,'[8] he once said. That he did. And they became his songs. All of them.

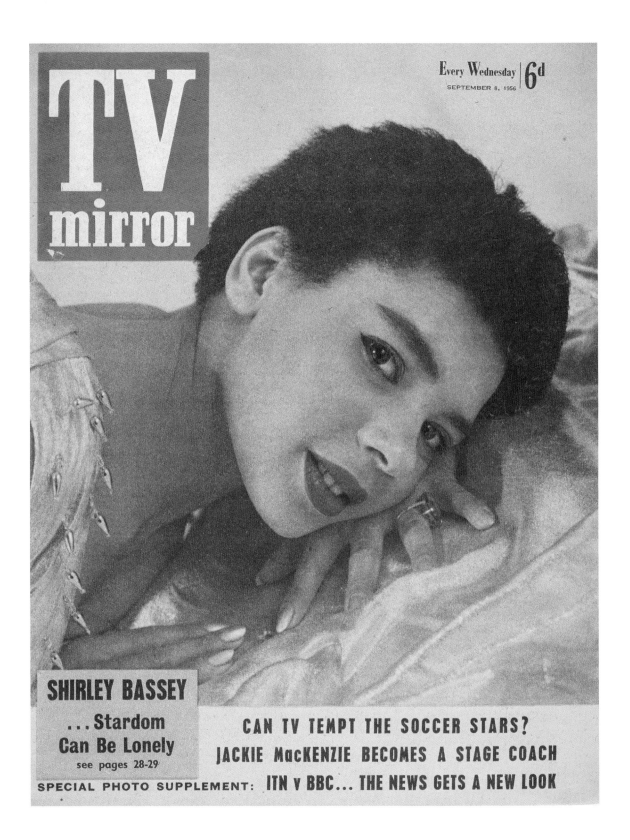

Every Wednesday | 6d
SEPTEMBER 8, 1956

TV
mirror

SHIRLEY BASSEY
...Stardom
Can Be Lonely
see pages 28-29

CAN TV TEMPT THE SOCCER STARS?
JACKIE MacKENZIE BECOMES A STAGE COACH
SPECIAL PHOTO SUPPLEMENT: ITN v BBC... THE NEWS GETS A NEW LOOK

ABOVE Shirley Bassey on the cover of *TV Mirror*,
8 September 1956.

Sophisticated Ladies: Winnie, Cleo and Shirley

STEPHEN BOURNE

The emergence of popular Black women singers and entertainers in British television, from 1936 to 1964.

Some Black celebrities have claimed that when they were growing up there were no Black people to be seen on British television. For instance, in *Rising to the Surface* (2022), Lenny Henry says that when his parents came to this country, there were no Black people on TV: 'This was in the days of black-and-white television. They should have called it "white-and-white television". If a Black person did come on, viewers thought there was something wrong with the set... The only Black people you saw on television in the 1960s were the Black and White Minstrels.'[1]

However, this was not the case, as demonstrated by the British Film Institute and the BBC when they funded a groundbreaking research project which pieced together the history of Black people in British television from its beginnings in the 1930s. This resulted in a two-part television documentary called *Black and White in Colour*, first shown on BBC2 in 1992. The project revealed that there were many more programmes featuring Black people in the early years of British television than had been anticipated. Themes explored in the 1950s and 1960s included decolonisation, the settlement of the Windrush generation in post-war Britain and mixed marriages. Racism was hardly absent, but the BBC's *Black and White Minstrel Show*, which ran for twenty years, coexisted with some outstanding programmes across all genres including two documentary series, *The Black*

Man in Britain 1550–1950 (BBC2, 1974) and *The Fight Against Slavery* (BBC2, 1975) and several editions of BBC2's innovative access programme *Open Door* (1973–83).

Indeed, as the research project discovered, the story began at the birth of television itself, in 1936, and unearthed a Black presence in the BBC's pre-war service, which was broadcast live from the Alexandra Palace studios in North London from 1936 to 1939. And yet, almost without exception, this 'secret history', though thoroughly researched until the project ended in 1992, has been ignored.

In the pre-war years, before the outbreak of the Second World War interrupted the BBC's television service, Black entertainers were given a high profile. Collectively they made an important contribution to British music and variety programmes. Some of the pre-war shows were influenced by the Black Broadway musicals and revues of the Harlem Renaissance. After the First World War, everyone wanted to shed their inhibitions and party. This led to the 1920s being labelled the Jazz Age. And it was the extrovert jazz singer Nina Mae McKinney who later became the star of two of the earliest BBC television shows: *Ebony* (27 February 1937) and *Dark Laughter* (5 June 1937).

Other Black women from the worlds of jazz and blues who were featured in pre-war BBC

television shows included the Americans Mabel Scott, Eunice Wilson, Alberta Hunter and Valaida Snow, and the London-born Dinah Miller. In 1939 the versatile Adelaide Hall, who had been a jazz innovator alongside Louis Armstrong and Duke Ellington during the 1920s, was seen with her Nigerian accompanist Fela Sowande in live transmissions from the Florida Club, her popular West End nightspot. Around this time, Adelaide made her home in London, joining another American expatriate, Elisabeth Welch, who had already settled here in 1933. Elisabeth's soft, lovely voice had already endeared her to the British public on BBC radio, including her own series, *Soft Lights and Sweet Music*. So, when she began her television career at Alexandra Palace, she was already known to many viewers.

After the war, the BBC reopened its television service on 7 June 1946. Shortly afterwards, on 18 July, its popular radio series *Serenade in Sepia* was transferred from Broadcasting House (radio) to Alexandra Palace (television). Its stars were the Trinidadian folk singer Edric Connor and the gifted London-born contralto Evelyn Dove, who had studied at the Royal Academy of Music. Other singers who were featured in the early post-war years were Minto Cato, Ida Shepley, Mable Lee, Maxine Sullivan and Josephine Baker, who made two appearances in 1948. In 1951 the Trinidadian calypsonian Mona Baptiste, who was one of the few women to arrive on the *Empire Windrush* in 1948, was featured in *Calypso Quarter*. Before the existence of videotape no technology existed to record for posterity any of these early appearances, though Nina Mae McKinney and Elisabeth Welch were featured in a couple of BBC demonstration films which have survived. The earliest known BBC telerecording (a live performance filmed from a television screen) dates from 1947: it is Adelaide Hall in an extract from *Variety in Sepia*, singing, dancing and playing her guitar – six minutes of pure magic.

ABOVE Winifred Atwell, 1957. She was a regular on television from her first appearance in 1946. OPPOSITE Adelaide Hall in the BBC's *Variety in Sepia*, 1947. It was filmed live in Alexandra Palace, London.

The Coronation of Elizabeth II in 1953 boosted the popularity of television hugely, and it spread to over fifty per cent of the population. A second channel, ITV, began broadcasting in 1955, aiming to be less highbrow – and thus more popular – than the BBC. By this time the Trinidadian pianist Winifred Atwell, popularly known as 'Winnie', had become one of Britain's most loved and accessible entertainers. In the era after the Second World War, her cheerful presence and her honky-tonk music brightened many homes. Winnie's records sold in their millions. She was the first Black recording artist to reach number one in the British 'pop' charts, and the first British artist to have three million-selling hits. Winnie was a successful Black woman but off-stage she was a shy, retiring person who transformed herself into a glamorous extrovert whenever she took to the stage with her piano. She was one of the first Caribbean artists to become a show business celebrity in an era when Black performers in Britain had more chance of success if they were American, and it was television that helped Winifred to become a household name in the 1950s.

ITV's output included many entertainment shows like *Sunday Night at the London Palladium* and these helped to nurture home-grown stars like Shirley Bassey, who had been born in Cardiff and enjoyed a meteoric rise to fame in the 1950s. Shirley made numerous television appearances on both channels. These gave her a high profile with the British public and helped to boost her record sales with such hits

In some ways Cleo was more highbrow than Shirley and never had the chart-topping success of her Welsh counterpart, but this did not prevent her from succeeding with the British public.

as the light-hearted 'Kiss Me, Honey Honey, Kiss Me' and the haunting ballad 'As I Love You', which reached number one in the charts in 1959. In 1957, when she visited Cardiff, the BBC produced a music special about the event called *Shirley Comes Home*.

A British-born singer, Cleo Laine made a number of television appearances in the 1950s. Cleo was extremely versatile and television showcased her as a stylish jazz vocalist as well as a supreme interpreter of popular songs. In some ways she was more highbrow than Shirley and never had the chart-topping success of her Welsh counterpart, but this did not prevent Cleo from succeeding with the British public.

Meanwhile, American entertainers kept coming. Talents as diverse as Eartha Kitt, Sarah Vaughan, the gospel singer Sister Rosetta Tharpe, opera's Leontyne Price and two Hollywood legends – Dorothy Dandridge and Lena Horne – all guest-starred on British television in the 1950s. Even the legendary jazz singer Billie Holiday, on one of her rare visits to Britain, found time to make a television appearance here in *Chelsea at Nine* in 1959.

By the 1960s a wide range of music and variety programmes had featured Black artists. However, racism was never far away. When Eartha Kitt and Cleo Laine were included in the all-star line-up for the BBC's 1962 Royal Variety Performance, they shared the bill (but not the stage) with the Black and White Minstrels, then at the peak of their television fame. But two years later, 1964 proved to be an extraordinary watershed year for Black women singers in British television.

1964 started with the show *Freedom Road* (ITV, 5 February), an impressive documentary with a concert format in which an outstanding cast of Black singers performed songs of protest from the days of slavery to the civil rights movement. Highlights included Cleo Laine's 'Strange Fruit', Pearl Prescod's 'We Shall Overcome' and Madeleine Bell's 'What Did You Do in School Today?', a duet with George Webb. The folk singer Nadia Cattouse also gave an emotionally charged dramatic account of Elizabeth Eckford's attempt to enter a white school in Little Rock. Nadia was also part of the 'folk revival' of the 1960s, and as such appeared in a number of television shows, often accompanying herself with a guitar.

Freedom Road was praised for its originality and won several international awards including the Golden Plaque at the Berlin Television Festival. Cleo Laine made another appearance in an innovative and critically acclaimed special: ITV's *Lyrics by Shakespeare* (6 April), in which she sang the Bard's words and sonnets set to music by several composers, including Duke Ellington and her musician husband John Dankworth.

By the end of the 1950s there had been a revolution in popular music with the rise in popularity of rock and roll. While artists like Winifred Atwell experienced a massive drop in their record sales, a new phenomenon surfaced: 'all-girl groups'. They were young, beautiful and glamorous icons for a new generation who

ABOVE Cleo Laine on *This is Your Life*, 1962.
She was married to the musician John Dankworth,
who also appeared on the show.

wanted music that broke away from the old styles, and excited them. Throughout 1964, several pop music programmes, such as ITV's *Ready Steady Go!* and the BBC's *Top of the Pops*, showcased all-female groups such as the Ronettes, the Crystals and the Supremes.

But the older stylists still found regular work. On the evening of 22 April, the sublime Ella Fitzgerald had her own music special on ITV, called simply *Ella*. She was also featured on the cover of that week's edition of the popular ITV listings magazine *TV Times*. When Sister Rosetta Tharpe returned to the UK she appeared in ITV's *The Blues and Gospel Train* (19 August), and Mahalia Jackson, one of America's finest gospel singers, appeared on BBC2 in *Mahalia Jackson Sings* (5 September).

The presence of so many Americans headlining their own shows on British television is best summarised by Ralph Harris, who produced *Lena* (ITV 1 November), a stylish music special starring Lena Horne. He explained that there were no opportunities for Lena or indeed other American stars, such as Ella and Eartha, to have their own music shows on American television at that time.[2] On this visit to the UK, Lena also topped the bill in the Royal Variety Performance, which was then televised on BBC1 on 8 November.

ABOVE The opening of singer Shirley Bassey's record shop in Hampstead, London, 17 November 1962. Bassey is shown with Sixties pop idols (left to right): Danny Williams, Shane Fenton and Jess Conrad. OPPOSITE Ron Moody and Millie 'My Boy Lollipop' Small in *The Rise and Fall of Nellie Brown*, 1964.

In 1964, music tastes had rapidly changed again, with the Beatles and the Rolling Stones practically revolutionising the music industry, but there was always room for artists like Shirley Bassey to wow audiences with songs like 'Goldfinger' from the popular James Bond movie.

In spite of the presence of the Black and White Minstrels, it is evident that some British television programme makers respected Black artists, embraced diversity and had an inclusive approach to television, unlike their American counterparts. This made it possible for artists like Cleo, Shirley, Ella and Lena to be showcased at their best in their own one-woman shows. However, it was rare for a singer or entertainer to have an original television musical created for them, but in 1964 the writer Robert Gould did just that when he made such a thing possible for his friend Elisabeth Welch, by then a television veteran.

Gould called it *The Rise and Fall of Nellie Brown* and he told the story of Selina, a young Jamaican girl who journeys from her loveless home in Liverpool to search for Lillabelle Astor, her famous relative who was known as the 'Broadway star who took London by storm'. In London, Selina discovers that Lillabelle is bedridden and cannot be visited. She is protected by her housekeeper, Nellie Brown, played by Elisabeth. The story ends happily when Nellie reveals that *she* is Lillabelle, masquerading as the star's housekeeper. For the role of Selina, a 17-year-old Jamaican called Millie was cast. Earlier in the year, this popular ska singer almost made it to the top of the British pop charts with 'My Boy Lollipop', and was featured singing the song in many television shows, but she hadn't acted before. Her lack of experience

and training posed a problem until Elisabeth Welch did everything she could to make her feel at ease. Elisabeth and Ron Moody, who was also in the cast, were, said Gould, 'thoroughly professional, generous to a fault, and it showed in their performances. To their credit they did not overshadow Millie at all, and everything worked out well. It is a lovely production and I am very proud of it.'[3] *Nellie Brown* was light-hearted, captivating and had some catchy songs. It proved to be a Christmas treat for television viewers when it was shown in ITV's *Play of the Week* series on 28 December. It was a fitting finale to a vintage year in Black British television.

A recording of *Nellie Brown* has survived but, from the 1930s to the 1960s, few examples of the appearances of *any* artist ever reached the archives: transmitted live, they vanished forever. It is depressing to think about what has been lost but, in addition to Adelaide Hall's 1947 appearance in *Variety in Sepia*, some of the titles that *have* survived include most of the 1964 programmes mentioned in this chapter: *Freedom Road*, *Ella*, *The Blues and Gospel Train*, *Mahalia Jackson Sings*, *Lena* and the Supremes on *Top of the Pops*. 1964 was an outstanding year of television treasures which should be revived and given the credit that is due to them.

Ambrose Adeyoka Campbell: West African Rhythm Brother

VAL WILMER

Ambrose Campbell's West African Rhythm Brothers were resident at the legendary Abalabi, a Nigerian nightclub in Soho's Berwick Street. His musicians were steeped in cross-cultural traditions they had picked up on the West African coast and on the high seas and in London they created fresh, new music that quickly became a magnet for London's most creative musicians.

Willie Roachford was standing at a bus stop in Edgware Road. It was two o'clock on a Sunday morning, it was cold, and Roachford was a long way from his Barbados home. A Nigerian musician, travelling home from a West End gig, saw this forlorn figure and stopped his taxi. A Londoner since the war years, he knew the all-night bus had stopped running. He also knew what it was like to be lonely and cold and offered the newcomer a lift. It was only then that he spotted the clarinet case Roachford was carrying. By the end of the journey he'd invited the youngster to share his room and also to play with his band.

You probably know Roachford, uncle of the Hackney-born singer-songwriter. He used to be seen on TV in the Kronenbourg adverts: the seasoned saxophonist applauding a young white pretender. Back in 1954, though, he was a novice – especially in Campbell's sphere.

Campbell's West African Rhythm Brothers were resident at the Abalabi, a Nigerian nightclub in Soho's Berwick Street. There was nothing grand about the place, but the basement was a far cry from the band's first London home, a hole-in-the-wall dive with penny gambling and a crate of brown ale on the floor.

London was riddled with bomb sites when the Alababi opened. The winters were cold, with snow that settled. In the dense fogs that were commonplace, the traffic often ground to a standstill, and when you blew your nose there was soot in your handkerchief. Forget about American fashions – men still dressed pretty drably and women made their own clothes.

The Nigerians were part of the scene, coping with rationing, the reality of coal-fires and sensory deprivation, finding substitutes for familiar foods until rare moments when visiting seamen materialised, bringing a taste of home. Yet out of hardship these musicians brought joy, their rhythms and light-hearted sound winning a new audience from people sick of wartime restrictions. They became local heroes, many years before Fela Kuti picked up his horn.

To play with the Brothers, Roachford abandoned a rigid police-band training he had undertaken. He knew nothing of the music but he 'Africanised' his clarinet, pitching it sharp to give his solos more edge. It fitted well and a few days later he was back with a friend. This was Harry Beckett, another Barbadian musician, who was to become a leading jazz trumpeter. Campbell was delighted. He had wanted a flute player, but with his horn tightly muted Beckett sounded just fine. The Barbadians stayed just over a year, that simple act of friendship

ABOVE The West African Rhythm Brothers rehearsing for Les Ballets Nègres in London, 14 October 1947. Third and fourth from left are the band's co-founders, Ambrose Campbell and Brewster Hughes.

and curiosity on Campbell's part leading to a productive and inventive relationship.

For Roachford and 'Bucketty', the bandstand was their schoolroom. Fifty years ago, English people learned lessons at the Abalabi too. Journalists, politicians, debutantes went there to dance to West African highlife and came away with much more. To Beckett, it was 'a novelty thing, the only club of its kind',[1] a warm, womblike setting where lazy, languid rhythms brought ease. The musicians dressed Latin American style, in matching Cuban blouses, and while Campbell sang in Yoruba, their dreamy and mellow polyrhythms developed around him. Brewster Hughes, a former schoolteacher from Ibadan, played laid-back lead on electric guitar.

The first time most Londoners saw Ambrose Campbell was VE Day: 8 May 1945. War in Europe was over and the whole city came out to celebrate. Men and women danced in the Trafalgar Square fountains and embraced complete strangers, and in the middle of Piccadilly an anonymous group of Nigerians arrived carrying drums and guitars. A little bruised and battered maybe – and far, far wiser than when they left Lagos to go to sea – they had learned to survive in war-torn Blighty and wanted to add three cheers in person. For these time-serving veterans of a difficult period, that day marked another step in the journey to becoming what they themselves called 'Englishmen'. To a newspaper reporter noting their presence they were 'West Indians'.

Soho in the 1950s has captured the imagination of London's chroniclers. In the 'official' version, skiffle and jazz, the 2i's café and rock and roll rub shoulders easily with figures such as the painter Francis Bacon. Seldom are they acknowledged to have rubbed shoulders with Africa. But they did.

Let's set the scene. Strolling through the Soho of the period you'd have found Black men wearing zoot suits in Gerrard Street where jazz clubs included the Zan-Zeba – King Timothy sang about it – and where Jamaica's 'Jumping' Sam Walker played booting tenor saxophone after hours. In Cambridge Circus you'd have run across a Nigerian percussionist carrying a big drum across his back. In Archer Street, where Africans and West Indians were among those seeking musical employment, you might glimpse glamorous Trinidadian singer Mona Baptiste on her way to cabaret fame. Had you followed any one of these figures, you could have ended up with your first taste of 'colonial cuisine'. Jazz fans of the day learned to eat curry goat in the company of Caribbean musicians, and with Nigerians, it was fufu and hot pepper soup. To English folk raised on a diet of meat and two veg, the significance of learning about cultural difference in this way cannot be overestimated.

In this milieu, Jamaicans Dizzy Reece and Joe Harriott played jazz with Britain's top modernists while Kitchener and Young Tiger, both from Trinidad, sang calypsos for traditionalist delectation. At the heart of it all – and to the pleasure of both sides – was the ubiquitous Ambrose Campbell, an African and the son of a preacher man. His musicians were steeped in cross-cultural traditions they'd picked up on the West African coast and on the high seas – but their own music developed in England. What other highlife bands then commonly used a piano? Campbell's did, and people related well to his inclusiveness, featuring some West Indians and some Europeans, as the WARB became part of the era's spiritual backdrop.

OPPOSITE Ambrose Campbell (left) looks on while Prince Buster poses for the *I Feel the Spirit* recording session, playing a talking-drum and wearing Campbell's *agbada*, a Yoruba gown.

A pragmatic man who experienced most things that life can throw at you, Ambrose enjoyed living day to day and shunned setting his sights too high or trying to get rich.

Campbell recalled the band's origins. It began in the misery of the blackout, in pubs and front rooms where, he said, 'we gather together and buy a couple of bitter and Guinness. I pick my guitar and start playing and a couple of boys would join in – just to cheer ourselves up.'[2] Soon afterwards, though, they were on television, accompanying Britain's first Black ballet company before travelling with them to Paris. Stage dancers sought them out when learning new steps, and in a period when Afro-Cuban rhythms were popular they were also hired by jazz clubs for 'The New Kick'. Anthropologists recognised their importance. In 1952 a critics' poll named them as significant for the future of British jazz.

Ambrose was well loved and respected by London's jazz community. Musicians went to the Abalabi and Club Afrique, its successor, to learn at the source – one perceptive listener likened the collective improvisation to Louis Armstrong's Hot Five band. Saxophonists Tubby Hayes and Ronnie Scott visited; years ago, Scott told me: 'Ambrose was a bit special, an expert in African music, a musicologist.' Kenny Graham, leading his own Afro-Cubans, was a regular but Phil Seamen, the most African of all English drummers, was Campbell's number one fan. He partied with musicians and their friends and passed on what he learnt – as the late Ginger Baker would have told you.

Although he played both guitar and percussion in London, Campbell started out singing in a choir at home in Lagos with his school friends. He dabbled on guitar but when the band was launched he was more at home singing or playing the tambourine. Ade Bashorun,

his bongos player, gave him guitar lessons but it wasn't until he studied with guitar guru Lauderic Caton that he concentrated on playing the instrument seriously.

Just as Ambrose knew anyone who was anyone, his own importance as a cultural figure was recognised by an astonishing array of people, from playwright George Bernard Shaw to Prince Buster (also a Campbell). Shaw was a sponsor of Les Ballets Nègres, with which the WARB were first heard in public, and although a vegetarian himself, he allegedly had chicken cooked for the band. Ambrose met his namesake at Melodisc Records and lent him the talking-drum and *agbada* seen on the cover of Prince Buster's debut album *I Feel the Spirit*.

Relying on the nobler aspects of human nature was part of Campbell's charm, although his capacity for trust could also be his downfall. Living at his own pace, he was often moved on – most landlords were not overkeen on midnight drumming – until taking up residence in Knightsbridge with a wealthy admirer, who was the son of a lord.

A soft-spoken man of great dignity, if he liked you, Ambrose called you 'my brother', 'my sister', regardless of race. His Yoruba name was Oladipupo Adekoya but among his friends he was 'Rosie', the name he'd adopted as a music maker in Lagos to protect his family's reputation.

All the bandsmen loved names, a necessity in Africa where names acknowledge both ancestry and personal qualities. Brewster Hughes was no exception. Already an accomplished guitarist when he joined the group, he became its spokesman. Abiodun Oke, Ignatius Oke or Ernest Henry Hughes had a string of aliases with which to puzzle officialdom. To the Black community he was 'Battling Brewster', a *nom de guerre* from his boxing days, but in England he became known as a tough guy who carried a gun. When leadership disputes arose between him and Campbell, Hughes formed the breakaway Nigerian Union Rhythm Group, later the Starlite Tempos.

Campbell and company established themselves against all the odds. They created a new African music but have been overlooked in paying homage to Franco, King Sunny Ade and Fela Kuti. With the piano of Adam Fiberesima – the ubiquitous 'Adams' of the discographies – and his Caribbean horns, Campbell established a pattern that others followed.

For English people growing up in the shadow of wartime deprivation, this 'sunshine' music was just what was needed. The atmosphere at the Abalabi and Club Afrique, and the warmth and friendliness of their African clientele, contrasted favourably with the restraint and stiff upper lip that got the country through a horrendous war but which, for some people, left something missing. Ambrose captivated everyone who heard him, and for many, his music – and life in the clubs – filled that gap. As a young English schoolteacher put it, 'I just loved it, the gaiety of it. It was sweet, an appeal to the soul. And the rhythm – compared to the English quickstep! It was very, very melodious and I really loved it, different and new.'[3]

In 1972 Ambrose Campbell did a disappearing act that left friends and admirers bemused. Record producer Denny Cordell, a long-time admirer, instigated the move. Cordell persuaded Campbell to join him and Leon Russell in Shelter, at their Los Angeles-based production company and studio. But with the studio awaiting

completion Russell took Ambrose on the road. It was fun for a while but when the partners split acrimoniously, Campbell was stranded. He continued to tour with Russell, who named Campbell as his spiritual adviser.

There were precedents for his involvement with American music – country music is not unknown in West Africa, where the singer Jim Reeves was a favourite – and elements of country can be heard on 'Sing the Blues', the WARB's first recording. Russell introduced Campbell to other musicians with whom he recorded as a percussionist, most notably alongside Bonnie Raitt on the Leon Russell/Willie Nelson million-seller, 'One for the Road'.

Among his many claims to fame is membership of an exclusive club that includes Louis Armstrong, Mark Twain and Dave Swarbrick. When Campbell's death was announced in Lagos, a three-minute silence was held in tribute, forcing him to fly out from the US to demonstrate that he was still on the planet. Small wonder then that when no one heard from him for years some Nigerian old-timers refused to believe the man was alive and well and living in Plymouth with his daughter – and with a gold record for that Russell/Nelson collaboration hanging on his wall.

Ambrose Campbell died in 2006, the year that Honest Jon's released the third volume of their acclaimed *London Is the Place for Me* series – it was appropriately dedicated to the music of Ambrose Adekoya Campbell. A pragmatic man who experienced most things that life can throw at you, he enjoyed living day to day and shunned setting his sights too high or trying to get rich. Ambrose never stopped writing and making music.[4]

Thanks to Ambrose Campbell, Lauderic Caton, Ade Bashorun, Harry Beckett, Pete Ford, John Jack, Ademola Johnson, Ilario Pedro and Jennifer Sikuade.

Number 50 Carnaby Street: A Unique Space and Place in London's Black Musical History

PAUL BRADSHAW

Carnaby Street rose to fame in the 1960s. A popular haunt of aspiring mods and chart-topping bands – the Beatles, the Rolling Stones, the Kinks, the Who – the street sold bold, new concepts of style announcing that a brand-new, post-war generation had arrived. The Swinging Sixties delivered a genuine sense of creative anticipation and that vibe was projected out into the country by a hip, monochrome TV show, aptly titled *Ready Steady Go!*

However, a decade earlier the shadow of post-Blitz London remained, and Carnaby Street was a famously shifty enclave of soot-stained buildings housing workshops, warehouses and tailors. In among this industry were a number of late-night establishments and 50 Carnaby Street hosted quite a few.

From 1936 it was the location of the Florence Mills Social Parlour, named after the Black actress Florence Mills and run by the charismatic Amy Ashwood, first wife of Marcus Garvey, the radical Jamaican-born Black nationalist and founder of the Universal Negro Improvement Association. It was Garvey who initiated the venture with Sam Manning, a pioneering calypsonian from Trinidad. It was part restaurant, part social centre, part jazz club, and a location where Black intellectuals and Pan-Africanists such as C. L. R. James, George Padmore, T. Ras Makonnen and the future president of Kenya, Jomo Kenyatta, could meet and reason.

In the 1940s it became the Blue Lagoon Club. It was said that guns had to be handed in at the door with your coats. The Blue Lagoon was superseded in 1950 by the short-lived 'modernist' Club Eleven. It took its name from the eleven aspiring bebop devotees (including John Dankworth and Ronnie Scott) who had united to create a space to explore the music of their idols Charlie Parker and Dizzy Gillespie. A drugs raid on the club quickly earned them headlines in the national press, and for a short time after that it continued to open six nights a week and act as a hub for any jazz musician working in the West End.

In 1952 the club was acquired by the former chef from the Caribbean Club, a Jamaican called Gus Leslie. He renamed the venue the Sunset Club and created a night spot that, despite the absence of a liquor licence, provided a home for a host of Windrush refugees and Black American servicemen on leave.[1] The Sunset was essentially a cabaret club and the Russ Henderson Steel Band – the first steel band in Britain, formed in late 1952 – played their first gig there.

In the mid-1950s the house band was led by the boisterous Trinidadian tenor-man Al Timothy. Apparently, the saxophonist's 'Jump Jive' repertoire was – to the ears of the proprietor at least – preferable to that of another short-lived resident and fellow Jamaican, Joe Harriott (see page 105). Maybe the avant-garde leanings of the now legendary alto saxophonist led him to stray, all too often, from the hits of the day.

OPPOSITE A dramatic moment from the dance floor at the Sunset Club in Soho, London, December 1951.

Additionally, the influential, multi-talented Trinidadian musician Rupert Nurse was a bandleader at the club from 1954.

Though a little rough and ready, the food was good and the Sunset regularly attracted visiting American artists who were performing at the nearby Palladium, such as Nat King Cole. Jazz greats such as Louis Armstrong, Lionel Hampton and Sarah Vaughan all visited the club.

Sadly, not long after Leslie finally secured a drinks licence in 1957, and was poised to move the club to the next level, the landlord refused to renew his lease.

In 1961 the club re-opened as the Roaring Twenties and was hosted by the soundman/DJ and – sometimes – bouncer Count Suckle. The music was rhythm & blues, soul and ska/bluebeat and live bands that played included the Beatles, the Rolling Stones and Georgie Fame. When Suckle left to open the Q Club, Lloydie Coxsone of Sir Coxsone Sound System took over. Coxsone returned to number 50 in the late 1970s/early 1980s, when it was renamed Columbo's.

In 2024, number 50 Carnaby Street is a Levi's clothing shop.

Kitch!

ANTHONY JOSEPH

Trinidadian Calypso Monarch and the Road March King, Aldwyn Roberts, aka Lord Kitchener, remains forever the face and the voice of the *Empire Windrush*.

The calypsonian emerges to face the mic and camera eye. He wears a wide-brimmed trilby, fawn brown, pinched at the crown, a polywool suit in indigo blue with wide lapels and padded shoulders. Black tie, criss-cross patterned with white near the knot. The camera operator sets his tripod on the roof of a car on the jetty below, and zooms the image of the calypsonian down to earth from the deck. What appears to be close in his lens is actually distant and this is why the film stock cannot capture the fine details of the calypsonian's face: the rigid bone, the cat-eyed blink. Instead, the image he records is dark and simple...

The now iconic footage of Lord Kitchener and his fellow travellers arriving at Tilbury in June 1948 frames them as a homogeneous group, arriving as blank pages waiting to be written. We are told (incorrectly) that '500 Jamaicans' have arrived, 'citizens of the British Empire coming to the mother country with good intent... discouraged but full of hope'. But by his arrival at Tilbury, Lord Kitchener had been composing and performing calypsos for almost two decades.

After losing both parents by the age of 14, he roamed as a troubadour through rural Trinidad, singing at wharves and waterworks for stevedores and labourers, and later as a chantwell or lead singer in the Sheriff masquerade band. He had left his hometown Arima in 1943, moving to Port of Spain, Trinidad's vibrant capital and Mecca of calypso, to pursue a profession in kaiso. One night, before performing at the Victory Calypso Tent, the veteran calypsonian Growling Tiger poured a nip of rum over his head and christened him Lord Kitchener. By 1947 he had been crowned calypso champion of Arima five times, and had established a reputation among his peers for innovation and lyrical skill. So when John Parsons asked him if he was 'really the king of calypso singers,' Kitch wasn't lying when he said, 'Yes, that's true.'[1]

In the *Windrush* footage, then, we should see Kitch as an urban griot, standing on the liminal gap between the Caribbean and England, serenading, or as we say in Trinidad, 'mamaguying' England. Not quite in England yet, he sings on the border. And even though he had never left the Caribbean before, he knows that London is the place for him, his town to run. The song is not a humble or naïve homage, but an assertion – colonialism's persuasion alone cannot account for it. When Kitch sings 'London Is the Place for Me', his throat is full of the revolutionary potential Louise Bennett-Coverley identifies as 'colonization in reverse'.[2]

In his novel *The Lonely Londoners*, Samuel Selvon makes serious humour of this liminal position, with Sir Galahad and Moses and 'the boys' occupying bedsits and basements deep within the city: inside, yet simultaneously as unwanted guests, socially excluded from English society.

And furthermore, how Kitchener know that London is the place for him?

OPPOSITE Lord Kitchener, seen here with steel pans in the background, *circa* 1960. He arrived on the *Empire Windrush* in 1948 with Lord Beginner and Lord Woodbine.

How he could say that London great when he know what colonialism is? Well, that is the art of the calypsonian, the zwill in the mad bull tail, while everything happening between waist and knee it have a long blade hiding in the lyrics and the melody.

What he wanted most was to hear his voice on the shellac, to see the stylus wind across the Wax… and we there behind him in the band, playing music like beast. Rupert Nurse there, Fitzroy Coleman. Lord, we shaking up like jumbie in that basement. And I look up through the one window it have in there and see the leaves leaving the big crab-apple tree, outside in the Manor grounds. It was autumn. I hearing motor car passing in the distance, train, people going about their business, and I say to myself, 'But wait, like England don't know we here at all.'[3]

In 1934, Portuguese-Trinidadian businessman and impresario Edouardo Sa Gomes paid for the Roaring Lion and Atilla the Hun to travel to New York to record for the Brunswick-ARC label. These were the first foreign recordings by Trinidadian calypsonians, the beginning of the commercialisation of calypso. But in seeking to broaden calypso's appeal and profit, the melody and 'tropical' rhythms of the music became the focus of marketing campaigns, not its political topicality and subversive undercurrents. Nevertheless, by the time of Kitchener's emergence in the mid-1940s, the recording industry had become an integral aspect of the genre's success.

From 1938, Sa Gomes himself recorded local calypsonians at his Radio Emporium in Port

KITCH AND COLLECTIVE Lord Kitchener (second from left) recording for Melodisc Records, with arranger Rupert Nurse (first left) and studio band including Al Timothy (tenor saxophone, far right), Russ Henderson (triangle), George Tyndale (tenor saxophone), Shake Keane (trumpet) and Clinton Maxwell (bongos), London, *circa* 1953.

of Spain. There are rumours that Sa Gomes recorded two early sides from Kitchener but these apparently were never released. In a 1995 interview Kenny Cooper, the Mighty Bomber, says that Sa Gomes offered to record him and Kitch after seeing them perform in the Old Brigade Tent, but when they went to the recording studio they met Lion and Atilla, who objected, asking Sa Gomes, 'How you could record these men? These is young singers. They now start. How you could give them record? So what about we, the older fellows?'[4]

Kitchener's first commercial recordings would be in London in late 1948, when he recorded eight songs at RG Jones Studios in Morden for Renico Simmons' Hummingbird label. Simmons, a Trinidadian boxer who had lost all seven of his professional fights, seems to have set up Hummingbird solely to record Kitchener. The recordings were aimed mainly at the Trinidadian and Jamaican markets in the UK and Caribbean. In the early 1950s Kitchener recorded for Lyragon and Parlophone. He played a starring role in a seminal Parlophone session at Abbey Road on Monday 30 January 1950. This session – the first major-label calypso recording in the UK – was well documented. In the following week's *Melody Maker* it was reported that the session was supervised by the jazz and skiffle producer Denis Preston and also featured a cocktail party with celebrity guests invited to 'witness' the recording. Lord Kitchener and another calypsonian and *Windrush* passenger, Lord Beginner, each recorded two songs that afternoon, accompanied by Cyril Blake's Calypso Serenaders. Kitchener recorded 'Underground Train' and 'Nora', while Beginner recorded 'Dollar and Pound' and 'Matrimony'. The band

comprised Freddy Grant (clarinet), Cyril Blake (guitar), Fitzroy Coleman (guitar), Brylo Ford (quatro), Neville Boucarut (bass) and 'Dreamer' (congas) – musicians who would continue to feature on hundreds of calypso recordings throughout the next decade.

On 15 March 1951 Kitchener made his first recordings for Emil Shalit and Jack Chilkes's Melodisc Records, an independent label based on Earlham Street in Covent Garden. Kitchener's recordings for the label between 1951 and 1962 are what consolidated his reputation as calypso's ambassador to Britain and the art form's greatest composer. The range of subject and style is wide: the call-and-response battle cry of 'Trouble' and the horn and percussion driven 'Alphonso in Town', which features the legendary Nigerian bandleader Ambrose Campbell, were militant jams designed for the road. There is the ribaldry of 'Too Late Kitch' and 'Tie Tongue' and potent comments on race politics such as 'If You're Brown', 'If You're Not White You're Black' and 'Africa My Home', written in Manchester, where he moved to in 1953. It was in Manchester that Kitchener became associated with Pan-Africanist activist and entrepreneur Ras Makonnen, who was to have a lasting impact on Kitchener's political growth.

In 'Nora' and 'Food from the West Indies' Kitch articulates the displacement and diasporic longing of his fellow West Indians. In 'No More Taxi' and 'Drink a Rum' they begin to build a home in the cold. Throughout, Kitchener is also able to keep up with events in Trinidad, remaining relevant and topical and sending music there, each year, just in time for carnival.

I used to beat pan for a side on Henry Street, a steelband call 'Dem Boys', and I remember Kitchener used to send down songs every year

Kitchener's recordings between 1951 and 1962 are what consolidated his reputation as calypso's ambassador to Britain and the art form's greatest composer.

from England. 'Mango Tree', we beat that. 'Old Lady' get beat. 'Nora', we beat that. But that man sing a calypso in England, in 1955, and he send the calypso down and it reach Port of Spain on Carnival Sunday. Imagine that. So when we in the barrack yard on Henry Street one of the boys come and he say, 'Ai, Kitchener now send down a 45.' And he bring it out with a lil' record player for we to hear it.

And on that record, one side had a tune call 'Constable Joe', about a Grenadian that paint a mule in Cumuto so he could thief it and all this kind of stupidness. But on the other side was a tune call 'Trouble in Arima', and when we hear that tune we bawl! And as pan men we want to play it.

But was Carnival Sunday eh, fellas painting costume, some painting pan, getting ready for jour vert in the morning, and my band captain was there in the yard, and he stand up and say, 'Who could play it? Allyuh feel allyuh could play it? You could play it Scholar?'

I say, 'Yeah man, I could play it, but what about the tune we done prepare to play?'

He say, 'Forget that.'[5]

By 1962 calypso's reign as the pre-eminent Caribbean music genre in the UK was being overtaken by ska, and Kitchener began a protracted path back home to Trinidad, moving there permanently in the mid-1960s. In Trinidad the grandmaster continued his reign, winning the Road March title eleven times – still an unbeaten record – and the coveted Calypso Monarch title in 1975.

He was recording until 1999, a few months before he died, three weeks before carnival.

1953: When we reach the studio and come to record, Rupert Nurse will just hand you the chart, and if your mouth slack or your knowledge fail, when the chart say blow G you blow B Rupert will just watch you cut-eye and smile to make you know he hearing. If you a semitone out he know, that mean don't do it again. He's a old army band man, he don't mess around. Al Jennings bring him from Trinidad with the All Star Band in 1945. 1–2–3 and he watching you frankomen in you face. Play B again, see what will happen.

Men like Willie Roach and Joe Harriott who like to play free had to straighten up and fly right. Because when it come to recording, Kitchener don't like to waste time, tape or money. He will hum the bass how he want it or he will play it himself if he have to. Sometime them English musician, their rhythm twist, they can't play calypso. It have a way Kitch does want the bass to rally with his voice. He play bass on 'My Wife Nightie' same way; the bass man couldn't swing the rhythm right, so Kitch say 'Gimme the damn bass lemme try.' And the try was the take.

But it was amazing to see, when he come in the studio, and he set up a tune, and he have pieces of paper, microphone there, how he loosen the tie, push back the hat and he going to sing. He will take a run through first and when he feel it ready he say, 'Right, let's do it.' And we leggo music – bram! An' he would kick out his foot and dance like he on stage, like he forget he in the studio.[6]

The Stage / Kitch!

101

Rockin' With Ray

VAL WILMER

The uptempo rhythm & blues of the Ray Ellington Quartet heralded the birth of British rock and roll.

Eight years before *Blackboard Jungle,* before jiving in the aisles gave teenagers a bad name and rock and roll a good one, Britain had a rock and roll band of its own. What they played was not strictly rock music, of course – the new white name for the uptempo blues had yet to be coined – but in 1948 the quartet led by drummer/vocalist Ray Ellington was just about the hippest band in the land.

You can forget about Bill Haley. Nine years before the chubby man with a kiss-curl got off the train at Waterloo and British teenagers gawped as the Comets' saxophonist Rudy Pompelli lay on his back and wailed, their elder siblings had already come face to face with a spectacle just as exciting but musically superior. The Ellington Quartet – German pianist Dick Katz, bassist Coleridge Goode and either Lauderic Caton or Laurie Deniz on guitar – were accomplished jazzmen, conversant with bebop. That meant they could improvise at will or play pretty, as well as rock the joint. And if the Comets' Al Rex grabbed the headlines by throwing his double bass around the stage, Jamaican born Goode beat him into a cocked hat when he jumped over his instrument while continuing to offer some of the finest bass-playing ever heard in this country.

Coleridge Goode, who continued to play into his nineties, often derived pleasure from

the first-time listener's reaction to his carefully preserved tapes of the group. Professionalism and attention to detail were crucial, he said. 'It had a freshness, I suppose, and a liveliness that other bands didn't have. And it was very rhythmic in contrast to the general ballroom thing. The quality of the instrumentation was good – what we did was certainly above the average dance band player's abilities.'[1]

Ray Ellington (1916–1985) became a household name in the 1950s on radio's anarchic *The Goon Show*. A natural comedian who exploited his robust voice and physique, he jousted weekly with Spike Milligan, Peter Sellers and Harry Secombe and sang dodgy numbers such as 'The Irish Were Egyptians Long Ago'. As a Black man he was the butt of some dubious jokes, yet importantly, he was also one of the team and an equal.

Before all that, however, the Ray Ellington Quartet topped popularity polls. Inspired by the comedy and interplay of Slim and Slam, the elegant Nat King Cole Trio and above all, Louis Jordan's rhythm & blues, they offered comedy and rhythm in equal amounts. And their musical significance was far greater than has been acknowledged. When they played such numbers as 'Five Guys Named Moe' or the zany 'I Didn't Know the Gun Was Loaded', they were helping to create a climate of receptivity for rock and

ABOVE The Ray Ellington Quartet, 1948: (left to right) guitarist Lauderic Caton, bass player Coleridge Goode, piano player Dick Katz, and bandleader and drummer Ray Ellington.

roll and the blues – and for Black popular music to come. 'The Three Bears', a CD compilation of tracks from 1948–9, confirms this claim.

The story began when South Londoner Harry Brown hung up his cloth cap and swapped his workman's muffler for a snazzy silk scarf. The year was 1933 and Duke Ellington had just visited London. Teenager Harry and the rest of the music world were agog. The youngster – son of an African-American comedian and Russian mother – had just started playing the drums and like most of his peers was uninspired by the 'milk-and-water' local jazz of the day.

Harry Brown responded to the Duke as a *soignée* and substantial role model. He changed his name to Ray Ellington and forged a reputation as a singing drummer, working in Soho nightclubs and dives. Serving in the RAF during the war, he made plans to form his own band.

With the guidance of Black American choreographer Buddy Bradley, he collared the house trio from a Piccadilly club called the Caribbean. In guitarist Lauderic Caton, a Trinidadian inspired by Lonnie Johnson and

Charlie Christian, he featured one of the first local musicians to amplify the instrument. Amplifiers, still an unknown quantity, were unpopular but Coleridge Goode – like Caton, an electronics enthusiast – employed one too. He also used a microphone to good effect while singing along with his bowed bass solos in the manner of Slim Gaillard's partner Slam Stewart. Then, when Caton dropped out due to ill health, his place was taken by the even more fleet-fingered Laurie Deniz, a Black Welshman who was responsible for some of the group's more boppish musical arrangements.

According to Goode, the dance halls, where most young people spent their leisure time, were the key to the quartet's early success. Three years after the war the wind of change was being felt. Staid ballrooms began to bow to the inevitable. Jiving was still banned in some places, but in certain halls, such liberating dancing became hailed as a feature.

Post-war youth was ready for something new. Presenting the band during the changeover of bands at such venues was a stroke of genius. With Black faces still a comparative rarity, dancers could not keep their eyes off the quartet. They loved Caton's beard and Ray's pencil moustache – and that was before the guys had played one note of music. With his looks, personality and stunning physique – it was said that when he had a suit made, he told the tailor to take the padding *out* of the shoulders – Ellington had plenty going for him, even without his stomping, fast-moving music. The quartet travelled the land, treading the boards and rocking the joint. They topped popularity polls and their records sold in quantities. They played for the dancers.[2]

Remembering Joe Harriott

SHARON O'BRIEN

On a cold January day in 1973, I stood at the graveside in a Southampton churchyard as the interment took place of the greatest musician I had ever heard and known: Joe Harriott. Only forty-six, he had died prematurely from spinal cancer, robbing music of an eclectic, visionary genius – and me of the man I loved.

To many people, Joe was an enigma: often misunderstood and way ahead of his time. Born in Kingston, Jamaica, he settled in London in 1951. You could find him playing with early bebop exponents such as Tony Kinsey's drummer-led band. He soon became resident musician at the Flamingo Club, playing stints with the likes of Ronnie Scott, Harry South, Laurie Johnson and later Stan Tracey. He played at the 100 Club with his group, the Quintet, which by the 1960s gained critical acclaim. Having built a solid reputation, he joined forces with bassist John Hart and ran the Country Club in Belsize Park, London, where he appeared with many star guests.

Joe sat at the heart of London's musical innovation. Most of his contemporaries, who seldom kept pace with his drive for perfection and ability to push musical boundaries, paid homage to the roots of all music.

I asked him once where his inspiration came from. His reply was that he was simply a vessel able to receive all that was given by a higher power. Joe saw his later free-form jazz as akin to the work of an abstract painter, and working with eminent poets such as Laurie Lee, Dannie Abse, Jeremy Robeson and John Smith challenged his approach to enhancing their words.

Outside of music Joe had many interests: politics, racial justice, bar billiards, philosophy, modern art and Indian food. His home in St John's Wood, where he lived for much of his time in Britain, was sparsely furnished: a photograph of Charlie Parker, a variety of records and books, his alto saxophone (which he named Betsy), packets of Rico 5 reeds, shoe-cleaning kits and copies of the *Melody Maker*.

Though he never returned to Jamaica, his principle of remaining a Jamaican never wavered. When Jamaica gained independence from the UK in 1962, Joe opted to have a Jamaican passport, which frequently caused problems as he crossed borders in mainland Europe.

And yet he had come a long way from the young child who had ended up in Alpha, the Catholic orphanage in Kingston, Jamaica, where he learned to play many instruments, read music and compose, alongside other fabulous musicians such as Harold McNair, Eddie Thornton and Rico Rodriguez, all of whom followed in Joe's footsteps and settled in Britain.

Joe left behind a huge body of recorded work; he is remembered as co-leader of the very successful Indo-Jazz Fusions, and for his work with Chris Barber and his groundbreaking *Free Form* album. But to me his exciting uptempo solos and beautiful ballad playing are what remains.

Joe was a passionate, kind, articulate and proud Black man. He was very spiritual and courageous, and remained optimistic even as his life was drawing to a close. I might never have become a nurse or a politician fighting for racial justice and representation for the Black community had I not known and loved Joe.

Today he is rightly revered by generations of jazz lovers. For me he will always be loved and admired for all he gave to me, even though it was more than fifty years ago.

JOE AND CO. The Joe Harriott Quintet on stage at the Marquee Club, London, 1961. (Left to right) Pat Smythe, Shake Keane, Joe Harriott, Tommy Jones and Coleridge Goode.

MALIK AL NASIR

While Beatlemania swept across the world, the Black roots of the Fab Four's music and their relationship to the Caribbean and African musicians in the Toxteth neighbourhood of Liverpool 8 were, at one point, literally airbrushed out of the picture.

When the *Empire Windrush* docked in Tilbury in 1948 with 492 migrants from the Caribbean, answering the call of a decimated post-war Britain that was struggling with labour shortages, the melodies of Trinidadian calypso, Jamaican mento, jazz and Dominican mambo came with them. While the famous Pathé footage of calypsonian Lord Kitchener singing 'London Is the Place for Me' continues to characterise their arrival, what remains lesser known is that 'Kitch' was flanked by two other calypsonians from 'the Young Brigade': Lord Beginner and the 19-year-old Lord Woodbine.

Like many on the *Windrush*, Harold Adolphus Phillips, aka Lord Woodbine, was a former serviceman. After lying about his age, the 14-year-old Phillips was recruited to the RAF and stationed in Britain during the war. He returned to his native Trinidad in 1948 and was immediately drawn to the volatile, outspoken and competitive community of calypsonians and pan men. It's thought that Woodbine earned his moniker due to a calypso that revolved around Woodbine cigarettes and after participating in

Lord Kitchener's prestigious calypso tent he earned a spot in 'the Young Brigade'. Together with Kitch and Beginner they set off to perform in Jamaica where, after six months, they boarded the *Empire Windrush* bound for England.

Upon docking in Tilbury – after some talk of the *Empire Windrush* being diverted to Kenya – Woodbine was forced to bed down in the 'Deep Shelter' in Clapham South. This was an underground bunker left over from the war, which was part of a network of dosshouses. This was a time when British landlords posted 'No blacks, no dogs, no Irish' in their windows. Leaving London behind, he briefly worked as a machinist in Wellington in Shropshire before heading off to Liverpool in search of his wartime sweetheart Helen (aka Ena) Agoro.

He had met Helen in the 1940s while playing music with other RAF servicemen at the Jokers Club in Liverpool 8 – an area that boasted around forty clubs within a two-mile radius. Once back in Liverpool, Woodbine recruited her to his band, the Cream of Trinidad. They married in 1949 and settled in the Toxteth area, where they raised a son and seven daughters. Alongside his musical career during the 1950s Phillips worked as a railway engineer, carpenter, decorator, gardener, builder, electrician and lorry driver.

Woodbine was a singer and a songwriter who played guitar and tenor pan. Along with fellow pan player Gerry Gobin they earned a place in UK musical history by forming – in 1955 – the very first professional steel pan orchestra in Britain: the All-Steel Caribbean Band. They

OPPOSITE Lord Woodbine with early members of the Beatles at the Arnhem War Memorial in the Netherlands, during a journey to Hamburg, 16 August 1960. (Left to right) Beryl Williams, Lord Woodbine, Stuart Sutcliffe, Paul McCartney, George Harrison, Pete Best.

would play regularly at Jokers, as well as in the basement of Allen Williams' Jacaranda – a coffee-bar complete with espresso machines and a jukebox. Woodbine's first club, Palm Cove, had opened in 1952. Three years later it was sold to Roy Stephens – a fellow musician and one of three brothers from Jamaica who had also arrived on the *Empire Windrush*. In fact, Stephens bought the whole block of five shopfronts and then demolished them to build his own Palm Cove Club where his band, the Caribbeans, were residents.

In among the Caribbean and African regulars of Woodbine's clubs and gigs was a group of scruffy, teenage Scouse lads: Paul McCartney, John Lennon, George Harrison and Stuart Sutcliffe. Both Lennon and Sutcliffe were at the Liverpool College of Art. This was the era of skiffle and emerging rock and roll, but McCartney and Lennon were mesmerised by the music of Woodbine's All-Steel Caribbean Band which featured musicians like Otto, Everette Everidge, Slim and Bones, and Gerry Gobin. Other influential Toxteth musicians were the Somali-Irish guitarist Vinnie Tow and Guyanese guitarist Zancs Logie. According to one local promoter,

ABOVE Queue down Matthew Street to enter the Cavern Club, Liverpool, *circa* 1963.

Through Woodbine, the Silver Beetles/Beatles performed as a backing band for strippers at their New Cabaret Artists Club and got to play on Monday nights at the Jacaranda.

ABOVE The Chants – who later became the Real Thing – at the Cavern Club, Liverpool, 1964; view from the back of the stage.

he witnessed Tow showing John and Paul the major–minor seventh chord progressions in Chuck Berry's music, while Zancs Logie was another willing and very visible teacher. He remained proud of how he'd taught Lennon to play his instrument.

Woodbine was busy promoting newcomers arriving in Liverpool, such as Derry Wilkie and the Seniors. He was keen to create a music scene where people could cross-fertilise musical ideas across the racial divide. In 1958 Woodbine took on managing the Jacaranda Club for Alan Williams. Lennon et al. would come to the club to bum food off Woodbine and offer to do odd jobs. Through Woodbine, the Silver Beetles/Beatles performed as a backing band for strippers at their New Cabaret Artists Club and got to play on Monday nights at the Jacaranda as well as at the New Colony Club. Woodbine effectively became their unofficial manager/promoter. However, due to his colour he struggled to get bookings and Alan Williams stepped in to help. On the advice of Gerry Gobin, who had taken the Royal Caribbean Steel Band to play in Hamburg, Woodbine and Williams organised for the Beatles to follow them. It was 1960 and the gruelling experience of playing over one hundred nights at the Indra Club and the Kaiserkeller forged the Beatles into a different band, one that was destined to take the world by storm.

When Little Richard, along with a young Billy Preston, performed at the Tower Ballroom in New Brighton, Wallasey on Friday 12 October 1962 the Beatles, who were now managed by Brian Epstein, were on the undercard. Also in the house was a host of young, Black Liverpudlian artists and Little Richard fans including Ramon 'Sugar' Deen and the Shades/the Harlems/

the Valentinos), Joey Ankrah (the Shades/the Chants) and Derry Willkie (the Seniors).

It was after this encounter that Paul McCartney invited the Chants, a Black doo-wop group featuring the late Eddy Amoo (who would later find global success with the Real Thing) to the iconic Cavern Club in Liverpool. Due to the club's racist door policy, which prevented Black and white teenagers being in the same space, they were forced to wait outside the Cavern until the afternoon session had emptied out. Once inside the deserted club, the Chants took to the stage to deliver a vocal harmony version of Gene Chandler's 'Duke of Earl'. The Beatles lost their minds. John Lennon took to the piano to work out the chords and before they knew it the Beatles were rehearsing with the Chants in Joey Ankrah's cellar and backing them on stage. Though Epstein had managed the Chants for a while, he had little time for this collaboration and as soon as the Beatles blew up, he dropped them from his roster.

In 1962, the Beatles' recording career was poised to take off. Ironically, it was at Woodbine's New Colony Club that George Harrison asked Ringo Starr to join the Beatles. In response to the sacking of Pete Best, Woodbine's daughter Carol Phillips declared, 'If my dad would have known the Beatles were kicking drummer Pete Best out of the band, I think he would have had something to say about it.'[1] After speaking to Pete Best, Carol added, 'Pete said, "I loved your dad, he was like a father figure to us. I think if he'd have known what they were going to do he would have said, 'No! No! No!'"' Best humorously added, 'John Lennon – Genius, Paul McCartney – Genius, George Harrison – Genius, Ringo Starr – Drummer!'[2]

Boom, Boom, Boom, Boom...

RICHARD WILLIAMS

Delving into the roots of the British rhythm & blues explosion that heralded the Swinging Sixties and gave birth to generation of raw, blues-based young bands that took the world by storm.

It was a virus of a very benign variety and the first to catch it were the young musicians whose elders – the members of what they called 'rhythm clubs' – had gathered in the 1930s to study and discuss the recordings of King Oliver, Louis Armstrong and Jelly Roll Morton, establishing the pattern of an obsession. Their successors, the first post-war generation, were a mixed lot, including an Old Etonian ex-guardsman (trumpeter Humphrey Lyttelton); the child of a Hertfordshire insurance statistician and a school headmistress (trombonist Chris Barber); the son of a classical violinist (singer and banjo player Lonnie Donegan); and the guitarist Alexis Korner, a refugee from wartime Europe whose father was an Austrian Jew and whose mother was of Greek, Turkish and Austrian ancestry.

Out of the traditional jazz bands in which they played came an offshoot called skiffle, and out of skiffle came British rhythm & blues. Not necessarily in a straight line, because that's not always how music develops, but with a clear lineage and common heritage. And the blues was becoming the universal language. Lyttelton had a surprise pop hit in 1956 with 'Bad Penny Blues', built on a barrelhouse piano riff. Barber used his popularity to bring Muddy Waters and Sister Rosetta Tharpe over from the US as his guest artists, introducing his young audiences to

the real thing. Donegan sang Leroy Carr's 'How Long, How Long Blues' and borrowed 'Midnight Special' from Lead Belly's repertoire. Korner and his harmonica-playing friend Cyril Davies formed a band called Blues Incorporated which became a seedbed for the whole scene.

For the next generation, born during or just after the war, it was like adopting a new language – one that seemed somehow more natural than their own. For Eric Burdon in Newcastle-upon-Tyne, John Mayall in Macclesfield, Brian Jones in Cheltenham, Van Morrison in Belfast, Mick Jagger and Keith Richards in Kent, Christine Perfect and Steve Winwood in Birmingham, Rod Stewart in Highgate, Eric Clapton in Surrey and Tony McPhee in Lincolnshire, to achieve a mastery of the blues – the latest version of the real blues, meaning the big-city rhythm & blues of John Lee Hooker, Howlin' Wolf and Jimmy Reed – was to serve an apprenticeship that bound them together and provided the platform for everything that was to follow.

The annual package tours by great blues artists became an institution, allowing audiences at the Fairfield Halls in Croydon, De Montfort Hall in Leicester and Manchester's Free Trade Hall to hear the likes of Sonny Boy Williamson, Lightnin' Hopkins, Sugar Pie DeSanto, Sleepy John Estes and Memphis Slim in a concert environment as unlike the rent parties and fish fries in which many of them had served their own apprenticeships as could be imagined. What did a Muddy Waters or a John Lee Hooker really make of the experience of being worshipped by throngs of white teenagers an ocean away from their homeland at a time when some

ABOVE American gospel musician Sister Rosetta Tharpe on Wilbraham Road Station in Manchester, England, filming the Granada Television special *Blues and Gospel Train*, 7 May 1964.

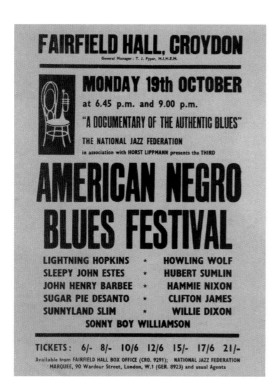

FAIRFIELD HALL, CROYDON
General Manager: T. J. Pyper, M.I.M.E.M.

MONDAY 19th OCTOBER
at 6.45 p.m. and 9.00 p.m.
"A DOCUMENTARY OF THE AUTHENTIC BLUES"
THE NATIONAL JAZZ FEDERATION
in association with HORST LIPPMANN presents the THIRD

AMERICAN NEGRO BLUES FESTIVAL

LIGHTNING HOPKINS	✶	HOWLING WOLF
SLEEPY JOHN ESTES	✶	HUBERT SUMLIN
JOHN HENRY BARBEE	✶	HAMMIE NIXON
SUGAR PIE DESANTO	✶	CLIFTON JAMES
SUNNYLAND SLIM	✶	WILLIE DIXON
	SONNY BOY WILLIAMSON	

TICKETS: 6/- 8/- 10/6 12/6 15/- 17/6 21/-
Available from FAIRFIELD HALL BOX OFFICE (CRO. 9291); NATIONAL JAZZ FEDERATION
MARQUEE, 90 Wardour Street, London, W.1 (GER. 8923) and usual Agents

LEFT American Negro Blues Festival, 1964.
OPPOSITE English singer, rhythm & blues and jazz musician Georgie Fame (second from right) performs live with the Blue Flames, including Phil Seamen on drums (left), at the Marquee Club in London, 1964. His 'Yeh Yeh' single was released at the end of 1964 and hit number one in the charts in January 1965.

states would not allow them to share a water fountain or a public swimming pool with their white fellow Americans? They were pleased by the phenomenon, of course, and by the fees and royalty cheques that came with it, but none of them ever really said how it felt, deep down.

Is it odd, bizarre even, that young white people from all over Britain – many of them from the middle classes – suddenly decided half a century ago in large numbers to reject their own culture, whether it be that of the music hall or the opera house, and to adopt instead the accents of the Mississippi cotton fields and the Chicago stockyards, singing songs that had their origins in plantations, penitentiaries and back-country juke joints? However strange it might seem now, at the time it felt the most natural thing in the world to lend your best friend your precious Muddy Waters *At Newport 1960* album so that they, too, could learn how to play guitar and sing to 'I'm Your Hoochie Coochie Man' and 'Got My Mojo Working'.

For a while it felt like a shared secret. You had to know the passwords to gain admittance

to this half-hidden world. The records and the information were not easy to come by. But that soon changed. When the blues purist Brian Jones persuaded Mick Jagger and Keith Richards to join him in the Rolling Stones, the interest in rhythm & blues was turbocharged. They were still singing the songs of Jimmy Reed and Bo Diddley, but with the kind of sex appeal that quickly turned them into pop stars. It was partly to do with looks: the handsome young Eric Clapton attracted a devout female following while performing the songs of Elmore James and Freddie King with John Mayall's Bluesbreakers.

Clubs all over the country started featuring rhythm & blues bands: Club a'Gogo in Newcastle, the Twisted Wheel in Manchester, the Mojo in Sheffield. The twin temples of the movement in London were both in Soho's Wardour Street. The Marquee, opened by the man who had founded the very popular National Jazz and Blues Festival in 1961, featured the Stones, the Yardbirds, the Pretty Things, the Downliners Sect and Manfred Mann – the bands that, loosely speaking, owed an initial allegiance to the guitar-based Chicago blues. Down the street was the Flamingo, with a very different vibe, owing more to jazz and hipster culture, where bands with Hammond organs and horn sections like Georgie Fame's Blue Flames and Zoot Money's Big Roll Band played songs from the repertoire of Ray Charles, James Brown and Mose Allison at all-night sessions to crowds that included West Indian immigrants and Black US servicemen.

For the white musicians and their audiences there was also a first experience of sharing the moment with Black musicians. Ronnie Jones from Springfield, Massachusetts sang with Blues Incorporated, as did Herbie Goins from

Ocala, Florida, who also led his own fine band the Nightimers, featuring Harry Beckett from Barbados on trumpet. The Jamaican trumpeter Eddie 'Tan Tan' Thornton and the Ghanaian conga player Nii Moi 'Speedy' Acquaye were members of Georgie Fame's band. Mike Falana from Nigeria played trumpet with the Graham Bond Organisation.

By this time certain promoters had spotted the commercial potential of bringing over American soul and rhythm & blues performers to tour the club circuit, meaning that audiences could see the likes of Little Stevie Wonder, Martha and the Vandellas, the Ike and Tina Turner Revue, T-Bone Walker and many others at close quarters. Some white kids even found their way into the shebeens – the (mostly) clandestine clubs in places where there were substantial West Indian populations. There the American soul-jazz sounds of Jimmy Smith and Jimmy McGriff were mixed with Jamaican dance music of Prince Buster and the Skatalites.

Even the Beatles had played their part. They were never a blues band – their journey from skiffle had come via the rock and roll of Buddy Holly – but they helped to popularise the Motown sound before it even had a name. The inclusion of covers of Barrett Strong's 'Money (That's What I Want)', the Marvelettes' 'Please Mr Postman' and the Miracles' 'You've Really Got a Hold on Me' on their first few albums demonstrated that they, too, were fluent in the language of rhythm & blues, allowing its raw emotional directness to undercut the image of beaming moptops in matching suits that was so carefully maintained by their manager throughout their initial rise to global fame.

For white teenagers in the UK, and then for white kids in France, Germany and the US – and just about everywhere this side of the Iron Curtain – the exposure to the sounds of Black America in the first half of the 1960s changed everything: not just the music on the radio and in the clubs but the way people spoke and felt more spontaneously, with a new sense of freedom – albeit a freedom that had come, when you thought about it, from someone else's slavery.

THE FRONTLINES

'On days like these we dance to us,
With the drum beat of liberation'
Benjamin Zephaniah

The Evolution of Frontlines in Britain as Spaces of Black Youth, Resistance and Rebellion

ISHMAHIL BLAGROVE, JR

By the mid-1970s, England's first generation of Black, British-born youth was coming of age. There was a rumbling undercurrent of discontent that was gathering momentum. They'd heard stories from their parents about the struggles and prejudices that they had endured since their arrival in Britain – and they were determined to bring about a change. They had found their voice and with clenched fists raised had embarked on a struggle to establish their presence in Britain.

This readiness would later manifest in the emergence of what became known as 'frontlines' across Britain. They were closely associated with the Black urban uprisings that ignited across English cities in the 1980s due to social marginalisation, racial prejudice, police persecution and their disproportionate use of the stop and search laws against Black inner-city youths. Tensions reached breaking point after a police raid on the Black and White Café on Grosvenor Road, St Pauls, Bristol, in 1980, resulting in rioting that ended with 130 arrests and 19 police officers injured. The following year Brixton ignited because of racial discrimination by the police and the increased use of stop and search that primarily targeted Black youths. Within a period of 48 hours 85 arrests had been made, 279 police officers injured, 56 police cars destroyed, scores of other cars torched and more than 100 buildings damaged by fire. Brixton was followed by other cities: Toxteth in Liverpool, Handsworth in Birmingham, Chapeltown in Leeds and Moss Side in Manchester. The riots were broadcast around the world and helped to firmly establish prominent Black communities in Britain and the presence of frontlines, particularly that of Brixton.

It was a moment when – for the first time in their lives – many marginalised Black youths felt empowered, felt their voices, their anger and their frustrations were being heard, albeit through the images of destruction of burning buildings, overturned police cars and urban chaos that were broadcast around the world. To some extent these uprisings were considered minor victories on the road to social justice and equality. Black youths had faced off with the powers that be and had lost their fear. Many of those arrested and imprisoned were released to a hero's welcome, and those who had distinguished themselves in the confrontations enhanced their names and status within their communities. It became a time to organise and reinforce community defences against further police and state repression. Popular cafés and liming spots became the frontiers of resistance, hubs for the newly emboldened youth who were to be the first line of defence for the communities under siege.

Frontlines as spaces of safety and socialisation far predate the urban tensions of the 1980s that brought them to national prominence. Though they may not have been known as frontlines at the time, various streets or a cluster of buildings in numerous towns and cities had been established as important nerve centres of communication, organisation and commerce wherever large numbers of African and Caribbean migrants had settled after the arrival of ships such as the HMT *Empire Windrush* at Tilbury Docks on 21 June 1948. Prior to the arrival of the *Windrush*, enclaves of the African and Caribbean community formed around the port areas of East London, Cardiff and Liverpool – areas where merchant seamen had established a presence in the boarding houses and cafés that serviced the ships that docked there.

Bell Street, situated off Edgware Road in central London, was a bustling commercial centre of activity from the early 1950s and provided for the needs of the growing West Indian and African population and many African-American servicemen who frequented the street. There, newly arrived immigrants could solicit advice from those who were more established in the country on what to expect in Britain – where rooms were available to rent, employment opportunities, which clubs were friendly to Black people, where house parties were held – and could catch up on the latest news from their respective countries. The street had eating spots, gambling houses, a speakeasy, barbershop, travel agents and other commercial ventures established by West Indian ex-servicemen who had served in Britain during the Second World War. The street contained the central ingredients of what would later come to epitomise a frontline, and it is considered by many to be one of the early templates from which frontlines began to blossom in other towns and cities across England.

Gambling houses played an integral part in the socialisation process for many West Indians, given that there were very few social venues where Blacks were welcome or felt comfortable. These gambling houses sold food and alcohol and played music until the early hours of the morning. At the height of its popularity, the gambling house on Bell Street attracted West Indian patrons from as far away as Liverpool, Bristol and Birmingham to gamble and socialise on weekends. Many of the blues dances, restaurants and Black-owned businesses that would later emerge across the country were inspired by or originated in these early gambling houses and barber shops. By the 1960s and 1970s, similar scenes and streets flourished in Railton Road in Brixton, Sandringham Road in Stoke Newington, Soho Road in Handsworth, Birmingham, and other enclaves where African and Caribbean people were concentrated.

A former patron of the Bell Street scene was Frank Crichlow, who had arrived in Britain from Trinidad in the summer of 1953 on board the SS *Colombie*. By 1959, after a stint at British Rail and embarking on a career as a musician, he opened his own speakeasy and gambling house called El Rio Café at 127 Westbourne Park Road in Notting Hill. The café was located at one of the furthest points east of Notting Hill, an area that had one of the most densely concentrated populations of West Indians anywhere in the country. The previous year Notting Hill had been the scene of fierce race riots where African and West Indian homes were petrol-bombed and pitched battles raged in the streets for days. The riots garnered international headlines and urgently prompted parliamentary debates surrounding the state of race relations in Britain. The same year that the El Rio Café opened saw the racist murder of Kelso Cochrane, a 32-year-old Antiguan carpenter who was stabbed to death by a gang of white youths while walking home in Notting Hill. The Notting Hill race riots of 1958, coupled with the racist murder of Kelso Cochrane in 1959, would later form the catalyst

by which the Notting Hill Carnival would be initiated by Rhaune Laslett, a local activist who in 1965 brought the different cultures and ethnicities of the community together as a means of easing racial tensions.

It was in this atmosphere of racial tensions that Frank Crichlow's El Rio Café opened its doors and became one of the major social hubs in the area. It was one of the few crossover venues where both Black and white, rich and poor patrons could mingle freely, listening to jazz and rhythm & blues music until the early hours of the morning.

The café gained national prominence – and infamy – in 1963 as a result of the Profumo affair, a political scandal at the height of the Cold War that seriously weakened Harold Macmillan's Conservative government. John Profumo, the Secretary of State for War, had been having an extramarital affair with Christine Keeler, a 19-year-old model who was also involved sexually with Captain Yevgeny Ivanov, a Soviet naval attaché and spy, and Lucky Gordon, a local West Indian hustler and part-time musician. Gordon was a regular patron of the El Rio, which was one of the venues frequented by Keeler, Profumo and the man who introduced them, Stephen Ward.

The El Rio Café would subsequently be the target of a number of police raids over the years, leading to Frank Crichlow closing down the venue and starting the Mangrove restaurant on All Saints Road in 1968. The new restaurant was an immediate success and boasted among its patrons the writer Colin MacInnes, actress Vanessa Redgrave, international celebrities such as Sammy Davis Jr, Dick Gregory, Diana Ross, Marvin Gaye, Nina Simone and in later years Bob Marley, as well as community activists, intellectuals, hustlers and card sharks.

The phenomenal success of the Mangrove restaurant led to resentment and further police raids on the establishment. A team of police officers from Notting Hill Police Station would often arrive unannounced and harass customers, at times overturning tables and sifting through the meals of patrons under the pretence of looking for drugs. After a series of such raids a demonstration was called which saw the community of Notting Hill march on several police stations in the area, protesting the harassment of the Mangrove restaurant and police brutality. During these protests the police kettled demonstrators and their heavy-handed tactics resulted in a number of arrests and charges, which culminated in what became known as the Mangrove Nine trials in 1971. Nine defendants – Frank Crichlow, Darcus Howe, Barbara Beese, Rhodan Gordon, Altheia Lecointe, Anthony Innes, Rupert Boyce, Rothwell Kentish and Godfrey Millet – were charged with various

ABOVE The Mangrove, the most famous Caribbean restaurant in London, All Saints Road, Notting Hill, 10 August 1970. The restaurant was repeatedly raided by the police, prompting a protest march to be organised by local residents.
OPPOSITE The Mangrove Nine: eight members of the Black British activists group, 16 December 1971. Front row (left to right): Rothwell Kentish, Rhodan Gordon, Altheia Jones-LeCointe, Barbara Beese. Back row (left to right): Frank Crichlow, Godfrey Millett, Rupert Boyce, Darcus Howe. Ninth member Anthony Innis is not in the picture.

offences ranging from assaulting police officers and affray to inciting a riot. The trial lasted fifty-five days and resulted in all being acquitted of the most serious charges. It became the first acknowledgement by the British judiciary of racial prejudice and discrimination within the Metropolitan Police. The victory helped propel Frank Crichlow, his Mangrove restaurant and the All Saints Road to national prominence and Crichlow became the leading figurehead and voice of the Black community in Notting Hill. However, this did not stop the police harassment of Crichlow and the patrons of his restaurant, many of whom would continue to be stopped and searched as they left his establishment.

Frustrated and facing financial ruin as a result of the damage done by the constant police presence and intimidation, Crichlow moved out the dining tables, brought in pool and table tennis tables and opened up his basement to card and dice players, in the process catering to a large number of marginalised Black youths who felt an affinity with Crichlow's experience at the hands of the authorities. They gravitated to the Mangrove and All Saints Road as a symbol of resistance and a place of safety. Crichlow became a father figure to the disenfranchised youth of the area, many of whom were experiencing problems both in their family homes and with the criminal justice system. Propelled by the musical success of Bob Marley and reggae music, Rastafarianism had gripped the imagination of the youth. Many adopted dreadlocks and notions of Black pride and resistance embodied in the philosophical teachings of the faith, while reggae music disseminated a history of slavery, colonialism, Black identity and emancipatory struggles. The tone of All Saints Road began to change as the youthful patrons adopted a more radical and confrontational approach towards the police, who, severely outnumbered by those who now congregated on the street, were ordered to retreat to the periphery of the surrounding roads and to only venture onto the street when absolutely necessary or to execute an arrest.

FREE SPEECH Darcus Howe addressing a rally for the Mangrove Nine in Notting Hill in 1970. Photograph by Sir Horace Ové.

The All Saints Road became a no-go zone for the police, and they faced the realistic possibility of being assaulted themselves, and having their vehicles destroyed.

Frontlines formed out of such scenes in towns and cities across the country, with individuals like Reggie Gutz from Notting Hill, Blue from Brixton and Doc Holiday from Handsworth assuming the role of enforcers and the arbiters of law and order. These streets were considered the frontlines of resistance by communities under siege from the police and adopted a quasi-command structure that contained captains, lieutenants and soldiers. Restaurants, minicab services, shebeens, gambling houses and other small businesses blossomed in this ecosystem, as well as the illicit trade in marijuana. Trade on such streets was so brisk that at times they were colloquially dubbed the Black Stock Exchange.

The origin of the name frontline to define these pockets of resistance is hotly contested. Some claim it originated from the All Saints Road in Notting Hill, while others argue that it specified Railton Road in Brixton years earlier. Nevertheless the term is widely believed to have come into broader circulation around the mid- to late 1970s, when the Black liberation wars took place in Angola, Mozambique, Zimbabwe and South Africa. Around this time Richard Branson's Virgin Records, which originally started in Notting Hill, launched its subsidiary reggae label Frontline in 1978, its logo a fist grasping onto a strip of barbed wire. That same year, Eddie Grant released his hit single 'Living on the Frontline', and Natty, a former member of South London's Sufferer Sound System, launched his sound system Frontline International.

By the time of the major urban uprisings across English cities in 1981, the term was already firmly established and in wide circulation, with patrons of respective frontlines forging communication channels and connections of mutual support and assistance. The All Saints Road frontline was arguably the most politicised and organised of all the frontlines, due to its many years of experience confronting the police and judicial system, as well as having a team of prominent lawyers and barristers at its disposal, including Gareth Peirce, Michael Mansfield, Paddy O'Connor and Paul Boateng – radical lawyers who were prepared to challenge the status quo and take on the establishment.

The All Saints Road frontline had a number of safe houses and expertise that known and respected figures from other communities could access when in need. Following the Bristol riots of 1980, individuals accused of rioting called on the assistance of Frank Crichlow and members of the All Saints Road frontline. They had already pleaded guilty but after acquiring the services of Frank's lawyers, the plea was retracted and a plea of not guilty was entered. At trial all the defendants were acquitted. Similarly, in 1985 after the Handsworth, Birmingham riots, the front cover of a newspaper featured James Hazell, Molotov cocktail in hand, with the headline 'RIOT'S MOST WANTED'. Through a network of contacts, James Hazell would find himself on the All Saints Road frontline, where he was sheltered in a safe house and given legal advice before turning himself in. Members of South Africa's African National Congress also sought refuge and respite in the network of the All Saints Road frontline's safe houses,

OPPOSITE All Saints Road, Notting Hill, 1981. Photograph courtesy of Rice N Peas Archive.

These streets were considered the
frontlines of resistance by communities
under siege from the police and adopted a
quasi-command structure that contained
captains, lieutenants and soldiers.

Darcus Howe and his Race Today collective,
who were based on Railton Road, intellectually
articulated the anger and discontent that was
being felt by Black youths.

and frontline soldiers would go on to provide protection to the Grenadian Prime Minister Maurice Bishop and US civil rights activist Al Sharpton upon their visits to Britain.

The events that led up to frontlines adopting a more radical and confrontational stance towards the police and authority can be traced back to the social discontent and uprisings of the 1980s. Following the New Cross house fire, which claimed the lives of thirteen Black people in what was suspected to be a racist arson attack on a house party on 18 January 1981, tensions were mounting within Black communities across the country. The lack of response and empathy from the police and government led to the 'Black People's Day of Action', a rally through London on 2 March 1981, that brought together more than twenty thousand people, with chants of 'Thirteen dead and nothing said!' Tensions were at boiling point and Black communities across the country were on high alert. The following month saw Brixton in flames, with Darcus Howe and his Race Today collective, who were based on Railton Road, intellectually articulating the anger and discontent that was being felt by Black youths. Other cities shortly followed with an equal frenzy of violence and destructive damage to public property. These events would emerge as some of the defining moments which frontlines played in mobilising the youth and would anoint their status within Black communities.

Brixton would again flare up and see street battles between predominantly Black youths and the police in 1985 after Cherry Groce was shot during a police raid of her home on 28 September of that year, as officers looked for her 21-year-old son Michael Groce in connection to a robbery and suspected firearms offences.

A week later Tottenham's Broadwater Farm ignited after Cynthia Jarrett died of a heart attack when her home was raided by the police after they arrested her son Floyd Jarrett under the pretext that he had been driving a car with a suspicious tax disc. In the violence that ensued, police officer Keith Blakelock was murdered. His death highlighted the deep animosity and tensions that existed between the Black community and the police. Following this uprising, Broadwater Farm gained national prominence and became Tottenham's frontline, with Dolly Kiffin, Millard Scott and Stafford Scott emerging as young leaders.

In later years frontlines succumbed to the crack epidemic that devastated many communities in the late 1980s. The streets had been infiltrated by Jamaican gangs, who brought with them an unprecedented level of violence rarely seen on the streets of England. The radical tone of resistance on these streets was muted, and replaced by a mercenary dog-eat-dog, *get rich or die tryin'* mentality. No longer were frontlines considered places of safety and refuge from the police; instead they began to implode, becoming gauntlets of arbitrary crime and wanton violence that marred the legacy of these once so important and integral spaces of Black resistance in Britain.

Frontlines are now a phenomenon of the past. In their day, they may not have appealed to everyone, but most benefited from their gains. They played an instrumental part in establishing a sense of empowerment that many Black people and marginalised communities now take for granted. Without them the road to the numerous victories achieved in race relations in Britain would arguably have been much longer.

OPPOSITE Crowds outside the Elgin pub on Ladbroke Grove as trouble flared at the Notting Hill Carnival, 31 August 1976.

The Frontlines / The Evolution of Frontlines in Britain...

Steel Pan

AYANNA VAN DER MATEN MCCALMAN

Direct from the slums of Port of Spain an ensemble of steel pan players (TASPO) represented Trinidad at the Festival of Britain. Russell Henderson's band paved for the way for the Notting Hill Carnival and for future steel orchestras like Ebony and Mangrove. Nostalgia opened the 2012 Olympics, while hundreds of schools host steel pan workshops and bands.

The history

More than seventy years after the arrival of the *Empire Windrush* and the Trinidad All-Steel Pan Percussion Orchestra (TASPO) performed at the 1951 Festival of Britain, the British steelband movement has expanded and suddenly, the possibility for some real change has emerged.

Undoubtedly at the forefront of the steel pan movement were two groundbreaking Trinidadian musicians – Sterling Betancourt and Russell Henderson – both of whom devoted their entire lives to advancing the musical art form within the London cultural scene.

Sterling Betancourt was a member of the Trinidad All-Steel Pan Percussion Orchestra (TASPO), a unique ensemble that was formed in 1951 under the auspices of the Trinidad and Tobago Steel Band Association. TASPO's membership initially consisted of one member from each of ten rival steelbands. It was an attempt to forge a degree of unity between the bands and to stem the violence that would often occur when they clashed.

Coinciding with the formation of TASPO, the residing English governor suggested that a steelband represent Trinidad and Tobago at the 1951 Festival of Britain. TASPO was the perfect contender. It was an all-star band and Betancourt – who had been the leader of Crossfire steelband from St James – along with eleven other players, set sail from for England.

They landed on 26 June and premiered their considerable skills on London's South Bank. Though rusted from the journey across the Atlantic, their pans were well tuned. An air of scepticism which permeated the audience was quickly put to rest when the band started playing and swung into a version of Perez Prado's 'Mambo Jambo'. The response from the press to TASPO's performance generated accolades such as 'first-class', 'wonderfully skilled playing' and 'virtuoso jazz'.

Steel pan had arrived in Britain and Sterling Betancourt decided to stay. The last surviving member of the TASPO era became the face of the steelband movement in the UK, with his 'traditional' steelband, Nostalgia, and decades of participation in the various carnival efforts taking place around the UK.

Russell Henderson arrived in the UK from Trinidad to study piano tuning during the same year TASPO arrived. He'd already had his own Russell Henderson Quartet in Trinidad, supporting calypsonians like Lord Pretender, Mighty Growler and Roaring Lion. Once in the

OPPOSITE The Trinidad All-Steel Pan Percussion Orchestra (TASPO), 1951. The band was formed to participate in that year's Festival of Britain.

The steel pan originated in the Caribbean twin islands of Trinidad and Tobago, and as a musical genre has spread across the globe, from its humble origins in the working-class ghettos of the islands.

UK he set up Britain's first steelband combo, which also featured the talents of Sterling Betancourt. They worked with Lord Kitchener and Young Tiger and played at the Sunset Club in Carnaby Street. Their Sunday afternoon sessions at the Coleherne public house in Old Brompton Road during the early 1960s attracted London's finest jazz musicians, including Joe Harriott and Shake Keane.

While it was radical journalist and activist Claudia Jones who would initiate the first of several roadblocked, town hall Carnival events to 'wash the taste of Notting Hill and Nottingham out of our mouths' (a response to the 1958 race riots), it was the Russell Henderson Steel Band that first took steel pan onto the streets of Notting Hill. That was 1964. Five years had elapsed since the murder of 32-year-old Antiguan-born Kelso Cochrane, but the dark shadow remained. Henderson had accepted the offer to play at a 'fayre' and children's parade organised by Rhaune Laslett, a retired social worker and community activist. As the band played and walked the streets, it turned into a street party. By 1966 it had begun to evolve into what we now know as the London Notting Hill Carnival, which annually attracts around two million people over the August Bank Holiday weekend.

The origins of the steel pan

The steel pan is a chromed circular metal musical instrument, which can be played individually or collectively (in which case it is known as a steelband or a steel orchestra). The steel pan was invented in or around the 1930s

or the early 1940s, and it has evolved into the present day's refined instrument.

The steel pan originated in the Caribbean twin islands of Trinidad and Tobago, and as a musical genre has spread across the globe. Its humble origins in the working-class ghettos of the islands were a development on the 'tamboo-bamboo', which itself gave way to biscuit tins, and later to dustbins. Eventually, good usage was made of the 45-gallon oil drums which had littered the oil-producing islands. Early migrants to the UK came with their steel drums, and did perform there, but it was the first steelband, TASPO, that led to the popularisation of the instrument here. Most of the early TASPO pioneers were pan tuners themselves, and Sterling Betancourt – the only member to remain in the UK after the tour was over – was one of the first pan tuners in the UK. After TASPO's performance, many pan tuners migrated to the UK, bringing with them their tools and pan-tuning skills. These included Michael 'Natsy' Contant, Dudley Dickson, Ezekiel 'Biggs' Yearwood, 'Zigilee' Constantine, Gerald Forsyth, Selwyn Baptiste and Victor Phillip.

Many (probably most) of the early steel pan musicians actually worked in the gig economy, going out as four-piece bands to perform at private events and at clubs where the novelty effect of this new instrument became very appealing to the British. As there were fewer pan musicians in the early 1960s compared to today, these early gig-men found economic security in the music performing arena, working almost all year round. Gerald Forsythe set up the Pan Players Academy in the early 1970s and set out to rally his fellow steel pan musicians

OPPOSITE Members of the Trinidad Steel Band demonstrate how a pan is tuned at the drum factory in Grays, Essex, 1972.

in the advancement of their art form. Later he became the coordinator within the Inner London Education Authority (ILEA), with overall responsibility of setting up steelband music classes in London's inner-city schools.

Steelbands in schools

Steel pan moved into UK schools in the late 1960s and early 1970s, through the work of Gerald Forsythe and Frank Rollock, and a resurgence of the steel pan followed, with community steelbands and new members joining the movement. Forsythe started the first school steelband at Islington Green School in 1969, drawing inspiration from steel pan projects in the US. He was approached by Islington Green School and later by the ILEA to select teachers suitable for the London Schools Steel Pan Project. The London Schools Steel Orchestra was set up to ensure that the gifted pupils could exhibit their skills to the wider British audience and show the versatility of this new instrument. More pupils joined the steelband movement and steelband moved from being a solely Black activity to an inclusive musical genre thanks to the ILEA and the Greater London Council (GLC).

Today there are hundreds of steelbands in UK schools along with regional education music services carrying out steel pan workshops all over the country. An improvement in the manufacturing technology and the increasing skill of pan-tuners have impacted on the tonal quality and the availability of good-quality instruments. With this new-found popularity came renewed interest in steel pan performances and in the annual UK steel pan Panorama competitions between orchestras, and steel pan music festivals which – particularly

those held in the main national concert halls – did much to advance the view that the inclusion of steelbands was worth serious consideration in the modern art arena. Previously segregation based on cultural difference had increasingly become a substitute for 'race', and for keeping the hierarchy in place. With the emergence of multiculturalism and anti-racist educational policies in inner-city areas, all ethnicities began playing the steel pan. It was no longer regarded as an instrument solely for Black children. The level of mainstream hostility to steelband inclusion fell away after the first European Steelband Festival (2000) and the ensuing World Steelband Music Festivals, and Pan Jazz Festivals. Top pan-jazz musicians like Samuel DuBois, Daniel Lewis, Rudy Smith and Anise 'Halfers' Hadeed paved the way for the younger generation of pan jazz musicians to follow.

Titans of the steel pan movement

Without a doubt, Ebony Steelband and Mangrove Steelband led the way in ensuring the popularity of steelbands in the UK. The rivalry between the two giants ensured that the annual steel pan competition – Panorama – became a keenly anticipated contest among steel pan enthusiasts. Mangrove Steelband had a history of fighting racism and discrimination against the Black population and had had its battles with the Metropolitan Police and the establishment. Ebony Steelband was seen as different, focused on their music, and their success rocketed in that early period. The contest for the title of National Panorama Champion of Steel, which takes place on Carnival weekend, has always pulled the largest audience of any UK steel pan competition and guarantees a fully enjoyable

OPPOSITE A float with steelband on the procession route at the Notting Hill Carnival, August 1995.

evening's proceeding. Anise 'Halfers' Hadeed, the arranger of Ebony Steel pan, holds the record with sixteen national championships under his belt. In 2023, the Panorama Championship was held on Saturday 26 August, with seven steel orchestras competing for the title, with more than five hundred musicians taking part, with thousands of instruments.

Steelband presence at the London Olympics 2012

In 2012 Nostalgia Steelband was approached by the organisers of the London 2012 Olympic Games to perform at the Opening Ceremony. The spectacle of the steelband musicians, along with a section depicting the Black presence in the UK, was a lasting tribute to this contemporary and visual performing Caribbean art form. Later that same year Brent Holder, a talented steel pan musician and bandleader, made an attempt at a world record, amassing the greatest number of pan musicians in one place, all performing the same tune: 'Brazil', a song made popular by Antônio Carlos Jobim. Brent Holder was able to put together a band of more than one thousand steel pans – and nearly as many musicians – which secured a place in the *Guinness World Records* 2013. The event brought together steelbands from all over the UK, and they gathered on the London South Bank, the same place Sterling Betancourt and the original TASPO had performed some 60 years earlier.

It seems that despite all the progress a serious argument was required to persuade not all, but a substantive number of the music establishment, that the steel pan deserved recognition by the established Western musical traditions. The definition of art in Western traditional culture risked encouraging an attitude to art that was ahistorical and elitist. Steelbands are now fully established in the school musical

curriculum, particularly in inner-city areas. Music bodies such as PRSSV Institute of Performing Arts and Heritage now offer children and adults learning non-Western (world music) traditions, such as steel pan, the opportunity to have graded performances in the competence levels of their chosen musical instrument (i.e. the tenor pan), and many teachers of the steel pan have gained teaching qualifications up to diploma level.

World steel pan day

In 2023 the United Nations proclaimed 11 August to be World Steelpan Day around the globe. This is extremely important for the steel pan fraternity in the UK, and many programmes were planned for the first World Steelpan Day. The community sees this as a recognition of how far the instrument has come since its invention. It remains the only non-electronic instrument invented in the last century.

Steelbands @ Notting Hill Carnival '23

Dallaway Steel Band
Ebony Steelband
Endurance Steel Orchestra
London All-Stars
Mangrove Steelband
Nostalgia Steelband
Metronomes Steel Orchestra
Pan Nation Steel Orchestra
Panash Steel Orchestra
Reading All Steel Percussion Orchestra
Real Steel
Southside Harmonics
St Michael & All Angels Steel Orchestra
Stardust Steel Orchestra
Steel Band In Motion
UFO Steelband

OPPOSITE Young people playing steel pan, Notting Hill Carnival, August 2000.

Mas bands

Mas Bands create and provide the costumes for Notting Hill Carnival. Each registered band has a new theme annually, and the general public are welcome to purchase a costume and join a band to 'play mas' on the parade route at Carnival. Each mas band is assessed by official judges at the judging point (south of Great Western Road) across both days. The winning mas bands are announced on social media.

Abir, Arawak, Arts-A-Light Mas 'The Bride'
Bacchanalia
Calabash Carnival Club, Caribbean Sessions
    Mas, Chocolate Nation Mas, Clement James
    Carnival Band, COLOURS CARNIVAL
D Riddim Tribe, DUKA's Mas Domnik UK Carnival
    Band, Dynamic Mas
Ebony Mas band, Elimu Paddington Arts, Elite
    Mass, Exotic Mas
Flagz Mas Band, Flamboyan Carnival Arts,
    Funatik Mas
Gemz Mas/Gemz Mas International, Glorious
    Backstage Arts
Hotwax carnival Ltd, Hype Mas
Invaders Mas, Island Mas
Karnival Mas, Karnival Mania
Lagniappe
Mas Africa, Masquerade 2K (M2K MAS)
Omnia Carnival, Oxypower Mas
People of Paradise Arts Carnival Group,
    People's World
Reign Mas Band
Soca Massive Fancy Sailors UK,
    Sunshine International Arts
Tears Mas, Tempos Mas UK, Trinbago Carnival
    Club & Inspirational Arts, Tropical Fusion,
    Tropical Isles, TTMudders
UCOM carnival (United Colours of Mas),
    Urban Touch, Utopia Mas UK
Vibrance Mas, Voice of Mauritius Mas UK
Xtreme UK

Notting Hill Carnival: Sonic Rituals of Resistance on the Streets of West London

PAUL BRADSHAW

Every August Bank holiday all roads lead to 'the Grove' and London's Notting Hill Carnival – a mind-blowing, community-led gathering with a history that now spans five decades. It is rooted in the Caribbean culture and the experiences of Britain's Black community. Carnival, as we call it, attracts around a million revellers, and while it might be number two to Rio de Janeiro, it is the biggest arts/street event in Europe.

The history of Carnival is long and has certainly had a few turbulent moments. Its very existence has been threatened more than once but it remains a symbol of cultural pride, and a symbol of resistance for a Black community that has fought hard against exclusion and racism. Carnival visibly stamps its cultural mark on the capital and its impact resonates through the inner cities of Britain as a whole.

The late Darcus Howe, political activist and broadcaster, maintained that, 'If there weren't race riots in Notting Hill I don't believe that we would have had the Notting Hill Carnival. If it wasn't for the murder of Kelso Cochrane, Carnival wouldn't have happened.'

Unlike the gentrified Notting Hill of today, post-Second World War Notting Hill was an impoverished hotbed of racial tension. In 1958, from 29 August to 5 September, gangs of working-class 'Teddy Boys' united with Oswald Mosley's Union Movement (formerly the British Union of Fascists) and the neo-Nazi White Defence League to attack and besiege West Indian households and residents in Notting Hill. It was in the wake of these riots, on 17 May 1959, that Kelso Cochrane was killed in a racially motivated attack just off Golborne Road.

Just prior to Kelso Cochrane's murder, in January 1959, Claudia Jones, a Trinidadian feminist political activist and pioneering journalist, put on a BBC-broadcast indoor 'Caribbean Carnival' at St Pancras Town Hall. It was to be the first of several indoor events in various halls dotted around the capital. As such, Claudia Jones is widely credited with planting the seeds for Carnival in London.

However, it was a children's street 'fayre' organised by a local resident and community activist, Rhaune Laslett, that would become what we now know as Notting Hill Carnival. In 1966 Laslett recruited bandleader and pan player Russell Henderson, along with Sterling Betancourt, Vernon 'Fellows' Williams, Fitzroy Coleman and Ralph Cherry, to take part in the outdoor event. Henderson's band had a strong following. They were regulars at Claudia Jones' indoor carnival events and when the steelband set off on foot from Portobello Road, a trail of locals spontaneously followed, dancing in the street to the sound of the pan. The first Notting Hill Carnival was officially born.

OPPOSITE Poster for Notting Hill 'Peoples Carnival', 1972. The first outdoor event was held in 1966 on the streets of Notting Hill.

PEOPLES CARNIVAL '72

TRINIDAD NORTH STARS

S.S. GOLBORNE SAILORS

open air dance
leave Portobello green
one p.m.

BANK HOLIDAY AUG 28

Under the guidance of Leslie 'Teacher' Palmer – Carnival director from 1973 to 1975 – the event took on new dimensions. Palmer is widely credited with getting sponsorship, recruiting more steelbands, reggae groups and sound systems as well as introducing generators and extending the route. He also encouraged traditional masquerade, and for the first time in 1973, costume bands and steelbands from the various islands took part in the street parade, alongside the introduction of stationary reggae sound systems. The template for Carnival as we know it now had arrived.

We've come a long way since then. There were riots along the way – 1976 was a milestone – and policing has been heavy-handed. However, Carnival Saturday continues to host the National Panorama competition between the various steel pan orchestras, while Sunday is always children's day. Live performances arrived in 1979 when Wilf Walker hosted a stage featuring reggae and punk bands. That paved the way for performances in the 1990s from hip-hop legends such as Jay

Z, Lil' Kim and Busta Rhymes. More recently Carnival stages have showcased Stormzy, Wiley, Craig David, Giggs, Major Lazer, Mr Eazi and Stefflon Don.

Steel pan still runs the roads while both live stages and 'trucks' (floats) have hosted performances from British-based calypso artists like Alexander D Great and De Admiral, as well as internationally known soca artists such as Bunji Garlin and Machel Montano.

While the spectres of commercial colonisation and political storm clouds continue to cast a shadow over Notting Hill Carnival, the Black community, from the Ends and beyond, will continue to make their flamboyant costumes, rehearse those steel pans and string up their sound systems alongside the peeps doing barbecued jerk chicken, currying goat and wrapping stuffed roti. Carnival will remain an annual, creative ritual of resistance that connects a people's past to the future.

For the first time in 1973, costume bands and steelbands from the various islands took part in the street parade, alongside the introduction of stationary reggae sound systems.

OPPOSITE Notting Hill Carnival first generation – Ladbroke Grove, 1969. Photograph by Sir Horace Ové. ABOVE Dancers and spectators at Claudia Jones' indoor Carnival, St Pancras Town Hall, 1959.

MANGROVE STEELBAND PANARAMA WINNERS LONDON CARNIVAL 198...

MANGROVE COMMUNITY ASSOC. WELCOMES YOU TO CARNIVAL '81

CARNIVAL Clockwise from above: The Mangrove, 1981, photograph by Adrian Boot; Norman Jay MBE, Notting Hill Carnival – Good Times, 1992, photograph by Tony Davis; Revellers at Notting Hill, 1979 and sound system outside the Mangrove, 1979, photographs by Adrian Boot; Step Forward Youth – Notting Hill Carnival, 1980, photograph by Sir Horace Ové.

GEORGE CLINTON
DOLBY'S CUBE

THE WALL POSSE Getting the best spot for the Wild Bunch set, St Pauls Carnival, 1986. Photograph by Beezer.

Carnival Days

BENJAMIN ZEPHANIAH

On days like these we dance to us,
With the drum beat of liberation
Under the close cover of European skies,
We dance like true survivors
We dance to the sounds of our dreams.
In the mirror we see
Rainbow people on the beat,
Everyday carnival folk like we.

Adorned in the colours of life
We let it be known that our costumes
Were not made by miracles,
We are the miracles
(And we are still here).
These giants were made by the fingers you see
(Too many to count)
Carried by these feet that dance
In accordance to the rhythms we weave.
On days like these we dance the moon.

On days like these we dance like freedom,
Like the freedom we carried in our hearts
When the slave driver was with his whip
When his whip was at our backs,
There is no carnival without us
And without carnival there is no us.
The colours of our stories joyful the eyes
And rhythm wise the body moves.

On days like these we dance the sun
We cannot make dis love indoors,
Or be restricted by the idea of a roof,
Dis soul, dis reggae, dis calypso,
Dis sweet one music we make
Is for all of us who work dis land
And cannot be contained by bricks and mortar,
It is we, the beat and the streets.

The passion has to be unleashed,
To rave alone is not today,
Dis is a beautiful madness
Dis is a wonder full place.
So play Mas citizen
Be the immortal bird you want to be
Bring hope and truth and prophecy
Or meet the lover in your mind,
Let us take these colours
Let us take these sounds
And make ourselves a paradise.
On days like these we can.

On days like these the elders say
Astronauts can see us dance
Glittering like precious stones
On dis rocking British cultural crown,
When Rio's eyes upon us gaze
And Africans are proud of us
With heads held high we say we are
The carnival, sweet carnival.

On days like these we dance to us,
On days like these we love ourselves.

OPPOSITE Manasseh Sound System,
Notting Hill Carnival, August 1992.
Photograph by David Corio.

Sonny Roberts: The Windrush Pioneer Who Shaped Modern British Music

CHARIS MCGOWAN

Anyone passing by 108 Cambridge Road in 1960s Kilburn would have been unaware that a humble, modest basement in the building was where an indelible era of Black British music was started: a space responsible for songs that went on to spawn numerous genres and influence some of the UK's biggest artists. That's because the basement was never envisioned to be a music studio – until Sonny Roberts first set his eyes on it.

An entrepreneurial spirit with a passion for music and skill for carpentry, Sonny arrived at Tilbury Docks on the SS *Manistee* in 1958 armed with his toolbox in one hand and some of his favourite records in the other. The few items he brought from his homeland, Jamaica, would be telling of the destiny Roberts would carve not only in his own life, but in British music at large.

Tall, polite and brimming with laid-back charisma, Sonny initially pursued carpentry in his new London home. He was a talented craftsman with a knack for woodwork and mastery in furniture-making. Before long he was contracted for some carpentry work by Chris Blackwell, who was running a fledgling Island Records from his cramped flat near Marble Arch. Blackwell, a white Briton raised in Jamaica, shared a deep love of Jamaican music with Sonny, and the two men quickly struck up a friendship.

All the while Sonny was busy making inroads in a different type of business: building sound systems. Souped-up mobile discos powered

by custom-built amplifiers and large speaker boxes, sound systems were an integral part of West Indian life in London. Routinely victims of racist door policies at clubs and social events, the community began to host makeshift dance halls in their own flats or houses. Roberts regularly attended these 'blues' parties, and was commissioned to make sound systems for the hosts. He also crafted his own sound system, lovingly named Lavender after his favourite wood polish scent. From the get-go, Sonny found ways to combine his carpentry skill with his passion for music.

On the sound system circuit he became acutely aware that his fellow Jamaicans shared a demand for music from home and would have to rely on hard-to-come-by imports to play at their parties. Roberts realised he could begin to produce in the UK and started to scout places to set up a studio, eventually finding the basement in 108 Cambridge Road – a corner building owned by Indo-Jamaican accountant Lee Gopthal, neglected and littered with leftover clothes and fabrics from Gopthal's former tailor shop. Sonny rolled up his sleeves to work on Planeton: the UK's first Black-owned studio, which opened in 1961.

In his memoir *The Islander*, Blackwell remembers Sonny as a 'very gentle Jamaican' with a vision: 'Inspired by the Busters and the Dodds, Roberts didn't want to merely import and sell Jamaican records; he wanted to record them. With home-grown enterprise, he got hold of a one-track recorder and some disc-cutting equipment and set up a makeshift studio.'[1]

OPPOSITE Sonny Roberts interviewed for BBC radio in his record shop in 1981.

150

In 1963 Roberts introduced Blackwell to Gopthal and before long Island Records moved into the first floor of 108 Cambridge Road. With both Planetone and Island on-site, Gopthal became enamoured with the music industry and wanted to play his part.

A few years later, sharing a love of sourcing and selling Jamaican and West Indian music, Gopthal and Blackwell co-founded reggae and rocksteady label Trojan Records, the label behind hits by Desmond Dekker, Dandy Livingstone, Ken Boothe, Nicky Thomas and Jimmy Cliff. Trojan Records is just another chapter of Roberts' larger-than-life imprint on British music.

David Betteridge, who was Island Records' Managing Director at the time, credits Sonny as having 'kick-started' Gopthal's interest in the music industry: 'He rented to Sonny, his interest in music originated there.'

Meanwhile Planetone was recording a number of hit successes of its own. The legendary ska trombonist Rico Rodriguez recorded his seminal reggae track 'Midnight in Ethiopia' in the studio. Other times, West Indian musicians would pack together in the studio and jam, seeking refuge from the cold. Sonny always made sure everyone was cared for – he'd cook up rice on a small stove to feed his guests.

'Sonny would cook up lamb soup, or stewed pork, and give them a little something. Some of them didn't have a job, y'know? Wages were small!' recalls his wife Monica Roberts. She first met Sonny in Planetone while chaperoning her adolescent niece Ornell Welsh, a highly skilled pianist. Over the groove of the blues and ska sounds, Monica and Sonny fell in love.

Monica Roberts remembers her husband was an accommodating and welcoming producer who was loved by the community. 'Sonny never

ABOVE Assortment of early Planetone records.

turned anyone away from the studio. Even if they weren't recording, they'd come sit and listen. It was like a home, a refuge.'

The legends that walked through the doors of Planetone included iconic reggae trombonist Rico Rodriguez MBE, who went on to record with the Specials and Toots and the Maytals, chart-topping soul singer Jackie Edwards, Millie Smalls of ska smash 'My Boy Lollipop' fame and rocksteady group the Marvels.

'My Boy Lollipop' was arranged and rehearsed in Planetone in 1963 before the final disc was cut in Olympic Studios off Regent Street, and was released in 1964. It was the first Jamaican song to go to number one in the UK, and sold over six million records worldwide. It was also the first of many global hits for Blackwell, who went on to launch the careers of U2, Bob Marley and Cat Stevens. Roberts' Planetone was part of this milestone, in what was only the beginning of Jamaican ska's global impact.

By 1965 Roberts had closed Planetone to focus on his more lucrative carpentry gigs. He had an infant child and there was another baby on the way: recording and cutting West Indian music was a passion, but it did not provide a stable income. But Roberts couldn't stay out of the industry for long; by 1970 Sonny opened a record shop, Orbitone, in Harlesden.

Orbitone didn't only stock ska, reggae and rocksteady music, but also Afrobeat and jazz. Anthony 'Chips' Richards, who worked in marketing in Trojan Records, remembers the place as 'a reliable shop': 'when you order music, by the next week you'll get it'.

Sonny pursued his love of Afrobeat in the studio and kept producing music. Working Monday to Saturday in the shop, on Sunday

he'd start to rent studio space and record with bands. In 1971, he produced the Nigerian band Nkengas' album *Destruction* – the first Afrobeat record ever made in the UK. The genre eventually evolved into Afrobeats, a style that went on to dominate UK charts. Richards remembers it as 'ahead of its time': 'He made a tremendous contribution to Black people's music in England. One of the giant heroes, he was a hard-working man, a man dedicated to the things you were doing and became successful as a result of his determination.'

Sonny's biggest hit came in a later phase of his career: Saint Vincent artist Judy Boucher's soft reggae single 'Can't Be with You Tonight' in 1986. It reached number two in the charts, held off the top spot by Madonna's 'La Isla Bonita'.

Multi-instrumentalist Lindel Lewis worked with Sonny on Boucher's album and remembers Sonny's animated vision: 'Every recording session with Sonny Roberts stands out for me,' he said. 'He always had an idea of what he wanted but didn't know what he wanted musically but he'd hum it, I'd play it and he'd say "yeah that's it." He wasn't a musician but he had ideas.'

A *Windrush* migrant with no musical background aside from his passion, Sonny Roberts made a great impact on British music, whether through Planetone, Orbitone, Trojan or his Afrobeat and Boucher ventures. Roberts never stopped pursuing his love for music with kindness, patience and warmth.

As Mykaell Riley, director of the Black Music Research Unit at the University of Westminster, sums up, 'He's a role model, which is really important retrospectively. His achievement was sticking with his passion in a calm and understated way, against all odds.'

Sir Coxsone Outernational: A Soundman's Journey

PAUL BRADSHAW

Acton Town Hall, West London. It's Friday night and it's the big cup clash... Beneath a web of cables, the dance is corked. The youth have arrived from every corner of the city and beyond. The four walls are lined with serious stacks of speaker boxes, and the air is vibrating with a combination of deep, soothing bass, crisp tops and wailing sirens.

A haze of herb smoke permeates every corner, swirls around in the heat from the amplifiers of the sound warriors who are sifting through their vinyl and their exclusive dub plates while mic-men are turning over fresh lyrics in their minds... the hotter the battle, the sweeter the victory. Jah Shaka – the Zulu Warrior – fills the room with crashing waves of sound and plaintive, conscious vocals. Alone at his control tower, stepping, mic in hand, this is his church and guided by His Imperial Majesty – Jah Rastafari – he's reaching out to the congregation. Another sound cuts in. Could be Quaker City, Midlands champion. Rootical. Heavy duty. Meanwhile in the Coxsone Outernational corner they are biding time, but pressure is mounting. Word is that Lloydie Coxsone has just touched down from Yard. He's on his way from Heathrow. Time is tight. When his distinctive presence suddenly appears through the crowd, it's like the Coxsone posse come alive. Festus and Blacker are ready. Lloydie delivers a stack of freshly cut dub plates. They are numbered from 10 to 2, the final one labelled 'Cup Winner'. And so it goes.

The clash is on and when that final dub plate drops, the crowd goes wild. The riddim is 'Drum Song' and later, we get to know this cut as 'Five Man Army'. The mic-man demands of those assembled, 'Ah who seh?' The crowd fires back. Coxsone takes the cup!

If I had to choose one word to describe Lloyd Blackford, aka Lloydie Coxsone, it would be *gravitas*. Coxsone is a tall, slim, Jamaican-born man whose angular features are framed by a crown of locks. Reflecting his nocturnal lifestyle, his eyes are often shielded by a pair of dark glasses. As the founding father and guiding light of the South London-based Sir Coxsone Outernational sound system he is an articulate, constructive and outspoken representative of the sound system fraternity in the UK. At the age of 78 he survives as the foremost repository of a history that has yet to be documented in the depth that it deserves.

In 1962, a teenage Lloyd Blackford was tricked into boarding a plane for England. His father and his brother had settled in London and like many other families who migrated to the UK in stages, it was his turn next. Upon arrival, he was greeted by one of the worst winters on record: 'It was black with snow!'[1]

Once settled in Balham in South London he had to find a job, and after months of futile visits to the Balham Labour Exchange he finally lost it and demanded: 'How come you have four boxes full of job ticket, and you can't give me a job out of them?' The clerk removed one of the cards

and then a couple more. They were all marked NCP: 'No Coloured People.' From another box he was shown another card marked NIP: 'No Irish People.' It was his first encounter with institutional racism in this country.

His first job was for Southern Rail, as a porter – he was given a 'big hat and a whistle'. Cricket and music were his passions. His first venture as a DJ was in his local shebeen on a modest two-speaker sound system called Queen of the West. He was paid £2 a session.

Through his brother he was introduced to a bigger sound called Barry Sky Rocket. Though he knew that the controller would never let him play the set, he seized the opportunity. He learned how to load the van and string up the sound, and learned all the tunes in Sky Rocket's record box.

'Back then, if you have a good tune you would play about six song and then you come back and play back the star song and the star song would rule most of the night. People dance the same way. There was a lack of music but we play what we had – Dan Drummond, Derrick Morgan, Eric Monty Morris, Jimmy Cliff, Roland

Alfonso, Tommy McCook – people really enjoyed themselves.'

However, a personality clash led Lloyd to quit Sky Rocket and invest the money he'd earned from working on the railway into his own sound: Lloyd the Matador. His childhood friend Clark Eugene, aka Festus, arrived from Jamaica in 1965. They joined forces to play blues and house parties around South London. Their reputation mushroomed and when an oversubscribed, roadblocked, old year/new year party spun out of control, their custom-built amplifier was destroyed: Lloyd the Matador was dead.

Following that new year's fracas, Lloyd was recruited by Duke Reid, a top South London sound capable of challenging North London sounds such as Count Shelly. Duke Reid had acquired a new residency at the Bedford in Balham and upon arrival at the venue (fresh from a game of cricket on Tooting Bec Common) Lloyd was accosted on the stairs by two white men. During a struggle his new mac was ripped and one of his assailants ended up at the bottom of the stairs.

What he didn't know at the time was that they were both police officers. And as the dance was finishing, the street was flooded with blue lights. Lloyd was arrested.

'They carried me down to Tooting Bec Police Station and plant me with a machete… They carried me to court knowing that I never had that weapon.'

That night he and Duke Reid had carried the amplifier down the stairs and as Lloyd was only wearing a shirt and trousers he clearly had nowhere to hide anything, let alone a machete.

ABOVE Coxsone's *King of the Dub Rock Part 2* LP.
OPPOSITE Blacker Dread, a dubplate and a young follower, 29 July 1981: Peace Dance in Railton Road Adventure Playground following the Brixton Riots. Photograph by Jean Bernard Sohiez.

Lloyd needed Reid to give evidence in court but despite numerous promises his boss failed to show. After a third hearing the judge declared he was not putting the case off any longer. Lloyd was jailed for six months.

Released from prison in 1968, Lloyd planned to build back his sound, based on the two big sound systems that ruled Jamaica, Duke Reid and Sir Coxsone. He was 'going to lick off Duke Reid head'. Lloyd took back his records from Reid's box and along with Festus and Glen Marcinick (who had two amplifiers) they launched Sir Coxsone. Together they built a successful residency at the Ram Jam in Brixton. They played in the West End at the Paradise in Derby Street and the Grotto in Chinatown: 'It was a little basement club where people go and dance, hippie people taking blues, pep pills. We just go on two speaker boxes down there and it was full every Friday night.'

Meanwhile, over in Carnaby Street, Count Suckle had left the Roaring Twenties to open the Q Club in Paddington. A succession of big names attempted to step into Suckle's shoes at the Twenties but it was Coxsone who got the job. Suckle had won a battle with the owners of the Twenties to allow his Black followers into the club and Coxsone inherited that door policy. He stayed for five years.

The Twenties was a controversial place, with a 1960s pop star celebrity reputation. It also serviced Soho's nocturnal community of pushers, pimps and hustlers and it was subjected to regular police raids.

At the Twenties, Coxsone spun the latest soul and funk alongside a selection that reflected the transition from ska to rocksteady to reggae. There was a fresh dynamic coming out of Jamaica. In 1972 Michael Manley – a modern-day Joshua – campaigned and won the election for the PNP (People's National Party). Armed

with his symbolic Rod of Correction and his own brand of democratic socialism, his vision resounded with the marginalised Rastafari. The singers and musicians responded. A spiritually infused Black consciousness began to permeate the music. It dealt with the legacy of slavery. It celebrated heroes and visionaries such as Paul Bogle and Marcus Garvey. It gave thanks and praise to HIM Haile Selassie. A new wave of songs steeped in ghetto-ology offered a livity of peace and love while supporting the liberation struggles in South Africa, Zimbabwe, Angola and Mozambique. The music of Bob Marley and the Wailers, Burning Spear, Abyssinians, Yabby You, Dennis Brown, Black Uhuru, Gregory Isaacs – so many artists – introduced Rastafari to the world.

Sir Coxsone reigned supreme as *the* roots and culture sound. A constant flow of JA record producers and artists passed through London and a visit to Coxsone was top of the list. By the mid-1970s there were dozens of high-powered sound systems operating across the capital. Sound clashes were a big draw and took place in clubs such as Four Aces or Phebes or in local town halls or youth and community centres such as Metro or Moonshot.

A host of serious sound systems operated in cities around the country – Duke Neville, Quaker City, Jungleman, Baron Turbo-Charged, Iration Steppers, Sir Yank, Jah Lokko, Enterprise Hi Fi – and Coxsone was the first London-based sound to take to the road, ready to entertain and show who was number one.

Lloyd Coxsone is proud of the teams that have run the sound over several generations: young men like Festus, Pebbles, Gunsmoke, Byron, Blacker Dread, Gappy Crucial, Harlesden, Duffus, Bikey Dread, Napthali, Country (aka Levi Roots), among others.

OPPOSITE Talent Contest at the Peace Dance, following the Brixton Riots, 1981. ABOVE Coxsone Sound System: Blacker Dread, Duffus, Bikey Dread at Peace Dance. Photographs by Jean Bernard Sohiez.

To run a good sound in the UK is teamwork. A young team of men, who are ambitious, record-crazy and have young ideas. I have seen a lot of good sound die 'cause they didn't build a team to manifest the work of the sound.

Coxsone sound boasted an unrivalled selection of music and custom-built equipment.

Coxsone Sound is the first sound to play stereo in this country, we play bass, mid and top. If you switch the bass off you'd only get the mid and the top playing and if you switch the bass and the mid off you'd only get the high top playing. We do all these things first and everyone follow. Coxsone is the first sound to put two eighteen-inch speaker into one box and everybody said, 'That's a waste of speaker,' but when that start to lick...

The first sound to play dub, Coxsone set the pace in equipment and pioneered the use of echo, reverb and equaliser in the late 1970s and beyond. The banks of amplifiers in evidence at any sound dance were testimony to a fixation with wattage rather than an ability to select and present the music.

'People can't dance to wattage,' asserts Lloyd.

Listen, the more you step up weight you lose quality. A man must be able to hear your vocal playing. I don't see sound that is rootin' down like bulldozer as good sound. I am more interested in sound quality and selection of music. If you play a song with a certain message you must find a next one with a message to match the first.

Lloydie Coxsone is no stranger to the studio. In 1975, he released Louisa Mark's seminal 'Caught You in a Lie' – a UK lovers' rock classic. He added to the repertoire of dub with the *King of the Dub Rock* LPs (parts 1 and 2). His Tribesman label also delivered 12-inch singles from Creation Steppers, Levi Roots and Fred Locks.

During the early 1980s you could catch Coxsone in residency at Colombos in Carnaby Street or at the Four Aces. Meanwhile, out on the street, tension was mounting. Aggressive policing in the form of stop and search was rampant within the Black community. Following the Metropolitan Police's invasive 'Operation Swamp 81', which saw stop and search numbers reach an unprecedented level, Brixton was set alight. By the summer, Black youth in every city and many towns were fighting back.

One chink of light during that dark time came on the day of the royal wedding of Prince Charles and Lady Diana. Lloydie Coxsone got together with his bredren – DEB music's Castro Brown – to host a Peace Dance in the adventure playground in Brixton's Railton Road. It was a beautiful day, as if all Brixton was there for the children's talent competitions, artists such as Eastwood and

ABOVE Coxsone's Tribesman imprint. **OPPOSITE** Coxsone Sound System: Box boys loading the truck... Naphtali, Duffus, Blacker, Bikey and unknown, 1979. Photograph by Jean Bernard Sohiez.

Saint, and the Coxsone Outernational's selection. There was no trouble and no police: they were all overseeing the royal wedding!

The 1980s saw a UK media panic focused on guns, cocaine and the arrival of the 'yardies'. The rude boys of the 1960s and the gunmen of the 1980s and 1990s have always been intertwined with Jamaica's music business. The complex and controversial world of dancehall is no exception. Errol 'Ranking Dread' Codling often appeared on the mic for Coxsone. The *Daily Mirror* later labelled him 'the most dangerous foreign national in Britain', while the Scottish *Daily Record* attributed at least thirty killings to the reputed Shower Posse enforcer.

Though the digital era of JA dancehall – ragga – was often associated with sex, violence and gangsters, it continued to have a major impact on music across the Caribbean and throughout Latin America. During the 1990s, Blacker Dread was the controller on Coxsone sound system, attracting visiting dancehall artists such as Nicodemus, Tenor Fly, Super Cat and Frankie Paul. From his shop on Brixton's Coldharbour Lane, Blacker was also producing and releasing the digital dancehall of the day. But all was not well, as we discover in Molly Dineen's documentary film *Being Blacker*.

'That is when Coxsone sound started to go downhill,' reflects Lloyd. 'The same standard was not there. So the crowd start to fall away. But we were a big team of people, and everybody was knowledgeable in their own right, so I don't think we could have stayed together forever.'

For more than five decades Sir Coxsone Outernational travelled the length and breadth of the UK and into Europe, through snow and rain, to entertain the Black community of every major city and numerous smaller towns along the way. They have a history that deserves to be told. There's a book and a film there. Ah who seh?

Jah Shaka: Spiritual Dub Warrior

VIVIEN GOLDMAN

Back in 1981, the *New Musical Express* produced a radical 'Sound Clash' feature, and representing the mighty Jah Shaka – who sadly transitioned to Zion on 11 April 2023 – was recording artist, author and journalist Vivien Goldman. These are her words.

It's something like seeing *The Wizard of Oz* for the first time; all that mighty, awesome thunder and noise of great rushing waters, then a faint start when you realise the tumult is coming from one man.

Shaka detests dealing in competition, but sound clashes are part of the game. Every sound system has its strengths, and all sound system followers have their favourites and there is a certain section of the population who love only Jah Shaka.

When the other sounds have done with their boasting and toasting, there would come a discreet hiss from the corner, and Shaka would mutter a title, or more often an invocation to Jah Rastafari, and the old-style heavy Bakelite-style head of his arm would lower to the vinyl. Then it might seem that the walls were tumbling down around your ears. Then it might seem that your body had never felt those rhythms to impel and overwhelm, you'd find your feet flashing like sparklers.

A crowd gathers round Shaka, watching entranced as if he was a conjuror. Sometimes he plays the vocal section straight, then he rides the rhythm until it disintegrates, you hurtle through the instruments like a dance of swop-your-partners, now whirling to the hi-hat, or fist-fighting with the bass. When the music hits, Shaka, well into the dub section now, looks like Lee Perry, swaying faster to a frenzy, bobbing and weaving as the music's penetrating. His hands seem to flash from knob to knob of his HH amp like lightning. A picture of Haile Selassie sellotaped above the deck acts as an inspirational icon.

Then come certain sounds, the sounds that mark out Shaka. A keening sound cuts you, trailing a tail like a comet. Shaka playing his harp, then syn-drum; he hits it with a drumstick or plays it with his hands, the abstract texture melodies that race like liquid neon through each vein. This is a music, a great improvisation, that goes beyond reggae or any other musical division. Almost beyond physical music, into the mystic; sheets of energy shooting from the barricading standing store speakers.

Some people complain, say Shaka carries too much weight, too much distortion. It's true, it can verge on pain when Shaka shakes a sound by the scruff of its neck till it gives up its secret. But he is an extreme artist. Unlike most sound system organisers, he stays alone at the controls, speaking only when the spirit says so, choosing the music that will re-charge the people's batteries like an orgone accumulator. If Shaka's sound sticks needles in your ears, it's like acupuncture, shaking up the sluggish circulation of the blood. He is a serious and dedicated man, who will only play inspirational music.

Shaka inspires the stepper dancers. When his turn comes round, the music hits new intensity, and the youths launch into gymnastic feats. As much mime as dance, the motions of stepping on stones over river currents, of peering through curtains and shinning up drainpipes, of finding your way from a fortress to freedom. These are guerrilla movements to complement Shaka's warrior style. Purposeful and athletic, with the frenzy of dervishes. It is no coincidence that Shaka cites Aswad, and Misty, the two warrior bands, as particularly crucial.

Such a stance is crucial in these times. Last Friday Shaka was making the rafters rattle like loose teeth in a South London Town Hall, playing a new Aswad dub. He cries: 'JAHOVIAH I', a long, warbled yowl that seems to span octaves, the cry he's adopted from the Twinkle Brothers' great 'Daniel' record. The warrior youth start to step with the crisp decision that marks a militant stepper.

Shaka named himself after the great Zulu warrior, the man who re-structured the Zulu armies in the early 1800s. He devised a new, lethal, fighting blade; imposed strict discipline, including months of celibacy at a stretch; divided the spoils of war radically, giving most to the poorest soldiers, and less to the rich. Jah Shaka says it's the Zulu's work he sets out to continue.

That same day, the papers report a seventeen-year-old skinhead Sieg Heiling in court as he's sentenced for the murder of an Asian youth, Akhtar Ali Baig. Another item next to it quotes Joan Lestor, MP, saying that many victims have no confidence in the determination of the police to seek out perpetrators of racial violence.

It's a warrior time, if you want to survive. Daily harassment of all kinds, the feeling of not being free to walk the streets; Shaka's answer, in the face of any argument, is repatriation to Africa.

'It's a complete solution. With the knowledge we've got over the years, we know the task. We

ABOVE Jah Shaka, Spiritual Dub Warrior, at the Dome, Archway, North London 1991. Photograph by Beezer.

BELOW and OPPOSITE ABOVE Jah Shaka plays the Rocket, London, 1990.
OPPOSITE BELOW Jah Shaka and full control tower, the Dome, London,
1991. Photographs by Beezer.

are not fighting to stay here. If I was to meet with the head of the National Front, it would solve a lot of problems.'

The man who inspires such fierce devotion does not like to talk about himself. 'It's nothing to do with my private life or my slave name, it's nonsense to bring yourself out into the limelight. I'm not involved with that. All I want to do is get on with my work, till such time as I leave the country.

'I don't know what the other sounds are doing, I only know what I am doing. It's nothing to do with what kind of speakers or amps I'm building; I'm only concerned with building spiritually.

'I spend a lot of time with the sound. Talking to the people is more important than the studio business. [Although Shaka himself is a musician and has just released his first record – 'Jah Children Cry' by African Princess on his own label.] I've got to bring people to remember that we, the Black people, have been forgotten. You could call us the forgotten race, as it says in the Bible. I take it very seriously. The people that are mentioned in the records I play – the Children of Israel – that is directly us.

'This is my most important job. People get depressed in this country. You have to give them something to hope for. There's a lot of pressure. People complain – they say the whole world is

upside down. People jump off buildings so as not to face earth as it is at this moment. The only thing to look to is God. People have tried everything else. Haile Selassie came to show us that everything we've been hearing about is not in the sky – there is such a place where we could be – Ethiopia.'

Shaka's views are controversial. He arrived from Jamaica when he was five; kept dances from when he attended the Samuel Pepys School in South London. He gives thanks that he was raised here: 'It's been like a college here for me.'

The first sound he checked for was Metro, who still build his amps. Shaka moves with twelve youths who help set up the sound, transporting the mighty, hand-carved speakers with their heavyweight thunder old American RCA boxes, and amps. Most of them are unemployed. They have followed Shaka for anything from five to seven years, devote their lives to his sound.

Between them the youths around Shaka number the several skills – carpentry, electrical and so on – necessary to maintain the sound. They are unemployed simply because work is scarce; but this is probably the most fulfilling job they could do. 'Money doesn't even come into it,' says one youth whose two brothers have also worked alongside the dub warrior for years. 'It's a message we're carrying, not just a sound.'

Those who followed Rasta as a fashion have moved on to roller disco. For the large hard core who are serious about their beliefs, Shaka is still here. When you hear Shaka play his sound, it's easy to believe his inspiration is divine.[1]

Bristol: Sound of the City

KEVIN LE GENDRE

During the height of the Black Lives Matter movement, the slave-owning legacy of Bristol was literally dragged over cobbled streets and dumped in the harbour. Journalist, author and radio broadcaster Kevin Le Gendre reflects on his time in Bristol and takes us on a tour of the city's thriving, innovative and effortlessly eclectic, Black music-inspired community.

In the early 1990s Black music buzzed all over Bristol. There was no shortage of clubs that played soul, funk, reggae and African rhythms, both live or on record, including Blue Mountain, Bierkeller, Lakota, Tube and Moon. Venues from east to west had something worth hearing. Away from the centre, there was culture. The Hen and Chicken – a very charming pub in Bedminster on the south side of the city – hosted comedy, theatre and jazz. The French gypsy jazz guitar legend Boulou Ferré did an unforgettable session there.

While at Bristol University I went to a lot of other gigs that have stuck firmly in my mind. Firstly, the Brand New Heavies at the Student's Union on Queens Road. In time-honoured fashion the Londoners did the college circuit, and they proved to be premier graduates of the JBs groove school, scoring highly for their infectious, tightly woven riffs and eye-catching retro attire that made us believe the 1970s had somehow stretched to the 1990s.

Secondly, a lesser-known outfit, QRZ?, appeared at the Thekla, a seminal club housed on a boat, the wonderfully named *Old Profanity*, which was permanently moored in the dockland area near to the Watershed arts centre. The band stood out because they had a brilliant rapper, M. C. Blak, a West Country MC of West Indian descent who delivered a seamless flow of thoughtful, truth-teller rhymes that locked in potently with a sharp rhythm section.

Even more interesting was the leader of the group: Larry Stabbins, a noted saxophonist-flautist from Bristol who had come to my attention in the mid-1980s as a member of Working Week, a key act of the Thatcher years that featured guitarist Simon Booth, vocalist Juliet Roberts and several African, Caribbean and South American players.

By the end of the decade acid jazz was gaining considerable media traction and Brand New Heavies and QRZ? were lumped in the new subgenre. There was never a precise definition of the music, bar a conscious embrace of the sound of the past, namely horns, Hammond organs and wah-wah guitars, but several of the acts did seek to fully engage with hip-hop, which was still in its infancy and represented the sound of the future.

Hence the presence of M. C. Blak in QRZ? opened up many possibilities. His verses and Stabbins's solos made a killer combination on tracks like 'This Is Calling You', a song that filled floors and also made you reach for the rewind when it was on a mix tape.

There should have been no surprise at this development given the fact that Stabbins had proved adept at handling limb-loosening samba

rhythms with Working Week, but his back story was also indicative of the rich and far-reaching history of jazz in Bristol.

As a youngster he played in several bands led by pianist Keith Tippett, a seminal figure in the avant-garde movement of the 1970s, whose boundless imagination stretched all the way to the fifty-piece orchestra Centipede, which in many ways was a cornerstone of radical British music. Tippett collaborated with the leading exponents of spontaneous composition of his generation but also nurtured younger locals such as another talented saxophonist, Andy Sheppard, and established the Seedbank Orchestra as a kind of workshop-rehearsal that welcomed mixed-ability players for gigs at Bristol Old Vic.

If Tippett's groups epitomised an independent spirit as well as musical originality, then Bristol produced other significant acts in the 1980s that drew on the history of African-American art music but also channelled the populist energy of funk and non-Western rhythms. Rip, Rig + Panic, its name taken from one of the landmark albums by legendary multi-reed player Rahsaan Roland Kirk, were an explosive, provocative combo in

which Mark Springer, Gareth Sager, Sean Oliver, Bruce Smith and Neneh Cherry created an audio-visual aesthetic that was worldly and political. Nods to French director Jean Cocteau and strong anti-establishment sentiment were part of their unique identity.

Then there were several groups that had an overlap of personnel but each fashioned its own individual sound from the crucible of dub, rock, post-punk and funk. The Pop Group had an anarchic banshee shockability, Glaxo Babies allied urbane lyric and staccato riffing and Maximum Joy crafted a loose, rangy groove that roughed up the polish of disco. The ability of these bands to make music that had elements of many genres without falling into any one in particular summarised Bristol as a vibrant, inventive musical hub.

Also interesting is what different individuals did once these combos broke up. In 1991 ex-Glaxo-Maximum Joy saxophonist Tony Wrafter made a single, 'Y Skate On Thin Ice (When You Can Dance)', that was notable for its contemporary form. It reflected the creeping permeation of mainstream Black music by hip-hop. Scratches, programmed drums and bulky bass were the backdrop for Wrafter's saxophone strains and a slew of rhymes by Michelle Pascal, who, along with Wee Papa Girl Rappers and Cookie Crew, was among the first women to bless the mic in this country. She was a pioneering MC.

ABOVE DJ Derek at his weekly DJ session at the Star and Garter, Bristol, 1984. OPPOSITE ABOVE The Ultimate Wild Bunch: (left to right) DJ Milo, Daddy Gee, Nellee Hooper, MC Willie Wee and 3D. The Dug Out Club, Bristol, 1984. OPPOSITE BELOW London vs Bristol: Newtrament vs Wild Bunch, Newtrament on the 1s and 2s, Red House, Portland Square, St Pauls, Bristol, 1985. Photographs by Beezer.

ABOVE Neneh Cherry of Rip Rig + Panic poses for a portrait in a squat on Ladbroke Grove in London, 1981. Photograph by David Corio.

For all its diversity, Bristol, like London, Manchester, Birmingham, Nottingham and Leeds, had unofficial boundaries drawn around its Black community.

By today's standards the Wrafter–Pascal collaboration is rudimentary, if not dated. But the point is that they were essaying new ideas rather than falling back on tried and tested formulas, and thus stepping on to a road of change down which others would later travel.

Furthermore, the monochrome picture sleeve of the 12-inch single, which showed Wrafter, a white man, side by side with Pascal, a Black woman, was a strong symbol of multi-cultural Bristol that could also be seen in the line-ups of QRZ? and Rip, Rig + Panic.

For all its diversity, Bristol, like London, Manchester, Birmingham, Nottingham and Leeds, had unofficial boundaries drawn around its Black community. And there was a wide range of perceptions of different locales. When I left the well-to-do area of Clifton, a landing point for many students, and relocated to Montpelier, a few eyebrows were raised because it was near to St Pauls, the hub of the Black population. This was the 'frontline' that had been the scene of civil disturbances in the early 1980s, just as had been the case in equivalent quarters in the aforesaid cities due to racial discrimination in housing, education, employment and policing. The cause and effect was on a loop nationally.

One person thought nothing of bluntly warning my new home was 'very ethnic'. Shocking as the words are today, they flowed freely in the early 1990s because of a lack of general recognition of unpalatable truths in Bristolian history. Colston Hall was a major venue and only those with the most prophetic minds might have imagined that three decades later the statue of the arts patron and slave trader after whom it was named would end up swimming towards infamy rather than glory in

the city's harbour, largely pulled under by the ghost of George Floyd. That wave of anger was still a very long way off.

In any case there was a distinct grassroots flavour to culture in St Pauls, which was vividly epitomised by the Malcolm X Community Centre. It was a community space in the real sense of the term insofar as it hosted anything from birthday parties to sound system dances and gave a graphic reminder of the role of culture as emotional and political sustenance to settlers form the Caribbean and their offspring who were born and raised in Bristol. At one life-enhancing session by the mighty selector Jah Shaka (see page 162) I was gripped not just by the heaviness of his dubplates but by the mass hypnosis created in front of a pair of giant speakers vibrating so much they looked like twin hearts pumping rhythmic electricity.

Other venues such as the Star and Garter were also crucial focal points for reggae, and Bristol laid claim to a rich heritage of bands inspired by Bob Marley, who had appeared at the legendary Bamboo Club in the 1970s (see page 190). Chief among them were Black Roots and Talisman, though singer Joshua Moses was another major talent on the local scene.

These artists gave voice to the stark reality of contemporary daily life for Bristol's Black population, broaching the stress of the 'dole age' and the strain of the sus laws.[1] Yet there was also an outlet for Caribbean tradition in the shape of St Pauls carnival, which, although lacking the national renown of Notting Hill, had a comparatively long history, and was fuelled by a similar energy and sense of release. To a

The Frontlines / Bristol: Sound of the City

171

These were not bands in the traditional sense of the term. They were sound systems. They had shifting collective personnel rather than the ages-old 'frontman'.

certain extent carnival was the key moment of my sojourn in Bristol precisely because the event took place in an outdoor space, in the streets, in the surroundings that were part of the history of West Indian migration that brought the gifts of song, dance, sartorial style – and spice buns.

While Black music in Bristol had an enviably rich pedigree, there was also something appealing about the relative lack of pretension and down-to-earth nature of the city's arts scene in general. I struck up many conversations with musicians, DJs and producers after a few chance meetings on the street or at the bar of a club devoid of 'A-list antics'.

Yet Bristol was not insular or parochial. There had long been connections between its artists and London's, as exemplified by the career of saxophonist Larry Stabbins. Furthermore, there was an upsurge of talent in the early 1990s that would make a significant breakthrough by engaging with a number of different figures, be they singers, rappers, players of instruments, producers or A&R from outside as well as inside the city. The excellent soul vocalist Tammy Payne and drum and bass icons Roni Size & Reprazent became two very significant Bristolian signings to Gilles Peterson's Talkin' Loud label.

A band that could also be described as a resoundingly British entity, being made both in the West Country and the capital, was Earthling. Producer Tim Saul was from Bristol, MC Mau from London, and vocalist Segun Lee-French, who had studied in Bristol, was from Manchester.

They created music that built an intriguing, often daring bridge between sampling, programming and live playing, soulful exclamation and film score extrapolation, a desire to match echoes of the past with reflections on the present.

Earthling were hard to pigeonhole and their debut album *Radar* remains a noteworthy document of a band that acknowledged the pervasive influence of US hip-hop while fashioning a UK aesthetic that had its own marks of distinction in both sound and word. Mau's most personal lyric nailed it, when declaring their confidence of self-identity.

Making the biggest commercial impact was Massive Attack. Their 1991 debut album *Blue Lines* is an important musical statement of the decade for its stylistic range insofar as it placed the methodologies of dub and hip-hop at the heart of a compositional world in which not one but many rappers and singers would have space to express themselves. Although 3-D, Daddy G and Mushroom were the nominal faces of Massive – all three of them Bristolians to the core – they made music by reaching out to collaborators *beyond* their locality. While Tricky, Willie Wee and Carlton were notable local MCs and singers, there were other brilliant vocalists: the deeply soulful Shara Nelson from London and Horace Andy, a reggae legend from Jamaica who was largely unknown to younger listeners and club goers who did not have the breadth of knowledge that Massive Attack had acquired

OPPOSITE Roni Size and Krust, Bristol Docks, 2000.
Photograph by Peter Williams.

from their previous incarnation as the Wild Bunch in the early 1980s.

Interestingly, a former member of the crew, Nellee Hooper, made a significant contribution to Black music in Britain by co-producing Soul II Soul, the London-based outfit that had enjoyed a run of major success in the late 1980s just a few years prior to Massive Attack's national emergence. This link between these two emblematic artists posed a challenge to the prevailing norms and models of the rock and pop industry.

After all, these were not *bands* in the traditional sense of the term. They were sound systems. They had shifting collective personnel rather than the ages-old 'frontman'.

They were initially successful as DJs and MCs who could draw audiences to dances and club nights, and had subsequently started to produce records in their own right, embracing new technological means to create beats that were able to fill the floor without completely turning away from the long-standing traditions of melody and orchestration.

Tellingly, Soul II Soul and Massive both had lush string sections *and* turntable scratches. Bristol was thus an integral part of a wave of progress, a spirit of newness, a dynamic of change that ran through Black music in Britain in the early 1990s. The city had a cornucopia of talent that was too good for the rest of the country, and eventually the world, not to recognise. Many visiting American artists would pick up on the vibrancy of the city and applaud both the intense engagement and profound knowledge of the local audience. When iconic vibraphonist Roy Ayers played Lakota, the first words he uttered on stage did more than move the crowd: 'We live in Bristol, baby. We're trying to make it, baby.'

PAUL BRADSHAW

Civil unrest. Conspiracy trials. Rock Against Racism. Riots. A decade of change?

The decade kicked off with the Old Bailey trial of the Mangrove Nine – a group of British Black activists tried for inciting a riot at a 1970 protest against the police targeting of the Mangrove, a Caribbean restaurant in Notting Hill in West London (see page 122). The 155-day trial was revisited in 2020 as one episode of Steve McQueen's *Small Axe* series on the BBC.

In 1974 the lights went out. Strikes by the miners led to flying pickets, clashes with the police, power cuts and a three-day week. During that year Dennis Bovell and his Sufferah sound system was playing at the Carib Club in Cricklewood, along with two other sounds, when the police stormed the dance. Bovell was arrested and accused of inciting an affray. He lost a year of his life during two trials at the Old Bailey. The first trial lasted nine months and culminated with the acquittal of nine of his co-defendants. A second trial lasted three months after which he was sentenced to three years in prison. Six months later, on appeal, the case was thrown out.

In the summer of 1976 Dennis Bovell was released from Wandsworth prison just in time to witness the Notting Hill Carnival explode. Tired of the racial profiling, sus laws and SPG (Special Patrol Group) harassment, the youth fought back: Babylon got a beatin'.

In August 1976, in response to a racist rant by Eric Clapton at a concert in Birmingham, David Bowie's espousal of fascism and the rise of racist attacks by the National Front, Rock Against Racism (RAR) was launched. Significantly their ever first gig featured Dennis Bovell's Matumbi.

The 'No Future' generation found their voice in punk rock. Using RAR's *Temporary Hoarding* fanzine and the music press to publicise the movement, activist groups sprang up around the UK. In conjunction with the Anti-Nazi League, RAR organised two carnivals, in London and Manchester. On 30 April 1978, one hundred thousand people marched six miles from Trafalgar Square to the East End of London for an open-air concert in Victoria Park. In Manchester, following a march to Alexandra Park (located between the vibrant communities of Whalley Range and Moss Side), forty thousand people came together to listen to Steel Pulse and the Buzzcocks.

During the RAR era, a new wave of politically motivated and Rastafari-oriented Black British reggae bands followed Bob Marley and the Wailers into the UK music mainstream. RAR provided a radical new platform for the music. The Cimarons, Steel Pulse, Misty in Roots, Black Slate, Aswad, Black Roots and Exodus all shared stages with their white counterparts. They were championed by the likes of John Peel; some

OPPOSITE Carnival Against the Nazis, poster, 1978, designed by David King. The Anti Nazi League and Rock Against Racism logos were seen everywhere.

TOM ROBINSON BAND
STEEL PULSE & X-RAY SPEX

**RALLY SUNDAY APRIL 30
11a.m.TRAFALGAR SQUARE
MARCH TO
VICTORIA PARK**

Anti Nazi League

CARNIVAL!!!!
AGAINST THE NAZIS!

ORGANISED BY ANTI NAZI LEAGUE, 12 LITTLE NEWPORT STREET, LONDON WC2, TOGETHER WITH ROCK AGAINST RACISM,
HACKNEY CAMPAIGN AGAINST RACISM, HACKNEY CRC, AND TOWER HAMLETS MOVEMENT AGAINST RACISM & FASCISM

signed to major record labels, appeared on *Top of the Pops* and had chart hits.

In August 1978, the confrontational approach of the National Front sparked the 'Battle of Lewisham'. It was an extremely volatile event and it was followed in April 1979 by the Southall riots. When the NF booked an inflammatory pre-election meeting in Ealing Town Hall it led to the mobilisation of West London's Asian community: three thousand protesters responded. They were met with a brutal response from the police. Blair Peach, an anti-racist activist and schoolteacher, was killed by a blow to the head. Dozens of protesters were injured, many with head wounds. Misty in Roots' manager Clarence Baker incurred serious head injuries at the hands of the police that led him to be hospitalised, in a coma, for over two months.

In May 1979 a general election was held and Margaret Thatcher arrived in Number 10 Downing Street. Waiting in the musical wings was the two-tone movement, who were to take on the legacy of RAR with songs such as 'Too Much Pressure' by the Selecter, 'Stand Down Margaret' by the Beat, and 'Ghost Town' and 'Racist Friend' by the Specials.

On 18 January 1981 a fire at a New Cross house party killed fourteen young Black people aged between 14 and 22. The pain was felt throughout the Black community and led to the Black People's Day of Action on 2 March. Over a period of eight hours, twenty

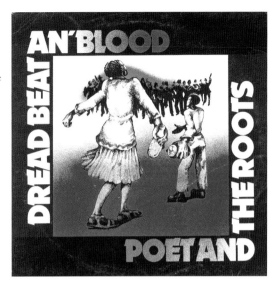

thousand predominantly Black people marched from South London and crossed the river to pass through Fleet Street. Placards read: 'Thirteen Dead, Nothing Said'. The tragedy will be remembered through the poetry of Benjamin Zephaniah's '13 Dead' and Linton Kwesi Johnson's 'New Craas Massahkah'. Both Benjamin and LKJ were no strangers to sharing Rock Against Racism stages.

In the wake of the New Cross fire, while anger was still simmering, the Met launched 'Operation Swamp 81' – a London-wide campaign against burglary and robbery. In early April a small army of plain-clothes police descended on Brixton. Over six days they stopped and searched nine hundred and forty-three people – arresting one hundred and eighteen predominantly Black youths. Over the weekend of 10–12 April 1981, after a stabbing incident outside the police station, rumours were rife and around two hundred youths turned on the police. Brixton was set alight. By the summer every major city followed Brixton's example.

OPPOSITE ABOVE Steel Pulse on stage at a concert organised by the Anti-Nazi League and Rock Against Racism at Victoria Park, Hackney, London, 30 April 1978. Photograph by David Corio. OPPOSITE BELOW Rock Against Racism Carnival, Leeds, 1981. Photograph by Syd Shelton. ABOVE *Dread Beat an' Blood* LP, on the Frontline label, 1978, and featuring Linton Kwesi Johnson.

BLACK BRITISH REGGAE A selection of bands that were formed in the 1970s, clockwise from top left: Black Roots, Bristol, 1983; Aswad, Brixton, 1981; Misty in Roots, London, 1979; Black Slate, 1981.

Black women at the Rock Against Racism concert in Victoria Park, London, 1978. Photograph by John Sturrock.

Missing Words: Pauline Black, a Black Women's Voice in Two-tone

CHARDINE TAYLOR-STONE

I became aware of the Selecter as a teenager, watching VH1 when it still played music videos. The slight fuzz on the screen, a video made in 1980 replayed on a 2000s TV screen, a glaring white background, the band dancing in sharp, black suits, the singer – Pauline Black – searing through the screen with a sweet vocal and a delivery that embodied fierce determination and intent. Her style mirrored the familiar image of 2 Tone Records as represented by the label's logo man and mascot Walt Jabsco.

Being mixed race – Anglo-Jewish/Nigerian – Black maintains she tried to embody a character that straddled both sides of her heritage; the two-tone scene 'felt like a good fit'. Fast forward to now and I find myself in conversation with Pauline Black, two Black women musicians from different generations who have carved out their space in a time when respective Conservative governments were dismantling the state to a point almost beyond repair.

Two-tone was a sound I strongly associated with a British childhood that combined both Black and white working-class cultures. When asked how the two-tone movement came about for her, Black comments: 'We all had the same beginning, we'd all been through the same school system, we'd listen to the same music...

we had the same references.' Combined with her knowledge of the civil rights movement and the Black Panther movement of the 1960s and 1970s, it meant, for her, that 'the time was ready for the public, the mainstream, to talk about racism.'

Despite the development of a shared youth culture, rock music remained the main voice for young people. But in 1976, in the wake of an incendiary racist tirade from Eric Clapton – an esteemed, blues-inspired musician who subsequently expressed deep shame at his Powell-ite rant – a new generation of aspiring musicians responded with a sound that better reflected the influences of their upbringing. It also gave momentum to a radical movement that swept the nation: Rock Against Racism (see page 174).

Inspired by Roxy DJ Don Letts, the Clash and the '77 punk generation spearheaded the reggae/rock collision. Two-tone, however, was a complete amalgamation of two cultures, the product of a new normal for a generation of kids from the Midlands who had fish and chips on a Friday and curry goat on a Sunday. It came from white teenagers who overheard their Black neighbours' ska and reggae records, who used the same slang as their Black classmates, who stood in the same dole queue as their Black friends. As Black reflects, 'As clichéd

We had to barricade ourselves in as people were coming for us with bottles and weapons. Fearing for your life in the back of Hatfield Polytechnic doesn't feel that empowering.

as it sounds, music is a universal language; relationships and other adult matters can appear complex to young people, so music is an easy tool to exchange ideas.'

Comparisons can be drawn with Britain today. Brexit, Trump and the rise of right-wing populism have led to an increase in racist rhetoric. The two-tone era followed an economic crisis and political instability and, like today, that left the white British identity, bereft of its colonial Empire, unsure of its place in the world. Although we are not back to the days where large groups

of skinheads would patrol the streets attacking – sometimes murdering – Black and Asian people, we still have disenfranchised white youths informed by ignorance and fear. Encouraged by alt-right influencers, young people, especially young men, look to easy targets to exert feelings of power in their local neighbourhoods and online rather than towards politicians. Black talks about the extreme violence she sometimes experienced on the road: 'We had to barricade ourselves in as people were coming for us with bottles and weapons. Fearing for your life in the back of Hatfield Polytechnic doesn't feel that empowering.' The need for unity had to be made

obvious because the divides were so sharp and the stakes, on the streets, so high.

Despite a commonly held belief that two tone led the mainstream to embrace multiculturalism, some form of cognitive dissonance continues to exist amongst fans, occasionally causing anger or confusion. Inspired by Malcolm X, Linda Bellos and other Black activists, Black continues to directly address issues such as racism or the government onstage. She vividly recalls one recent gig where the band had projected images of Boris Johnson with a Pinocchio nose as a backdrop: some fans took serious umbrage and walked out.

This *we just wanna dance* attitude towards Black musicians is the result of an unconscious bias, where Black musicians are infantilised into just being wholesome entertainers, patronised with the assumption they have nothing more to contribute to their art form than rhythm – a good beat for white people to dance to. Ska music may be oriented towards dancing but any real fan of the genre knows that the music itself came from a time when Jamaica was beginning to assert itself as an independent nation. The joy of the music embodies those aspirations. Jamaican musicians have never been afraid to comment on the political situation in Kingston or in the 'motherland'. Rudeboy classics such as Dandy Livingstone's 'A Message to You, Rudy' and the Wailers' 'Simmer Down' directly addressed the increase in gang and party political violence in Kingston. From my own cultural background in Trinidad, political commentary is a key component of calypso and soca. Denying the political voices in our music misunderstands our culture entirely.

OPPOSITE Pauline Black with the Selecter on tour in the USA, 1980. Photograph by Ebet Roberts. ABOVE The Selecter on the 2 Tone Tour, 1980. Photograph by Virginia Turbett.

BELOW Pauline Black, Suggs (Madness) and Neville Staple (the Specials) on the 2 Tone tour, Brighton, 1979. Photograph by Chalkie Davies.
OPPOSITE The Selecter's first single, 'On My Radio'. The double A-side featured 'Gangsters' by the Specials on the other.

A new generation of Black-led alternative bands like Bob Vylan and Nova Twins deliver overtly political lyrics that express their experiences and feelings as modern-day Black Britons, but like the Selecter, then and now, they are often confronted with heckling fans telling them to 'get on with it'.

With knowing nods of acknowledgement based on our mutual experiences, we talk about the oppressive racist and sexist structures in the music industry, how fickle it is. Black comments: 'I remember coming into a record company office one day and suddenly the kids had moved away from wearing black and white to wearing New Romantic kilts and make-up.' She remarks that this probably suited the budgets of the record company. Sending a seven piece band like hers on the road is a lot more expensive than a synth duo/group. It's also arguable that the Thatcherite aspirations of some New Romantic groups made them less controversial to market. 'It shouldn't be the backdrop to how music was made but unfortunately it is,' Black responds.

In contrast to the message of equality, Black also points out that in the past the majority white, male, two-tone bands would get paid more than her band and others with a lot of Black or women members. Despite all this she holds onto a memory in which she felt real solidarity, standing on stage at Hammersmith Palais. It was a benefit gig with John Lydon and Linton Kwesi Johnson in the audience. The bill included the Specials and the Mo-dettes. A group of skinheads were doing Nazi salutes at the stage. 'If you needed a greater reason for

you to be doing something, you just needed to look at them,' says Black. 'So we stopped the gig and asked the audience, "Do you want us to continue?" Everyone said, "YES". So, we said we would go off stage whilst these people were thrown out, then we'd come back on stage and play for you. We got such a resounding cheer you felt like there was a reason for doing this.'

We end our conversation on the importance of how we as Black women in alternative music can use our platforms and how having a microphone with an ability to hold an audience gives us the opportunity to be heard when often we are not. At this point, I feel her look me directly in the eye with all that strident energy she displayed in that first video I saw all those years ago: 'If you are given a platform, given a microphone, if people don't understand what it is you are on about – tell them to fuck off!'

Di Great Insohreckshan

LINTON KWESI JOHNSON

It was in April, nineteen... eighty one
Down 'n on dee ghetto of Brix-ton
Dat deh Babylon dem cause such a fric-tion
Dat it bring about a great insohreck-shan
And it spread all over deh nay-shun
It was truly an historical occas-sion
It was event of deh year and I wish I had been der
When we run riot all over Brixton
When we mash up plenty police van
When we mash up the wicked one plan
When we mash up the Swamp 81, fi what?
Fi make deh rule of dem understand
Dat we nah take no more of dem oppression
And when me check out deh ghetto grapevine
To find out all dat I can find
Every rebel jus a revel in dem stohry
Dem ah talk bout deh power and deh glory
Dem ah talk bout deh burning and the looting
Dem ah talk bout deh smashing and the grabbing
Dem ah tell me bout deh vanquish and deh victree
Dem said deh babylon dem went too far
So wha? wi ad woz fi bun two kyar
And one or two innocent get marred, buh wha?
Thas how it go sometimes in a war, in star
Thas how it go sometimes in a war
Dem say we burn down deh George we coulda burn da landlord
We burn down deh George we never burn da landlord
When we run riot all over Brixton
When we mash up plenty police van
When we mash up the wicked one plan
When we mash up the Swamp 81
Dem say we commendear car and we gather ammunition
We build wi barricade and deh wicked catch afraid
We sen out wi scout fog oh fine dem whereabout
Den wi faam-up wi passi an wi mek wi raid

Well now dem run down deh plan 'call to action'
But dem plastic bullet an' dem water can-non
Will bring a blam blam, will bring a blam blam
Nevermind Scarman... We bring a blam blam

ABOVE Linton Kwesi Johnson, Railton Road, Brixton in 1979.
Photograph by Adrian Boot.

The Bamboo Club

TRACY DURRANT

In the face of racial hostility and police harassment, Bristol's Bamboo Club opened in 7 St Paul Street and provided the community a space that embraced food, dominoes and live performances from local, US and Jamaican artists, hosting one of the earliest UK performances of Bob Marley and the Wailers.

Tony and Lalel Bullimore founded the Bamboo Club in 1966. It was a pioneering West Indian entertainment centre that hosted icons like Bob Marley and Jimmy Cliff until its closure by fire in 1977. It was opened against the backdrop of the 1963 Bristol Bus Boycott which led to the Race Relations Act 1965, when there was still racial discrimination in public places. The Bamboo Club provided a space for respite. According to club member Sonia Burgess, 'You couldn't just walk into a pub, you'd probably get beaten up. Up town often the guys on the door would tell you that the club was full – they had reached their quota of Black people.'

Reflecting on the club's beginning, one former employee of the Bamboo Club, Yvonne Mills, shares: 'I remember first meeting Tony Bullimore. He asked my mum about entertainment spots for Black people.' Her mum explained that there was nowhere for Black people to go and enjoy themselves. Soon after, despite local opposition, the Bamboo Club was opened on 28 October 1966.

The contrast between inside the club and the outside world was stark. Yvonne Mills is clear that the police didn't like the idea of a Black club. 'Most nights, they'd [the police] turn up with their riot van, claiming they heard of a fight – even when we were just setting up. Police presence deterred some people, especially the older generation. Despite the racial tensions outside, inside the club the atmosphere was fun, inclusive and loved by many people from all backgrounds.'

Larry Stabbins, respected avant-garde saxophonist and co-founder of Working Week, honed his skills at the Bamboo with the white soul band the Franklin Big Six: 'We played there a lot, we had a Thursday night residency during the winter of 1966–67, we'd play Motown, Tina Turner covers. It was the first place in Bristol where Black and white people could go together. It was generally mixed and there were no problems there.'

LEFT The legendary Bamboo Club in May 1968. It brought some of the biggest names in Caribbean music to Bristol, including Bob Marley and the Wailers. OPPOSITE Bamboo Club flyer, February 1977. DJ Hank was the Bamboo Club's resident selector.

There was something for everyone at the Bamboo. 'The Cave' was dedicated to the domino players, 'the Basement' was where resident DJ Hank Durrant played and 'Upstairs' was dedicated to the live acts.

The roster of artists that played the club is impressive: John Holt, Burning Spear, Mighty Diamonds, Gregory Isaacs, Skatalites, Jimmy Cliff, Dennis Brown, Alton Ellis, Toots and the Maytals, Derrick Morgan, Desmond Dekker, Ben E. King, the Ronettes, and Bob Marley and the Wailers all performed and contributed to the club's legendary status.

'I saw Desmond Dekker perform "The Israelites" just days after he went number one on *Top of the Pops*; the club was packed and his performance was excellent,' recalls Alfred Durrant, a club member and regular.

Sonia Burgess reflects on the time funky US rhythm & blues star Joe Tex performed at the club: 'I won the skinny leg competition, I won some dollars.'

In 1972 Bob Marley was so impressed by the Cimarons' rendition of his song 'Duppy Conqueror' that they were invited to do three shows with the Wailers, one at the Apollo in London, one at Bouncing Ball in Peckham and the third gig at the Bamboo Club, Bristol.

'We didn't have a van. We fit everything into these two cars and we drove to Bristol,' recalls Locksley Gichie, guitarist with the Cimarons. 'The atmosphere was laid back and cool. It felt safe there. They were always so good to us, giving us food and drinks. The Bamboo Club led to more gigs.'

'A lot of bands came to the Bamboo Club, some from Birmingham, Manchester, London,'

adds Basil Russell, who worked at the club and performed in the Atlantic Rollers. 'Me and Tony used to go to Pama Records in Harlesden when we wanted to book bands.'

Bristol reggae musician Jashwa Moses won the 'Search for a Star' competition held at the Bamboo Club and went on to record 'Africa (Is Our Land)' at the Berry Street Studio in London, produced by Dennis Bovell.

Domino tournaments would draw in crowds from across the UK. The Bamboo Club was the founding centre for the Bristol West Indian Cricket Club, Bristol West Indian Football Club and the Western Star Domino team. It also hosted an annual children's Christmas party. Yvonne reminisces: 'From curry goat to rum punch, the restaurant had it all.'

The Bamboo Club was more than just a nightspot; it emerged as a pivotal community centre and a symbol of unity, bridging people from different cities, countries and cultural backgrounds. The recounted experiences not only highlight the importance of having access to such inclusive spaces but also illustrate how they can transform communities. They create a sense of belonging, safety, and radiate love and joy within the community.[1]

TOP Outside the Reno. **ABOVE LEFT** Founder Phil Magbotiwan and his wife.
ABOVE CENTRE Linda Brogan, Sabina Quarcoopome and David Palmer in the Reno.
ABOVE RIGHT UPPER Reno regulars at the Moss Side Carnival. **ABOVE RIGHT
LOWER** DJ Persian at the Reno. You can take a deep dive into the Reno here:
https://thereno.live/home and https://www.youtube.com/@excavatingthereno1959.

The Reno: Digging Deep into Moss Side's Musical Past

PAUL BRADSHAW

The man behind Moss Side's legendary basement club, the Reno, was Phil Magbotiwan. Originally from Nigeria, he settled in industrial Manchester. A qualified and skilled engineer, he gradually invested his money in property and in 1962 acquired a building in Princess Road.

Like all major cities during the 1950s, Manchester was rife with racial tensions and setting up the Reno was far from simple. After being refused a liquor licence Magbotiwan continued to use the building as a refuge for African seamen unable to get beds for the night. According to his daughter, Lisa Ayegun, 'There was no drinking. Just a metal urn with tea and John Player's cigarettes, so the seamen could wake up, have a cig, have a brew and then go.'

Once the liquor licence was finally obtained, and in order to operate freely, he then had to deal with interference from the local police to ensure the club would not be raided and shut down early.

In the early days the club hosted live music that sometimes featured Lord Kitchener, who had taken up residency in Manchester. Above the Reno was the Nile. Both clubs stayed open until 5 or 6 am six nights a week. The Nile was reggae and African music – live and DJ'd – while the Reno, in the basement, played strictly soul and funk. The DJ who remains synonymous with the Reno is DJ Persian, who had the dance floor packed playing the latest imports purchased from Manchester's Spin Inn Records.

Lisa and her sister and brothers worked in the club from a young age and she recalls, 'The Reno was full of more people with afros, suits and dancing. The Nile was full of people with dreadlocks, wanting to whine and slow dance all night... My dad only liked Nigerian music.'

During the Reno's heyday, 1971 to 1981, it was visited by Muhammad Ali (who had met Phil Magbotiwan at a boxing match in Montreal) and Bob Marley along with globally famous cricketers such as Clive Lloyd. One regular at the Reno until it closed and was demolished in 1986 was a young Linda Brogan. Her father was Jamaican and her mother Irish. In 2016–17, Linda organised an 'Excavating the Reno' project with Salford University Archaeology.

Of her own experiences she says, 'The first night I ever went down to the Reno, there were many mixed-race people there. I hadn't seen anywhere else like that – it felt like "my place". Everyone has a place that has made them feel like that, and for me, it is the Reno. The music was always absolutely rocking... it was really hard NOT to dance. This was a place where you'd hear records every night that got you moving!'[1]

In the eyes of some it was a place to avoid. The Reno's clientele reflected the community and it had its rough side. That said, for the regulars it was family, a close-knit multi-generational community. They even had their own football team: Afroville.

In 2016, Linda Brogan – now an award-winning playwright – set out to collect Reno memoirs and explore the connection she still felt with the club. Determined not to let the bulldozers erase her own history along with that of others from her generation, in 2017 she literally excavated the site of the club to deliver an exhibition at the Whitworth (2019–20) and a website.[2] For that, we give thanks!

Our Casablanca: A Short Story

ANTHONY WRIGHT

The Casablanca was once a church. To us, it was our church. After all, what is a church but a building to guide and teach its flock, a place of sanctuary, a place of magnificent, profound storytelling conveyed to you by people in whom we trust?

Knock it down. Get rid of it along with the slum houses. Rebuild. Start from scratch. What's the use of this place but a home of drug dealers and other such vices? These are the questions that those with the power asked. But we, the people who used the Casablanca, always believed: destroy this haven and you murder the community. We feared this outcome daily. That is why narratives like the one below, which portray the spirit of the Casablanca, need to be told and preserved. Only then will the characters within such stories continue to grow with each generation and become the myths and legends that help lead and teach our younger generations.

Music came from within: Renford's story

The waft of fish and chips and static atmospheric music filled the bare room, illuminated only by a naked bulb. Renford swayed to the beat alone. It was his nightclub. Some would call it a dive but soon it would be filled with his people, a space where they relived their youth, laughed, loved and faced life's blows together, unified by the music of their choice.

Boy me strong like lion, he shouted to himself as he flexed his still athletic-looking body. But

the truth, in the form of a coughing fit, was a fact that could not be denied.

Renford waited patiently in the doctor's surgery. He hated any medical place, seeing doctors as charlatans no better than the Obeah men back home.

Hello Renford, said the doctor. *I have your results*.

Results, countered a nonchalant Renford, *Country Man 'gwan' mash up Conquer Sound tomorrow, Sah! It no contest*. The doctor raised his voice.

It's serious! It's c—

Cancelled! Shouted Renford as he grabbed his hat and ran out of the surgery. *Babylon can't cancel de dance!*

You can't run from cancer! screamed the doctor to Renford's 70-year-old back that moved faster than any 70-year-old's back should move. As Renford left the doctor's, he took a bow to those waiting in the room of doom and gloom, ending his pending relationship with chemotherapy and such. Choosing to live, doing what he loved best, skanking and self-medicating with Jah herb and reggae along with his bredrin at his beloved Casablanca Club.

Renford's treatment was to begin at tonight's planned sound clash. Rumours abounded that the treatment was due to be terminated by the *undesirable, ever-present forces of Babylon*. The sound system crew were the only real family Renford had ever known in the UK. Music had been his parents. Music protected him whenever trouble had knocked on his door. The Casablanca

Doors flew open, uniforms of blue invaded the club. The sanctuary of the darkness now had become a dungeon of terror. Batons swung. Boots penetrated speakers.

was his baby, that he had created, nurtured, and he would need his family now more than ever.

The kinetic motion of Renford's dance attracted the crowd like moths to light. Angelic butterflies and mystical birds penetrated his high frequencies, his arms and hands plucking these supernatural creatures out of the atmosphere. Rasping trumpets of Zion occupied the central locality, a realm where Renford's African grandparents had insisted the innocent spirits dwelled. At some stage Renford shifted into a trance-like state akin to a spiritual possession as the operator teased and threatened to drop the boom, the bass. Renford called out, cried for redemption. Only the primordial spirit of music could communicate with Ronford or the other swaying black, brown and white bodies that succumbed to the meditating rituals of the Casablanca dance floor. The bass thumped and shook. Sweat mixed with smoke. Night mingled with day, day mingled with night, reality with fiction. The Casablanca knew no boundaries or constraints.

A single tweeter box vibrated and, like the dancers, was moved by the rhythm fantastic. Slowly the tweeter box danced dangerously close to the edge of the booming bass bin. Below this, Renford gyrated, oblivious to the danger above. The box crashed onto the dreadlocked, balding head of Renford. Those who observed the spectacle raised heads concerned, though not disturbed enough to kill their vibes. Renford stopped dead, for ten seconds at most, did a sign towards the heavens and proclaimed to all: *fear not my bredrin! Me nor de dance done yet.*

Renford proceeded to catch butterflies even more vigorously from the air. It was then another sound was heard a sound, soundly ignored, a familiar commotion oft heard at the Casablanca.

First it was a tap, then a banging. Fierce voices boomed, agitating the minds of the subdued dancers. Doors flew open, uniforms of blue invaded the club. The sanctuary of the darkness now had become a dungeon of terror. Batons swung. Boots penetrated speakers. Truncheons did for the amps. Music ceased to play; a deadly silence fell. Renford carried on skanking while those around him were frozen in time and space. Renford's voice rang out as if he was speaking in tongues, as if communicating with the spirits of his African forefathers.

Suddenly, frozen bodies thawed, the people, black, brown and white, danced free and His Majesty's finest stopped the violence and made for the ringleader, Renford.

The crowd sang and hands clapped as Renford's zombielike body fell to the floor as he repeated *Where there were no drum, music came from within, a clapping of hands and a stamping of feet leading the souls to freedom with every beat*. The evil force retreated as the congregation lamented.

Renford's wake was held at his beloved Casablanca. A banner on the wall proclaimed: 'Leading the souls to freedom'. People of Tiger Bay knew that despite the club's destiny, its inevitable demolition, with singing and clapping of hands, the spirit of the Casablanca – just like that of Renford – will live on eternally.

Black Music, Black Vinyl... Enter the Record Shop

GARTH CARTWRIGHT/2FUNKY ARTS

Across the nation, from as far back as the 1920s, the people's passion for Black music fuelled an army of record shops that provided community hubs and cultural power plants that have helped shape the Britain we know today.

That music of Black origin has played a huge part in shaping almost every genre of British music-making over the past century is a truism. What is less noted is how British record shops served as community hubs and cultural power stations from the 1920s into this century – especially specialist record shops that were devoted to the ever-changing currents of Black music. As migration from Britain's colonies in the Caribbean and West Africa increased in the post-Second World War era, the Black British record shop served as a mix of trading post/cultural attaché/youth club/oracle for the new communities who were putting down roots across the UK while still strongly connected to 'home'. These Black music record shops – which range from those set up by white British fans of jazz, blues and soul to 'dub shacks' – where sound system operators queued on a Saturday morning to purchase that week's 45s (fresh from Jamaica's recording studios), through to myriad dance music shops (soul, funk, rap, house, techno, jungle, dubstep, grime) run by an assortment of black, white and Asian DJs, have all helped shape British music-making, street fashion, vernacular and entrepreneurship.

Some of the shop staff were teachers – in the truest sense of the word – while others could be miserable, rude and intimidating. No matter, British record shops whose focus was Black music helped shape our society into the more inclusive, multicultural one it is today. And for this – and the music they championed – they should be celebrated.

The earliest Black music specialist shops opened in the 1920s. By then 78 records were the medium by which people listened to music and early African-American jazz, blues and spiritual recordings won over music lovers across Europe, none more so than in the UK. The first notable British Black music shop was Levy's of Whitechapel – renowned as the 'hot music' emporium (jazz often being described as 'hot music' then) and boasting 'over 100,000 records from all over the world'. Levy's stocked jazz and blues 78s alongside releases by the East End's Jewish artists and music from the colonies: calypso from Trinidad and palm wine music from the Gold Coast (now Ghana). Levy's shop became a hub for jazz fans and musicians – pioneering New Orleans clarinettist Sidney Bechet hung out there in the 1920s, while Ken Colyer, an icon of 1950s trad jazz, got his first jazz 78s here – and Levy's extended into running record labels, promoting concerts (including Duke Ellington) and much else. Many other British record shops would follow suit.

OPPOSITE Woman in a London record shop, 1983. Photograph by Richard Saunders.

Immediately following the Second World War Dobell's Jazz & Blues shop opened on central London's Charing Cross Road. Owner Doug Dobell championed African-American music to such a degree that Louis Armstrong, Horace Silver and B. B. King (among other notables) would visit when in town. Across the UK other Black music emporiums opened: the Diskery in Birmingham, Manchester's Hime & Addison – and while jazz and blues records never sold in significant numbers, their influence and inspiration was huge. And they brought young white and Black Britons together.

By the mid-1950s the Windrush generation were opening their own record shops, notably Theo's Records in Brixton and the Calypso Shop in Ladbroke Grove. The former was run by Jamaicans, the latter by Trinidadians and both represented their new communities – Theo's provided Claudia Jones with office space to publish the *West Indian Gazette* while the Calypso Shop served as a frontline hub during the Notting Hill race riots of 1958. Not long after, a Jewish couple, Rita and Benny King, would open R&B Records in Stamford Hill, specialising in West Indian music and releasing 45s they licensed from Jamaica. By the mid-1960s London-based Jamaican Lee Gopthal (see page 150) was financing West Indian record shops across London – Desmond's in Brixton was celebrated as 'the Blue Beat shop' (Jamaican ska being known then as 'blue beat'), while Gopthal's Music Land and Muzik Zone shops sold rhythm & blues and rock alongside West Indian music (Gopthal would go on to operate Trojan Records, a pioneering UK reggae label) and employed Black staff – a rarity then on the UK high street.

By the mid-1970s reggae and dub shops would exist in every British city with a Black community: Dub Vendor, Intone, Daddy Kool, Pecking's Studio 1, Don Carlos (where UB40's members bought the records that would shape their sound) and many more ensured that the UK became an epicentre for Jamaican-inspired music-making. At the same time specialist dance shops opened

By the mid-1950s the Windrush generation were opening their own record shops, notably Theo's Records in Brixton and the Calypso Shop in Ladbroke Grove.

to cater to a new generation of Black and white funk and soul fans – Northern Soul was named such by Soul City record shop in Covent Garden, and specialist record shops in Manchester, Wigan and other north-west towns and cities championed the genre. As with the reggae shops, the dance shops were operated by Black and white music aficionados and did a great job at making music available that was rarely heard on radio or covered in the music press. At the same time the music of Africa's many cultures became available to British listeners via Sterns African Record Centre. Originally a small shop selling short-wave radios and kettles on Tottenham Court Road – with a back room dodicated to imported African records to cater for African students at the nearby School of African and Oriental Studies – Stern's grew into a European epicentre for African music, recording, licensing and reissuing seminal African albums alongside touring artists.

Rap, house and techno led to a new generation of Black music record shops opening in the 1980s as youths embraced the new American underground sound. These shops often specialised in white label 12-inch 45s that were produced exclusively for club DJs. Sheffield's FON record shop helped launch UK rave via employees who founded the Warp record

label. Croydon's Big Apple Records employed DJs who invented dubstep while Rhythm Factor (in East London) was the grime scene's initial focal point. Roony Keefe, aka Risky Roadz, who documented the grime scene's early years, says: 'Without Rhythm the scene would be very different now. It was more than just a record shop, it was where everyone congregated and spoke about ideas.'[1]

This remains true of the best record shops today – as it was way back when Brian Epstein, manager of Liverpool's hugely successful NEMS Records, first encountered the then unknown young Beatles: they were rowdy customers buying American rhythm & blues 45s they would often cover. With Epstein as manager the Beatles changed the world – not bad for a partnership that began in a record shop.

OPPOSITE Levy's Record shop, Whitechapel, circa 1950. The store was a very early source of 'hot' music (jazz), originally selling klezmer and swing music to an East End clientele.
RIGHT American jazz pianist, composer and Blue Note recording artist Horace Silver outside Dobell's jazz record shop, Charing Cross Road, London, circa 1969. Photograph by Bob Baker.

OPPOSITE Left to right: John MacGillivray, Martin 'Redman' Trenchfield, Donald 'Papa Face' Facey and Noel Hawks outside the Dub Vendor Record Shack in Ladbroke Grove not long after it opened in 1981. Photograph by Chris Lane, courtesy of Noel Hawks. ABOVE Reggae musicians (left to right) Delroy Witter, Ken Murray and (first right) Desmond Bryan in the Into Reggae record store, Willesden, London, 3 October 1975. Photograph by Duncan Baxter. BELOW George 'Peckings' Price (right) at Peckings' Studio 1 record shop, Askew Road, London, 22 October 1984. Photograph by David Corio.

The Art of Buying Reggae Music: A Back-in-the-Day Journey From Dalston Junction to Tottenham High Road

PAUL BRADSHAW

Back in 2011 I was chatting to a friend visiting from Senegal about reggae music in London, and the realisation that all the reggae shops I used to frequent between Dalston and Seven Sisters no longer existed prompted me to write this piece – a journey in more ways than one.

The post-1980s generations of inner-city Black British youth have created their own groundbreaking genres of music. Soul II Soul gave us 'A happy face, a thumpin' bass, for a lovin' race'. The junglists went worldwide creating drum and bass. The two-step/garage crews went dark creating grime. At the time of writing it feels like we are in the midst of a 'post-dubstep' meltdown, with Appleblim and Shackleton at the helm. Genres aside, it would be safe to say that all this music has a strand of reggae in its DNA.

Despite the overwhelming impact of the digital revolution on the whole music industry and the advent of Ableton Live for DJs, vinyl is still in the mix. Those who religiously frequent actual record emporiums must, I believe, feel that they are necessarily tapping into the source... into a tradition of buying tunes... and there's a skill to that!

With that in mind, what follows is a personal reflection on my own initiation into the world of reggae music and the knowledge and etiquette employed in the purchasing of those magical pre-release singles that used to arrive from Jamaica every week.

It was around 1972–73, while at art college in the leafy, conservative backwater of Cheltenham, that I started buying Jamaican music. The early 1970s were responsible for a wave of astonishing soul and jazz albums from Marvin Gaye, Curtis Mayfield, Donny Hathaway, Stevie Wonder, Parliament, Miles Davis, Charles Mingus, Pharoah Sanders and Alice Coltrane. I was attuned to it all.

However, inspired by the groundbreaking writings of Carl Gayle/Jah Ugliman in *Black Music* magazine I headed off to Gloucester, the nearest city with a Jamaican community, in search of *Version Galore* – a compilation which united the lyrical talents of 'toasters' like U-Roy, I-Roy, Big Youth and Dennis Alcapone – and the mind-blowing instrumental LP *This Is Augustus Pablo*. In a humble reggae emporium in Barton Street I found what I was looking for but as I gazed upon the selection of music available I realised I had much to learn.

It also was in Gloucester that I first encountered a 'sound system'. A visit to a blues dance run by a local soundman called Skinny and an encounter with the mighty Sir Coxsone at the Jamaican Club in Gloucester were a point of no return. The impact of hearing the music on 'sound' took on a metaphysical dimension. Nothing could have prepared me for the weight and power, the bass and tops, the mic men – the toasters – of Coxsone Sound System. It was a supersonic and spiritual experience. I became a Coxsone follower.

During the 1970s, liberation struggles raged across southern Africa and post-independence Jamaica was caught up in tribal warfare between two main political parties – the Jamaican Labour party (JLP) and the People's National Party (PNP). A rich vein of reggae music emerged during these troubled times that cultivated the mysterious, apocalyptic vision of the Rastafari. The music transmitted a call for love and unity in the face of Babylon and declared allegiance to HIM Haile Selassie – Ras Tafari. This music threw up questions that required answers. Who was Marcus Mosiah Garvey? Who was Paul Bogle? What is livity within Rastafari? Basically, the Marxist-rooted history that I was familiar with required serious revision, especially in relation to the legacy of the transatlantic slave trade and Black nationalism.

I graduated to the metropolis in the autumn of 1974 and settled in E8, between Mare Street and Dalston Junction. I had arrived in reggae music central. Driven by the songs and music of the Wailers, Yabby You & the Prophets, Big Youth, U-Roy, I-Roy, Gregory Isaacs, Dennis Brown, Augustus Pablo, the mind-bending dubs of King Tubby and the drums of the Mystic Revelation of Rastafari, I would roam the High Road from the Junction to Seven Sisters in search of new acquisitions and elusive, mythological masterpieces like Lee Perry's *Blackboard Jungle Dub.*

I would begin my journey in Dalston Lane at Java, a stone's throw away from the legendary Four Aces nightclub. Freshly opened, this most alluring little 'record shack' was run by two respected session musicians, drummer Jah Bunny and bassist Floyd Lawson. Also behind the counter was a most stylish and knowledgeable youth called Lenny. The style and pattern of

the day was the unbuckled woven ites gold and green belt, the Gabicci, Clarks and a rakishly offset Baker Boy. I was overly keen and my attempts to look relaxed and 'down' in this one hundred per cent Black environment were initially the butt of 'nuff jokes.

That said, Java and its successor M&D Records, which was run by Lee Hall – a *selectah* and salesman par excellence – went on to become my second home. It was there that I gained a serious education in this music and the deep culture that underpins it. I learned to listen and reason and how to deftly peel an orange using a ratchet knife.

Before settling in London I'd buy what I'd read about. It was only when I arrived in London that I fully grasped that reggae was essentially a singles market. Initially, I hadn't a clue what a 'Pre' was – I'd simply heard that some shops kept a selection of exclusives under the counter for their regulars. As my knowledge expanded so the search for a specific tune would sometimes take me on a mission beyond Java or M&D to other local shops which had their own label or reputed speciality.

Music City in Ridley Road market was always an enticing prospect on a Saturday. The shop had direct links to the prolific Trojan Records. The covers of brilliant albums like Dennis Brown's

ABOVE Outside the Four Aces club, *circa* 1990. Photograph by Alan Denney.

Intel-Diplo
H.I.M.
BABYLON QUEENDOM
Peter Tosh

JUDGE I O'LORD
(I.N.R.I.)
TAPPA ZUKIE
Produced by Lloydie Slim
℗ 1976
Marketed by
BLACK WAX
Carol Elizabeth
Lox 8
LOX8A
LOCKS

TREBLE
Published by
Tropical Music
M.C.P.S.
℗ 1975
CCC 01A
A Sound Stracs
Production
Mfg. & Dist. by
Tropical Records
I Man a Grass Hopper
P. Henry/G. Chung
PABLO MOSES
Arr. & Prod. by Geoffrey Chung

ORTHODOX
12 TRIBES OF ISRAEL
12 Tribes Production
Arranged by
Pablove Black
Backround Vocals
Dan Hudson
Geo. George Beaufort
AFRICA AWAITING IT'S CREATORS
(D. Hudson)
EWAN NAFTALI

ATTACK
Made in England
Copyright
Control
℗ 1974
ATT-8066
(ATT 8066A)
LOVE IS OVERDUE—Pt. I
(Gregory Isaacs)
GREGORY ISAACS
Producer: A. Ranglin

STEP FORWARD YOUTH
(L. Corty)
PRINCE JAZBO
Arr./Prod. by
P. Jazbo
Made
in England
45 r.p.m.
Copyright
Control
A
CS057
Count Shelly

ROCKERS
INTERNATIONAL
Prod. by
Arr. by
Time:
PL 1178
'35 ORANGE ST
Phone 661
OR 20663
HUMBLE YOURSELF
(Winston Richards)
Asher & Trimble

TUFF GONG
RECORDS
5002-A
Wailers Prod.
Recorded in
Jamaica, W.I.
45 RPM
KINGSTON 12 SHUFFLE
(Bob Marley)
BOB MARLEY & HUGH ROY
THE WAILERS

CONCRETE JUNGLE
45rpm
CJ 750(A)
Published 1976
JAH HEAVY LOAD
I. JAHMAN

THIRD WORLD
STEREO
IS 8663
WAA8162V1IS
RE I
Time-4:90
©1978 Island
Records Inc.
Mighty Three
Music-BMI
NOW THAT WE FOUND LOVE (Edit)
(K. Gamble/L. Huff)
PRODUCED BY THIRD WORLD
and THIRD WORLD
for CAVLIP PROD. LTD.
EXECUTIVE PRODUCER:
CHRIS BLACKWELL
Island Records Inc.

SUN & STARS
Promoted and
Distributed
by Atomic
Records
Phone
021-773-1811
021-773 4671
Made in England
Arr. & Prod. by
W. Thompson
STA 3 A
℗ 1975
BEST DRESS CHICKEN
W. Thompson
ALIMANTADO

MORE
CUT
MCT 001
A
45 R.P.M.
K & B
MUSIC LTD
℗ 1976
Made in
England
RUN, RASTA RUN
(D. Curtis)
AFRICAN STONE
Produced by Dennis Curtis
K & B Records
Tel: 70-68854

Just Dennis, Big Youth's *Screaming Target* or Ras Michael's *Nyabinghi* hung in the shop window. The speakers outside the shop projected the music of Al Brown covering Al Green or the sweet sound of Ken Boothe's chart-topping 'Everything I Own' or maybe a touch of 'Skenga' – a scattering of 'Irie Feeling'. The sounds of young Jamaica rose above the vibrant hustle and bustle of Black and white working-class shoppers and the cockney mantras of the various vendors. It always felt good, especially as Ridley Road market had a dark history of hosting volatile racist gatherings by Oswald Mosley's British Union of Fascists and the National Front – the forerunner of the BNP.

Having partaken of a patty or a bagel, one would trod on from Ridley Road. Once back on the High Road, in the region of Arcola Street one might be tempted to deviate slightly from the mission and check out a mom-and-pop record store that was owned by some local white folks. Along with the top twenty hits of the day they stocked a positively arresting selection of Nigerian juju from the likes of Sir Shina Adewale and King Sunny Ade.

However, to get back on track we cross the High Road and head for the shop of Ephraim Barrett aka Count Shelley, a pioneering and popular local sound system operator who in the early 1970s was the resident DJ at the fabled Four Aces. His reputation as a soundman and selector ensured that he was always ahead of the game. His shop was always stocked with the latest singles along with an array of albums and seven-inch singles on his own Count Shelley label. He released music from UK-based artists like Honey Boy, Gene Rondo, Roy Shirley and Laurel Aitken as well as JA stars of the day like Delroy Wilson,

Alton Ellis and Prince Jazzbo. Confirming Count Shelley's vision it was he who first released Tapper Zukie's majestic *Man a Warrior* – an LP that became the stuff of legend due to the writings of Penny Reel, a youthman of Stamford Hill origin who also roamed that same High Road.

Moving on from Shelley's one had to resist stopping off at the Astra Cinema – now the Aziziye Mosque. Back then it specialised in separate screenings of 'adult films' and classic Hong Kong martial arts movies: *Shaolin vs Lama*, *Iron Monkey*, *The 36th Chamber of Shaolin*. An afternoon session would normally be empty apart from myself and a posse of Black youth who were either unemployed or bunking off school. Most likely these were the same youth who took the moves of snake, monkey and praying mantis kung fu onto the dance floor of Jah Shaka's sessions at Club Noreik.

The next stop on Stoke Newington High Street is a shop I associate with Pepe Judah from the

12 Tribes of Israel organisation. However, this shop was actually home to one Leonard Chin and his Santic label. He arrived in London from Jamaica around the same time as I did and set about releasing the music he'd recorded with Gregory Isaacs, Augustus Pablo and Horace Andy. Seeking out his compilation *Harder Shade of Black* was a must. It featured a cover shot taken on Hackney Downs and delivered a brace of excellent vocal and dub tracks.

Leonard Chin's JA roots credentials are impeccable but he was also quick to respond to the rise of UK lovers and enlisted a new wave of up-and-coming local singers like Carroll Thompson, Jean Adebambo and Trevor Walters. At the same time Anthony Brightly, the keys player with Stoke Newington-based Black Slate, began recording home-grown, Black British lovers to release via his Pure Silk imprint and to play on his sound, Sir George, which enjoyed a hugely popular residency at Cubies in Dalston Junction and Phebes in Amhurst Road.

From Stokie it was always tempting to hop on a double-decker to Stamford Hill and touch down at the most excellent R&B Records. While London's Orthodox Jewish males strutted their stuff and did their runnings in their white stockings, black silk coats and extravagant fur hats, a more modest Jewish couple, Benny and Rita King, plied the post-Windrush generation with some serious music.

Amazingly R&B Records opened back in 1953 and, following constant requests for Jamaican 'blues' records, they contacted legendary sound man and producer 'Coxsone' Dodd in order to buy the music directly from Jamaica. The early 1960s saw them launch their own R&B and ska beat labels, satisfying the tastes of the Jamaican community along with the style-obsessed Mods who'd discovered the music in clubs like Count Suckle's Roaring Twenties in Carnaby Street. However, by the early 1970s Benny and Rita had given up the labels and were distributing pre-releases from JA to thriving shops around Britain like Black Wax and Don Christie in Birmingham.

My fondest memory of Rita and Benny was asking Rita – who was like your gran – if they'd got Burning Spear's *Marcus Garvey* LP. It had just been released in JA on Jack Ruby's Fox label and the buzz was massive. Lenny at Java had a copy and it was most definitely not for sale – they were awaiting a shipment. I couldn't wait, so here I was at R&B Records. Rita said, 'Burning Spear? Marcus Garvey? No! Do you have this?' And put an album on the turntable.

The first track was 'Door Peep Shall Not Enter' on what was Burning Spear's debut LP *Studio One Presents Burning Spear*. It starts with singer Winston Rodney's call to the 'most high' Jah Rastafari, in an unforgettable voice that still sends a chill down the spine.

It was one of those record-buying moments, an experience that I can only compare to hearing Coxsone Dodd's mother spinning the Gladiators' 'Roots Natty' in the Brentford Road shop in JA. There's a feeling... it goes through the whole body to the crown of the head... maybe it's something in the voice... something ethereal. Spear could do that. He did it in the Rainbow theatre in Finsbury Park at his first London concert. He walked onstage and as his voice gathered power to the sound of 'Fr-r-e-e-d-o-o-o-o-o-o-m...' the whole of the Rainbow stood up in unison... One time! Deep!

And so, back to R&B Records... without even knowing it I'd paid, thanked Rita gracefully and stepped back out into the street in a quietly euphoric daze.

OPPOSITE Muzik City record shop in Ridley Road market, Dalston, London, 1973. Photograph by Martin Mayer.

I was sucked into the shop. I'd help out with mail order, idle away the hours, sipping on a bottle of Guinness and listening to music new and old. It was a hub of news from Yard.

It was rare that I would progress beyond Seven Sisters and onto Tottenham High Road. This is an area I associate with Jah Bones and RUZ (Rasta Universal Zion), Club Noreik – where Jah Shaka was resident – and, of course, the legendary Fat Man Hi Fi. However, the release in 1974 of an extraordinary album by Keith Hudson called *Flesh of My Skin, Blood of My Blood* had me scouring the High Road in search of Brent Clarke's Atra Records. I'd heard the opening cut of 'Hunting', with its cascading Rasta drums, stinging electric guitar and spaced-out mix and was on a mission.

There was a serious mystique surrounding this LP. It was marketed like a pre-release, so you had to track it down before it potentially vanished. Upon locating the shop I was overjoyed to sight a copy of the said LP. From the sleeve design to its lyrics, *Flesh of My Skin, Blood of My Blood* was a radical and conscious venture. I also walked with a freshly pressed copy of Hudson's classic *Pick a Dub*. It was a good day.

Back in Dalston, when Lee took over Java and renamed it M&D Records my wanderings diminished. Whenever I was passing, I was sucked into the shop. I'd help out with mail order, idle away the hours, sipping on a bottle of Guinness and listening to music new and old. It was a hub of news from Yard. As I said earlier, Lee was a controller and skilled *selectah*. The man had a nice little amp and pre-amp, a couple of superb Tannoy speakers and some discreet, uncased tweeters tucked away in the corners of the shop which gave that little extra lick of tops.

Word would go out when a shipment of pre-releases was destined to reach the shop. It would be packed. There was a sense of deep community. Most people knew each other, had gone to school together, they raved in the same dances but might have followed different sounds. There was mad musical knowledge amongst those gathered. For many this music signified a deep ancestral, spiritual, cultural connection to their roots in the Caribbean.

On those days, you had to stand firm and hold a place where Lee could clearly see you signal that the tune was to be added to your pile. Hesitate, and all you'd hear was the words, 'It done!' He would work the buyers, soundmen and punters, dreads and baldheads. These were geezers who knew their music, had refined tastes and swiftly recognised an intro from a tune dropped in the dance the previous weekend, and when all that new music had been reduced to 'no more takers' he would start on the revives, the Studio One – the head cornerstone.

Lee was the master and at those sessions he would ensure that whatever money you had in your pocket would be seriously dented. That was how it was and you'd step into the night with a righteous bowling walk, clutching a brown paper bag full of pres on an array of enticing labels: Clinch Records, Studio1, Music God, Prophets, Black Solidarity, Youth Promotion, Marlion's Victorius Steppers, Black Ark, Tuff Gong, Heavy Duty, Channel One, Crazy Joe, African Museum, Yard Music, Intel Diplo, Soul Syndicate, Solomonic, High Times... Jah Guidance...[1]

OPPOSITE Classic albums of the era.

JULIET FLETCHER

**British gospel music (BG or BGM) has had a
distinct and evolving narrative over the past
fifty years, weaving a multi-layered, complex
story: community-rooted while becoming
an emerging industry sector. In contrast to
the more renowned figures associated with
American gospel, British gospel's world-class
artists, musicians and producers may not be
household names, but their influence and
contributions are.**

This narrative, still in its formative stages of
telling and retelling, unfolds uniquely, drawing
from the experiences and knowledge of
individuals like me: I'm a child of the Windrush
era, brought up in the Black Majority Church
(BMC) and a pioneer of British gospel. My
fifty-year eyewitness perspective focuses on
conveying the BMC's role in placing British
gospel within British Black music's central story.

Reasons: how and why

The term 'British gospel' came into regular use
during the latter part of the 1990s, emerging as a
reflection of a forty-year experience influenced
largely by US gospel and Caribbean music. It
signifies a maturation process, a realisation
that the British gospel scene had developed
its own distinct sounds, a profile and history
with legacy offshoots. This evolution occurred
with the integration of second- and third-
generation children into a Black British identity,
embracing ownership of their Caribbean (and
latterly African) roots and of music previously

considered 'worldly' and 'unacceptable,'
compared to its 'sacred' use.

The BMCs in the UK, from 1948 to 1979,
primarily comprising migrant Caribbean
communities, faced traumas and tensions, as
well as the imperative to contribute to Britain's
transformation. The first generation, resourceful
and resilient, laid multiple foundations, enabling
a subsequent wave of African migrants, arriving
in significant numbers between 1980 and 2000,
which caused a phenomenal growth of BMCs
and a meaningful change in the perception of
gospel music (and Black music) styles.

In his autobiography, Olaudah Equiano said,
'We are almost a nation of dancers, singers
and poets': this is lived out in the African
diaspora of faith communities; it is how we
have functioned and overcome diversity; and
our ability to survive is in the freedom of music,
song and dance.[1] I, for one, believe it is God
given. Although this trait in us has been mocked,
misused and abused, it has saved our lives. And
right now, considering the world's mental health,
its capacity is to save the world.

Most BMCs came into existence because
of rejection and racism experienced in or by
established traditional indigenous churches
that Caribbeans were used to in their island
homelands. Be it known that some BMCs
saw themselves as Christian missionaries
in outreach to a Britain that was losing its
Christian values/virtues.

BMCs seriously underestimated their
creative potential; some argue that it was the

Black Majority Churches in the UK primarily comprised of migrant Caribbean communities. They faced traumas and tensions, as well as the imperative to contribute to Britain's transformation.

ABOVE The United Church of God, Austin Road, Handsworth, 1986.
OVERLEAF Annual National Convention of the Black-led Churches in England, Bingley Hall, Birmingham, 1983. Photographs by Vanley Burke.

The 1980s to the 1990s was known as the golden age of British gospel, because every element of the music seemed to blossom, whether it was choirs, soloists or groups of various configurations.

music that propelled their visibility and helped sustain their relevance.

Music is at the heart of a typical church event. Certainly, the construct of BMCs as I have experienced over decades is with children involved in expressing themselves through recitations, small plays or skits, musical instruments and vocal singing. Hence individuals and countless others such as Benjamin Zephaniah (writer/poet), Mica Paris (singer/presenter/actress) and Ian Oakley (composer/arranger/MD) all had their early experiences in church. Creative maestros routinely pass through on their way to worldwide prominence.

BMCs are therefore a veritable hub of community life in music, arts and culture. Mostly, their exclusive critical uniqueness functions with inclusive openness. This awareness is making the future of BGM exciting.

The gospel scene: from yesterday to today

British gospel music in popular culture and entertainment occurred within the first ten years of the establishment of Black-led churches. It happened before anyone realised it.

The BMCs' dominant sounds throughout the early years were: spirituals, hymnody, country and calypso. Dominant sounds on the British gospel scene from the 1970s onwards were US traditional and contemporary gospel RnB/soul, reggae, hip-hop, rap Afrobeats, grime.

A critical contemplation: the (i) Caribbean-led BMC leadership had to consider how their music was used and viewed by (ii) young people of the

church (iii) the music industry (commercial) and (iv) formal education systems. The problem was that there was no relationship between BMCs and the music industry. Young people in the middle had a right- *and* left-hand relationship with both sources. Since the right hand didn't know what the left hand was all about – and vice versa – that was the cause of much of the ignorance and tension that ensued. Within BMCs, the music of the church was seen as sacred – solely to worship God. In the music industry, the Black Church was (and some would say still is) about providing entertainment and a never-ending talent pool. For gifted and talented young people, the natural progression and now proactive expansion of the gospel music scene was and is a critical solution; a solution for all those creatives who rightfully credit BMCs as their source and ongoing inspiration. It gives room for the music that belongs to 'the House' – where quality and creativity is sustained and 'sacredness' retained. But, should anything cross over – 'Oh Happy Day', for example – well, cool.

I believe the Lord placed our music into the culture of the day: for example, the now-famous and influential Soul Seekers were the first successful electric-pop-style gospel band in the 1950s; family group the Singing Stewarts were very popular on both TV and radio from the 1960s to the late 1980s; the Heavenly Hopes was the first gospel group (followed by the Doyley Brothers – referred to as 'Britain's answer to the Jackson 5') to participate in the national television talent show *Opportunity Knocks* – the equivalent of *The X Factor* or *Britain's Got Talent*.

The 1980s to the 1990s was known as the golden age of British gospel, because every element of the music seemed to blossom, whether it was choirs, soloists, groups of various configurations – both *a cappella* and instrument-based, female, male or mixed – all seemed to have a moment to shine in that precious period, and were in demand by commercial record labels such as Virgin, Island and Polydor. British gospel was due to be the breakout genre and source of new stars. Unfortunately, it didn't quite happen in a sustained way. However, various key things did occur:

- The blossoming of world-class musical directors, producers, composers, songwriters and arrangers – many of them award-winning in various genre spheres.
- The rise of world-class musicians and backing vocalists that became the backbone of the pop industry to the present day.
- The range of internationally acclaimed gospel directors and choirs/vocal ensembles with experience in television, film and theatre.
- Peripatetic music tutors with a gospel background in the education system transformed the quality of singing in schools and this has continued in an explosion of community choirs. Add to this choral projects with agencies like the NHS and other public, third- and private-sector bodies.
- The increase/plethora of dedicated, globally connected media platforms and social media networks.
- BGM influence and leadership increased as a first choice throughout Europe.

Around 2004, fusions and variations of 'the gospel sound' arose. Unpredictably, US gospel has opened up to British and African music styles and events. The Gospel Music Industry Alliance (GMIA) – the UK body officially representing the genre – has linked with the US-legislated annual marking of September as Gospel Music Heritage Month.

Karen Gibson and the Kingdom Choir's gospel rendition at the royal wedding, Stormzy's transcendent choir collaboration at Glastonbury, Lawrence Johnson's (LCGC co-founder) arrangement of Stormzy's 'Crown' and Femi Koleoso's success (rooted in church music) with jazz fusion Ezra Collective at the 2023 Mercury Prize all showcase the genre's diverse impact and exemplify its significance. Despite tensions, BGM, which is centred on goodwill, hope, love and faith, prevails. Their journeys reflect the genre's enduring influence, promising future success for those embracing and leveraging their roots in this rich musical tradition.

We must position ourselves to retain authenticity of the form, protect and preserve, direct and discern, consolidate and control all that we have and who we are within Black music and the wider streams. The spirituals (gospel) is the root cry, our eternal marriage to the blues, our birthing of jazz and soul; our musical (grandchildren and great-grandchildren) expansions within Western spheres; as we now realise our connected relationship to our motherland Africa we walk in the 'promised land' of endless/limitless possibilities. Established media bastions like Premier Gospel and *Keep the Faith* magazine champion growth and the ambitious potential of the genre.

Of course, I'm a Believer! We are on the cusp of a new era. GMIA stands as a bridge between BMCs and the creative industries, to teach/learn/interpret, to ensure that we remain there in our purest forms, variations and most importantly in our own right!

ABOVE Judy Mowatt, 1979, photograph by Peter Simon in
Kingston, Jamaica. Judy was a solo artist and one of the I-Threes.

Rasta Women, Rastafari and Roots Music

RASHEDA ASHANTI MALCOLM

Celebrated writer, activist, teacher and Black Business Woman of the Year Rasheda Ashanti Malcolm reflects on her own faith and livity within Rastafari and the sense of pride, identity and spiritual consciousness provided by roots reggae music.

Back in the 1960s, 1970s and early 1980s, the mention of Rastafari would create the image of a black-bearded male, with long, roped, tangled dreadlocks, undoubtedly with a marijuana joint – or spliff as it is commonly called – hanging from his lips, nodding in time to the sound of reggae roots music. This stereotypical image is what the media perpetrates about our culture. Now, mention the Rasta woman and the image that emerges is one of a humble woman, a housewife whose only role is within the home, rearing the children and giving spiritual upliftment to her family.

My experience and way into Rastafari happened at the tender age of 14, when along with another teenage friend I attended a Rastafari conference held twelve miles from my home in Hertfordshire. Up until that moment, my knowledge of Rastafari was my glimpse of young Black men and teenage boys who donned red, gold and green hats (called crowns) with dreadlocks tucked away, and who loved and danced to reggae music.

During the conference, a Rasta woman stood up to speak, and she was referred to as 'queen'. She wore African print trousers, with a knee-length dress over them, her locks resting on her shoulders and a colourful scarf wrapped around her head. She looked like a warrior, and in my eyes, she epitomised beauty – the kind of organic beauty that enhanced identities and ignited pride.

The next time I was to see a Rasta woman that amazed me was the arrival of the I-Threes – Judy Mowatt, Rita Marley and Marcia Griffiths – on my television screen. The I-Threes were integral to the sound of Bob Marley and the Wailers, and a powerful onstage presence. Both Rita and Marcia had released music in their own right, but when Judy's self-produced 'Black Woman' arrived in 1979 on her own Ashandan record label, that was, for me, the Rasta women's anthem. Only Bob Marley's 'No Woman No Cry' came close. I became an admirer of Judy the instant I heard 'Black Woman' because it told our story, the length of time we have been labouring, rooting us back to biblical times, and highlighting the strength of women. We all knew the words and sang our hearts out to the melody. Years later there wasn't a Rastafarian home you could visit or an event or dance you could attend and not hear 'Black Woman' bellowing through the speakers of the sound boxes. Then with the release of Rita's first album in 1980, *Who Feels It Knows It*, which included the popular song, 'One Draw', it was evident that Rasta women had carved out their own musical trajectory.

Roots music emerged as a subgenre of reggae music, which took an anti-imperialist stance in the 1970s, reflecting support for liberation movements such as the Rastafarian faith. Roots

music was heavily influenced by the Rastafarian lifestyle and was certainly embraced by the movement as a device of activism. It was most popular on the African continent and still plays a pivotal role in the Rastafari movement. It is a strong tool for storytelling and spiritual upliftment, even translating into a mode of praying for many of us. Through roots music, the stories of our history and the trials, problems and conquests are relayed. The music is used to explore, expose and condemn inequality, oppression, and political and colonial treachery.

On the other hand, reggae artists used roots music to encourage unity and love, and to bring joy to the hearts and souls of people across the globe. Judy Mowatt, Rita Marley and Marcia Griffiths toured the world with Bob Marley and the Wailers. Their voices, their songs, touched millions of people. The ideologies and views of the Rastafarian community were transmitted globally by a wave of Jamaican artists including former Wailers Peter Tosh and Bunny Wailer alongside respected, award-winning artists such as Burning Spear and Black Uhuru – a vocal

trio that included the short-lived, luminous presence of Puma Jones, and Queen Ifrika. Their lyrics echoed a call for equal rights and justice, and death to Black and white oppressors. They declared 'unity is strength' and offered 'one love'.

Roots music will go down in our history as recounting the hopes, sorrows and challenges of everyday people living in the ghetto areas of Jamaica, and on the streets of inner cities like London, Birmingham, Manchester and Bristol. It provided a sense of pride and boosted self-esteem, while educating the community about their history prior to slavery.

We're now in the midst of a new generation of roots artists emerging, carrying on and upholding the genre's traditions and values. Female artists such as Koffee, Lila Ike, Queen Omega and Jah 9 have breathed new life into roots reggae, and are as respected as their contemporary male counterparts Chronixx and

ABOVE Bob Marley in concert in Munich in 1977. He is accompanied by the Wailers' vocal trio, the I-Threes: Marcia Griffiths, Judy Mowatt and Rita Marley. **OPPOSITE** Sound system dance in Wolverhampton, 1978. Photograph by Chris Steele-Perkins.

Protoje. As a result the genre remains relevant and continues to resonate with audiences around the world with its message of anti-colonialism and pan-Africanism.

Popular UK sound systems like Jah Shaka and Jah Youth (Roots Ambassador) took roots music even further and have had a profound influence on various musical genres worldwide. Roots has provided a solid foundation for the development of related genres such as dub, dancehall and lovers' rock. Roots reggae's distinctive sound and lyrical themes have been incorporated into hip-hop, punk rock and electronic music, and its far-reaching impact is a testament to its universality and its unique ability to connect with listeners from diverse backgrounds.

The Rastafarian lifestyle, hand in hand with roots music, is seen to give back dignity to our history because it is written and told by us and not the bystander, the outsider. Roots music not only offers entertainment in the form of storytelling, but it is a place where Rasta

women and men retreat for spiritual guidance, education, self-development, self-awareness and self-actualisation. Ideally, and as clichéd as it may sound, Rastafari is a lifestyle that many of us see as using music to curate the perfect environment, the perfect world for humans to thrive peacefully, progressively in love and harmony. The proof is in the music.

Lovers' Rock

LISA AMANDA PALMER

From the mid-1970s to the close of the 1980s, the reggae sub-genre of 'lovers' rock' took young, Black women into the national charts, became the home-grown sonic cultural expression of a generation and, in turn, influenced the music of Jamaica.

Lovers' rock is a popular genre of romantic reggae that blends the deep bass lines of roots reggae with the soulful melodies of African-American soul and RnB. This distinct soundscape of Black working-class music emerged in London during the politically turbulent mid-1970s and consolidated itself in the years that followed the traumatic New Cross fire and the rebellions that swept through many of Britain's inner cities in 1981. It resonated with predominantly young Caribbean-rooted performers and audiences who were actively exploring the meaning of their heritage and identity within an openly racist and hostile environment.

Lovers' rock was a vital part of the soundtrack that counteracted the systemic and structural forms of racism that impacted the lives of young, inner-city, Black teenagers facing poverty and economic marginalisation – a generation of young people frequently demonised in the mainstream media as lawless muggers and irresponsible single mothers. 'Lovers' was home grown – written, sung, played, produced, consumed and performed in the UK – and it successfully captured the cultural politics of romantic love, Blackness, gender and sexuality.

These iconic, joyful and intimate love songs were played widely in people's homes, on cassette tapes, in clubs, on sound systems, at blues parties and on local pirate radio stations. It's a genre that is associated with young Black teenage girls, like the late Louisa Mark, whose 'Caught You in a Lie' is considered to be the first definitive British lovers' rock single. Released in 1975 on Safari records in the UK and in Jamaica by Gussie Clarke, the single was produced by Sir Lloyd Coxsone, a hugely significant and leading figure within the development of reggae sound system culture in the UK.

Louisa Mark was 15 years old when she went into the studio to deliver her rendition of 'Caught You in a Lie', a track that was originally a 1967 African-American soul B-side by Robert Parker about a two-timing lover. Growing up in West London, Mark had featured as a guest vocalist on Dennis 'Blackbeard' Bovell's Sufferer sound system and it's fitting that the backing track for 'Caught You in a Lie' was laid down by Matumbi – the British reggae roots band that bass-man Bovell had co-founded in 1971. Her later recordings with producer Clement Bushay, for the Trojan label, included songs such as 'Six Sixth Street' and 'Keep It Like It Is', which, alongside 'Caught You in a Lie', continue to be played as lovers' rock classics.

Like other UK producers, Dennis Bovell was in search of a distinctive form of 'Black British' reggae that went beyond merely imitating the songs being produced in Jamaica. He and guitarist John Kpiaye – alongside husband-and-wife team Dennis and Eve Harris – are largely credited as the original architects of the British lovers' rock sound.

Lovers' rock became an important platform for many Black women performers, including Ginger Williams, Janet Kay, Carroll Thompson,

ABOVE 'I'm In Love with A Dreadlocks' by Brown Sugar, released on the Lovers Rock label in 1977.

Jean Adebambo, Joy Mack, Kofi, Caron Wheeler and Sandra Cross. Janet Kay scored a huge hit in 1979 with the track 'Silly Games' which reached number two in the UK national chart. Kay is noted for her soaring high-pitched vocals on both 'Silly Games' and her earlier cover of the Minnie Riperton classic, 'Lovin You', produced by Jamaican reggae singer Alton Ellis.

This music has a distinctive Caribbean genealogy. Versatile Jamaican roots and lovers' rock singers such as Sugar Minott, Dennis Brown and Gregory Isaacs enjoyed mainstream success in the British charts. However, they also received much more international recognition than their counterparts in the UK despite the fact that many male singers in the UK reggae scene such as Vivian Jones, Winston Reedy, Victor Romero Evans, Peter Spence and Peter Hunnigale were hugely popular on the UK reggae touring circuit. Bitty Mclean and Maxi Priest are two of very few British lovers' rock

singers to have entered the UK national charts. Priest is perhaps the most successful lovers' rock performer of all time with his pop-infused hits like 'Wild World' and his most successful recording, 'Close to You', which hit number one on the US *Billboard* Hot 100 chart in 1990.

Although lovers' rock was, and remains to this day, an integral component of reggae music's vernacular, these romantic love songs were often characterised as being apolitical, in contrast to the unmistakable Black liberation politics of Rastafari-infused roots reggae. Many of the early performers of lovers' rock were young teenage girls and this reinforced the idea that it was a 'soppy,' 'soft', feminine set of romantic songs, performed by young women to entertain female audiences. However, many of the young women in the lovers' rock scene did not shy away from the politics of race, racism, gender and Black freedom. Lovers' rock girl groups such as Brown Sugar and 15 16 17 were instrumental in establishing what would later be known as 'conscious lovers'. This style of reggae blended themes of romance, sexual desire, Rastafari and Black consciousness in tracks such as 'I'm In Love with A Dreadlocks', "Black Pride' and 'Black Skin Boys'. Indeed, conscious lovers was a form of lovers' rock that spoke directly to the tensions and synergies between Black politics and Black erotic desires constructed through heteronormative ideas of love.

In recent times there has been a resurgence of interest in lovers' rock which has brought international attention to this lesser-known genre of Black Caribbean British music and culture. Most recently, Steve McQueen's five-part series *Small Axe*, which aired on the BBC in the autumn of 2020, featured his much-anticipated and critically acclaimed film entitled *Lovers Rock*. McQueen's film showcased a radical extended

scene playing Janet Kay's 'Silly Games' with a cameo appearance from Dennis Bovell. The late Menelik Shabazz's documentary film *The Story of Lovers' Rock*[1] also examined how lovers' rock music defined a generation. John Goto's photographic publication *Lovers' Rock* uses the genre to curate a series of portraits of young Black people from the Lewisham area of London taken during the 1970s. Sonia Boyce's ongoing project, *Devotional* (see page 228). which was part of her award-winning exhibition at the Venice Biennial in 2022, features lovers' rock singers to redress forms of systemic amnesia that obscure the cultural contributions of Black British female singers more broadly to British music.

Black women performers in the lovers' rock scene were the voices that defined the sonic cultural expression of a generation of children born in the UK following the period of post-war migration from the Caribbean to Britain. However, the legacy of lovers' rock is now intertwined with and perhaps superseded by the music forms that had originally given shape to the genre. Today, for example, lovers' rock tracks are much more likely to be performed by contemporary Jamaican reggae artists including Beres Hammond, Sanchez, Jah Cure, Gyptian, Etana, I Octane, Tarrus Riley and Morgan Heritage. The influence of conscious lovers can also be traced in the aesthetics and themes of US hip-hop and RnB artists such as Lauryn Hill and her album *The Miseducation of Lauryn Hill*. Other RnB performers such as John Legend and Jazmine Sullivan have both recorded lovers' rock tracks.

This resurgence of historical, cultural, musical and artistic interest in the genre makes it an ideal time for wider audiences to understand the significance of lovers' rock's Black female vocalists in the history and making of reggae and contemporary popular music in Britain and beyond.

OPPOSITE House party, 1983. Photograph by Richard Saunders.
ABOVE Lloydie Coxsone in the studio with Simplicity, *circa* 1981. Photograph by Jean Bernard Sohiez.

223

Carroll Thompson: Back on Easy Street

ANGUS TAYLOR

It's a picture that captures a moment in history. A young Black woman wearing a large brown fur coat sits on the bonnet of a white car on a North-west London street. Her legs are crossed. She is not looking directly at the camera. She has a faraway look in her eyes, as if dreaming of something or someone that brings a faint smile to her lips.

The woman's name is Carroll Thompson. The street is Milton Avenue in Harlesden – reggae music's capital outside Jamaica. And the picture is Des Bailey's now iconic cover shot of Carroll's 1981 LP *Hopelessly in Love* – a high point in the hotly contested, distinctly 'Black British' reggae subgenre called lovers' rock. It harks back to a time when British reggae avoided the male-dominated, mystical and pan-African preoccupations of its Jamaican counterpart in favour of a return to romantic love. When young girls from London could be stars in reggae's thriving second city of culture.

But like many pictures, the *Hopelessly in Love* photo only tells half the story. Carroll wasn't from Harlesden. The car belongs to her executive producer Anthony 'Chips' Richards. The fur coat isn't hers either. And Carroll's enigmatic expression is a dazed look of mild embarrassment about it all.

'I'm looking very sheepish...' laughs Carroll forty years after the shot was taken. She's giving an interview to mark the album's four-decade anniversary reissue by North-west London's Trojan Records. 'I just felt really weird and uncomfortable. I'd never had a photoshoot before. I just sat down and they put this coat around me and they went click click click. There was no conceptual thing about it but it turned out to be a real sort of ghetto fabulous, back end of Harlesden. I never thought I'd still be talking about it forty years later...'

Of course no one would be talking about the picture without the music it marketed. Co-produced by Carroll and Bertie Grant, and executive-produced by Richards, *Hopelessly in Love* struck a winning lovers' rock formula of dreamy, precise vocals and tasteful arrangements. Recorded at East London's Easy Street studios, it featured some of British reggae and jazz's finest musicians. And – unusually for an art form often associated with soul covers – songs written or co-written by Thompson herself.

Carroll had been writing songs since the age of nine or ten, growing up in Letchworth, Hertfordshire. She was raised by her grandparents, to whom she credits her love of music. Her grandfather had come over from Jamaica in the 1950s, as part of the Royal Air Force, based in Henlow. He ran 'blues dances' – unlicensed parties playing ska, rocksteady and reggae. Carroll's grandmother was known as 'the bell of Trelawny' – the family parish – due to her singing voice. She was active in the local New Testament Pentecostal Church and enrolled Carroll in piano lessons. 'She got me on the piano as early as she could,' says Carroll, 'from about six or seven. It really helped with the songwriting. I used to write a lot of poetry and then put that to the music. That classical training – as much as I didn't like it – it really helped!'

OPPOSITE Carroll Thompson. *Hopelessly In Love* LP, 1981.

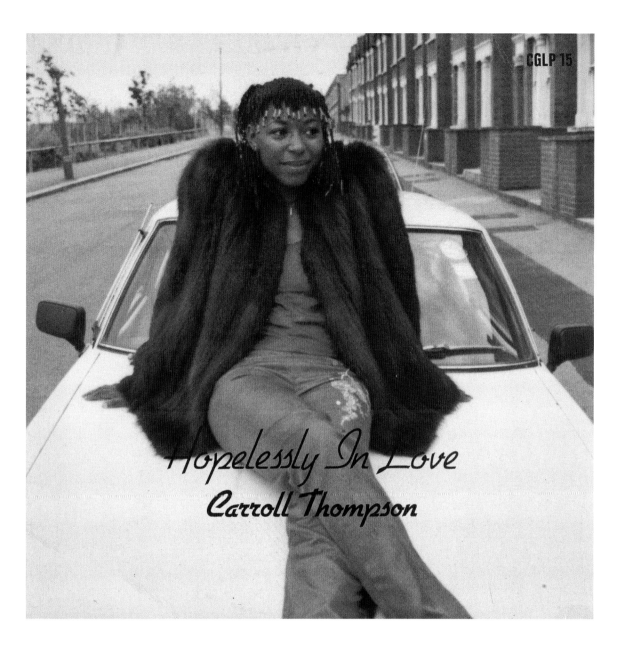

Hopelessly In Love
Carroll Thompson

Her first composition was, naturally, a gospel song, called 'I Know He Is with Me'. But as secular music was allowed in the house ('you couldn't tell my grandfather he couldn't listen to Desmond Dekker,' she laughs), she very soon fell in love with Ella Fitzgerald and, on the reggae side, Dennis Brown.

Her initial recordings as a teenager, however, were not reggae or jazz, but pop. She auditioned for a group named Sugar Cane, put together by Frank Farian, the mastermind behind Boney M (and later, more controversially, Milli Vanilli). She

sang a cover of 'Hot Stuff' by Donna Summer at a studio in Bond Street. The Sugar Cane project then paused for a while, and by the time Farian wanted her back she was already having success in the burgeoning lovers' rock scene.

Carroll first became aware of lovers' rock in 1975 when she heard Louisa Mark sing her cover of Robert Parker's 'Caught You in a Lie' (the result of sound system owner Lloydie Coxsone's brief but productive association with producer/ engineer Dennis Bovell). 'I just knew... this is a British sound. This could be my next-door neighbour.' When Janet Kay hit number two in the pop charts in 1979 with the Bovell-penned 'Silly Games' '[it] just sort of sealed it for me. It felt attainable.'

Her way in, ironically, came via a visiting Jamaican producer. Leonard 'Santic' Chin had made his name in the early 1970s roots era, recording his distinctive, rickety, crab-like rhythms for Horace Andy's 'Problems' and Freddie McKay's 'I'm a Free Man'. By the late 1970s he'd moved to London and was looking for a smoother, more soulful sound. Carroll was working as a trainee accountant in Knightsbridge and got chatting to the receptionist on the floor below. 'She said, "My uncle's from Jamaica and he's looking for some young Black English voices".'

Carroll sang into an answering machine tape recorder, and Chin liked what he heard. He encouraged her to write her own songs. 'I really thank Leonard for saying, "Carroll, do you have anything original?" Not many producers were asking these girls that were coming into studios whether they wrote music. There was no care or attention for a lot of the female singers. Because most of the songs in the chart were covers. Apart from myself and Jean Adebambo. Sandra Cross wrote a few songs as well. And Janet did write a few but they were album considerations more so. But not an entire body of work where they are all original.'

Carroll's classical training gave her a keen understanding of a composer's rights. She insisted Chin credit her as songwriter. 'I think there might be one pressing that had his name alone on it. But it was rectified very quickly. By the time we went to the second press it did have my name on.'

Both records, 'I'm So Sorry' and 'Hopelessly in Love', became local hits. They attracted the attention of Bertie Grant, who formed a production – and romantic – partnership with Carroll, as C&B Productions. Grant was a trained engineer who had strong connections to London's top musicians. Just as fortunate was the financial investment from former Trojan marketeer 'Chips' Richards of Carib Gems Records, the driving force behind the idea that Bertie and Carroll create an album. He put up the money to record at Easy Street, freeing Carroll from the need to work a 9 to 5. 'It was unheard of and an unbelievable experience for me, for which I will forever be grateful. I gave up my job in Knightsbridge and was in the studio from day till night-time. So my life became the studio.'

'We were just like little teenagers let loose in a state-of-the-art recording studio,' she laughs. 'Because Easy Street was a really good rock studio. Eddie... the guy who ran [it]... he made a bit of money and made the studio. So this was a proper rock studio and all of a sudden he was completely overwhelmed by all these mad Jamaicans, right? He didn't know what hit him! He was quite happy because there was so much weed in the place.'

Easy Street became a magnet for musical talent. The original Santic-produced single of 'I'm So Sorry' used most of the roots group Black Slate – so bassist Ras Elroy Bailey and drummer Desmond Mahoney were hired for the album. Jah Bunny from the Cimarons and Matumbi also played drums. Jamaican legends Vin Gordon and Sowell Radics contributed trombone and guitar respectively. Cleveland Watkiss sang on harmonies. Guitarist Alan Weekes brought his jazz chops to the sessions. 'He was able to bring in all these chords that I loved. I could concentrate on melody. We grew up on jazz through to reggae to pop through to Motown and Philly. So we had the same musical palette. We were able to construct some wonderful songs together.'

Like all good reggae songwriters, Carroll drew her lyrics from lived experience. 'No You Don't Know' was based on another life-changing event: becoming a single mother at 17. 'That was definitely autobiographical. Being in love so young and having a child with your very first boyfriend. He just wasn't ready for that. And neither was I really. So you're left with a lot of heartbreak and disappointment at that age because you're not really sure what life is, you're not really sure what love is. When you're 17, love is just attraction.'

The cryptic 'What Colour Are You', with its playful Rasta references to red, gold and green, came from her in-studio banter with Ras Elroy. 'He was always flirting with me. I said, "Listen, you know I'm going out with Bertie, it can't work." So he said "Yeah, let's write a tune then!" So it was like that. We wrote this flirty song. He would say "Are we going to go on a first date? What colour would you wear?"'

The album would eventually go on to sell thirty-five thousand copies. But it didn't bring immediate financial success. 'I was recognised a lot more,' Carroll recalls, choosing her words with care. 'But the actual business around the album was very difficult. But apart from that it did change me. It made me determined... I was not going to go back and study accountancy. I was going to be a musician.'

By the 1980s, lovers' rock had attracted some of Jamaica's top singers to come to London and record. Carroll would duet with Sugar Minott on the 1983 single 'Make It with You'. Sadly, support from the major labels that had embraced Bob Marley and roots reggae was less forthcoming. 'There was a roadmap for roots music... but

lovers' rock was a bit of an anomaly. It wasn't soul, it wasn't going with the roots and it kind of got lost in the cracks...'

Yet in a way, Carroll found that her lovers' rock achievements did lead her to a wider audience. Trinidad-born British soul singer Billy Ocean heard 'Hopelessly in Love' and asked Carroll to tour with him as a backing vocalist. This opened the doors to engagements with US legends, including Stevie Wonder, Michael Jackson and John Lee Hooker. 'Billy just plucked me out of obscurity. He was a fan of the album. He was blowing up and invited me to do his world tour. Had I not done that album then I would never have started my trajectory in this industry the way I did, working with so many fantastic musicians in many genres.'

And the reputation of 'Hopelessly in Love' continued to grow. Today Carroll is asked to sign copies of it by adoring fans after her concerts. Even the ambivalent cover photo led to some interesting encounters. When she was doing the shoot, 'There was a little girl looking out of the window at me. I was thinking "Just hurry up and take this photo please!" A couple of years ago a woman came up to me and said, "I've been wanting to meet you all my life. I was that little girl who was looking out of the window the day when you were taking that photo."'

Lovers' rock may not have been properly supported at the time, but its power has endured. It's loved by new generations of people all around the world. 'They do because most of the biggest hits in terms of reggae are all lovers' rock,' says Carroll. 'From Aswad through to John Holt, it's all lovers' rock. I think people understand romantic reggae now and they get the lovers' rock for what it was. It's just a different approach but good songs, good arrangement, lovely beat. I mean you can't beat that, can you?'

TEJ ADELEYE

One day in 1997, while on a residency in
Manchester, the acclaimed British artist Sonia
Boyce was crossing the road when she was
pulled into the memory of a song she hadn't
heard for over a decade.

It was the Jamaican vocalist Susan Cadogan's
reggae cover of 'Hurts So Good'. Recorded by
Lee Scratch Perry, it reached number 4 in the UK
singles chart. 'It was a song me and my friends
loved, and we loved singing it together,' she
shares over Zoom. 'I don't know what triggered
it that day, but I started singing to myself. I
went back to the studio and wrote down all the
words – it's kind of about a sadomasochistic
relationship, which I was too young to
appreciate at the time!'

It was a moment that sparked her curiosity
about 'the relationship between memory and
music, our emotional attachments and how
we seem to store up internal archives – sound
is a way to capture that'. Two years on, Boyce
was invited by Foundation for Art and Creative
Technology (FACT) as part of an outreach
programme partnering artists with local
organisations with the aim of making original
work. She was partnered with the Liverpool
Black Sisters, a grassroots activist organisation
established in the 1970s to provide support for
Black women across Merseyside. It was initially a
six-month project, where a small group of women
would gather regularly to explore collective
histories through music. 'During the first session,
I asked if they could name a Black British female
singer. My hope was that we would then play a
record, or sing together.'

But what followed were ten very awkward
minutes of silence. While Black singers from
America were easily named, no one could
recollect a Black British female artist. Eventually,
someone remembered the Nigerian-Welsh
powerhouse Shirley Bassey. 'We all got up and
sang "Big Spender",' she remembered. 'There
was a lot of singing, laughter and jollity. Then,
very unexpectedly, participants went home and
asked their families, friends, work colleagues if
they could think of anyone – it slowly started to
gather pace. By the end of the six months, we
had forty-six names.'

The names didn't stop coming. People would
turn up to artist talks and events with plastic
bags of ephemera: records, posters and books.
The project became known, aptly, as *Devotional*.
'Something about the gathering of names
seemed to touch a very personal nerve – I think
people have a real desire to contribute to public
knowledge,' she observed.

Boyce emerged as a seminal figure in
the 1980s, as part of the Black British Arts
movement. It was a renaissance moment, with
collectives putting on their own shows and
setting their own agendas about art in relation
to race, gender, politics, aesthetics and identity.
Boyce featured heavily in her own earlier
interdisciplinary works, and at the age of 25 she
became the first Black artist to have their work
purchased by the Tate Gallery. Decades later, she
would go on to become the first Black female
Royal Academician.

By the 1990s she was less interested in being
the sole subject of her works: 'I needed to shift

ABOVE Sonia Boyce, *Devotional Wallpaper and Placards*, 2008–20, *In The Castle of My Skin* at MIMA, Middlesbrough Institute of Modern Art.

from that position. Since then, my work and methods have been more about a collective context,' she reflected. She drew inspiration from the Brazilian conceptual artist Lygia Clark – who worked with objects to create participatory experiences as part of a clinical arts therapy practice that made space for addressing trauma and exploring agency. These threads – of objects, transformative processes and collaborative participation – also run through *Devotional*, and its latest iteration *Feeling Her Way,* which won the Golden Lion at the 2022 Venice Biennale.

Back in 2005 *Devotional II* was installed at the European Union headquarters in Brussels, and is owned by the British Government Art Collection. Over nine metres high, the piece is a dazzling column of multi-coloured stripes featuring the names of eighty-four Black women artists along a timeline. In 2007, Boyce was invited to do an installation at the National Portrait Gallery, which featured portraits of some of the women in the growing *Devotional* collection. On this occasion, Boyce spent two weeks drawing the names of almost two hundred women by hand on the walls of the gallery. In need of a more sustainable way to share the project, she turned to a beloved medium – wallpaper – upon which she printed the names of around two hundred women, grouped by different decades. Each name is surrounded by concentric black circles with waved lines that appear to move, each one seemingly emitting its own pulse.

As Boyce puts it, the collection signals 'a call to pay attention'. It serves as a working intervention, not only asking how we care for these women's memories, but also calling us to pay attention to the on-going conditions,

processes and power relations that shaped their lives. The recent Black Lives in Music report underscores the continued impact systemic racism has on the mental health and income of Black women working across the music industry.

To quote Saidiya Hartman, Boyce's creative approach to caretaking for collective memory – and therefore the present – generates 'a dreambook for existing otherwise'.[1] It's an archive of dreams, filled with endless examples of Black women pursuing their own artistic impulses. For instance, Boyce points to the journey of the Somali-British punk prophet Poly Styrene as 'stepping outside of the very constrained imaginings of what one could be as a Black woman'; and the evolution of artists such as Joan Armatrading, who recently scored her first symphony.

This dreaming impulse found realisation again at the Venice Biennale, where she collaborated with soul singer Poppy Ahjuda, jazz vocalist Jacqui Dankworth, Swedish experimental act Sofia Jernberg and singer-songwriter Tanita Tikaram, who were all guided by the composer Erroyln Wallen. Reflecting on the place of sound in her work, Boyce shared, 'There are all these complex things happening when sound touches you, [you can use it] in therapeutic ways, to keep people present in the present, as well as keeping them connected to their past.'

The group first gathered at Abbey Road studios, where they growled like lions, practised breathwork and declared themselves to be queens while leaning into the creative freedom of improvisation. Videos were made from this recording session, and stills from the film were fashioned into wallpaper adorning the gallery walls. There was more ephemera from the

Devotional collection, which now has over four hundred names and an as yet uncounted number of items. The earliest record is currently the singer Rachel Baptisite, nicknamed the 'Black Siren', who toured Ireland in the eighteenth century. Each room of the exhibit featured video performances of the artists in solo, duet and group formations – with the sound from each room bleeding to form a collective chorus resonating across time.

Much of the ephemera displayed at the Venice Biennale was purchased from charity shops in the six-month period before the show, and Boyce made the choice to keep the cheap price stickers of different items. 'There are many archives that are happening throughout this work,' she reflected. 'One of them is the journey of these distributed objects, the production that's gone into the music, the advertising, someone's choice to buy and discard that music... all of that can result in something that's [priced at] 20 pence.' In foregrounding the question of value in her work – which includes how Black women are valued in society at large – Boyce uses the collection to point to value systems outside of industry validation, outside the social processes that have enabled particular kinds of devaluation to take place and outside 'official' records of history.

'Archival practices have historically been tied to the law,' she shared. 'It's about what gets recognised by the state – and who speaks legitimate history. Whoever keeps the archive keeps control of a certain narrative.' *Devotional* keeps its gaze on people who may not historically have been recognised by the state or historical records. In doing so, she practises what she has named elsewhere as 'unearthing as an act of solidarity', creating a history from below – an open-ended archive structured by feeling and a sensitivity to experiences that have been rendered invisible. 'There is an unacknowledged sense that women of colour have been here in plain sight, but not seen, for centuries. They're just there, present, making a cultural life, but also not there at the same time. Their ability to do something significant, build the richness of our cultural life, and then very quickly disappear from our consciousness is repetitive,' she shared.

The collection points to the histories of empire, migration, class relations and trade that have made the UK a nexus point for Black cultural production for centuries, unsettling fixed ideas of Britishness, nation and diaspora in the process. Boyce uses a politically Black framework for the project, featuring women of African, Caribbean, Asian and Arabic descent. Having an open-ended collection creates space to explore complexity, tension and evolving conversations between groups: there's room to discuss the colourism, misogynoir and anti-Blackness which have long plagued the music industry.

At its heart, this collection is one that foregrounds relation – the relationship between the public and artists, our collective implication in the social relations that structure our lives and how we can creatively negotiate them. Boyce still plans on creating the participatory experiences for us to collectively feel our way forward: 'My greatest desire would be to build a museum, as an artwork, of these women who have changed the sound of the UK.'

Transitions: The Sound of Young Black Britain Goes Worldwide

PAUL BRADSHAW

Against a backcloth of a global hip-hop revolution, UK club and rave culture consolidated itself during the 1980s and tribute needs to be paid to four key players/collectives that shaped a fresh and enduring template for Black British music and culture.

A Wag Club regular, Nigerian-born Helen Folasade Adu, aka Sade, went from stage to studio to be voted the face of 1984. Her debut album, *Diamond Life*, delivered a cool blend of jazz-tinged Brit-funk and UK lovers' rock combined with a hint of melancholia and tangible sexiness. It won her a 1985 BRIT award for Best British Album of the Year and launched a career that has generated six albums and record sales worldwide in excess of fifty million.

Jazzie B – the Funki Dred – initiated the truly radical Soul II Soul in 1982. Conceived as an umbrella organisation, it included his sound system, a clothing line, a record shop in Camden, London, and a record imprint. From 1985 to 1989, Soul II Soul ran their legendary party at the Africa Centre in Covent Garden. Soul II Soul's mantra was all about happiness, love and bass, and in 1989 they scored a UK top-ten hit with 'Keep On Movin''. The group's debut album *Club Classics Vol. One* dropped in 1990, peaked at number one on the UK albums chart and went on to sell over four million copies worldwide. 'Back to Life (However Do You Want Me)' hit the UK number one spot and went top five in the US. That same year Soul II Soul won a Grammy award for Best RnB Performance by a Duo or Group with Vocal. They have sold over ten million records worldwide.

Meanwhile in Bristol, the Wild Bunch had emerged as a hip-hop collective, but as they morphed into Massive Attack in 1988 their roots reggae/sound system sensibilities came to the fore – not least through their decision to recruit the distinctive voice of Studio One veteran Horace Andy. Also brought in to supplement the original trio of Robert '3D' Del Naja, Andrew 'Mushroom' Vowles and Grant 'Daddy G' Marshall were vocalists Neneh Cherry, Shara Nelson and rapper Tricky. *Blue Lines* dropped in 1991 and ushered in the spacey, bass-heavy concept of trip hop while going double platinum in the UK. Massive Attack have since sold thirteen million records worldwide.

Pirate radio promoted Black music in all forms and was key to the thriving club and warehouse party scene. Norman Jay MBE was a founding member of Kiss FM and, along with his brother Joey, ran their own Good Times sound system – a valuable and radical addition to Notting Hill Carnival. Deeply familiar with the NYC soul and funk scene, he used his groundbreaking Kiss FM show to pioneer the UK rare groove scene and broke down the doors with his legendary Shake and FingerPop parties. His High on Hope parties took him into the 1990s with a paradise garage-style mix of deep house and disco. Respected worldwide, in an online interview with DJ History, Norman Jay maintained, 'We've learned a lot from America in thirty or forty years. Acid jazz could only have come from England. Rare groove could only have come from England. Jungle, drum and bass... We are now making music that the Americans used to take for granted years ago with jazz, RnB, hip-hop, house. We're creating our own and challenging them.'

OPPOSITE Sade and the band perform on *Saturday Night Live*, 14 December 1985.

SOUL II SOUL Live at the Palladium, New York, USA, 1990.
Photograph by Catherine McGann.

CYBERSPACE

'a human internet rooted in the dance floor and tapes, across airwaves, record shops and computers'

Monique Charles

Jazz Warriors: The Legacy

KEVIN LE GENDRE

Today's thriving, diverse, musically eclectic UK jazz community continues to reach for the sky, to organically elevate the music of a generation, and that requires us to step back to the mid-1980s, and to encounter a group of young, aspiring Black British jazz players. Schooled in reggae and jazz-funk, they regularly met up in the Atlantic in Brixton where they gave life to a big band – the Jazz Warriors.

Black British musicians of Caribbean descent have long had a complex relationship with the homeland of their parents. The *yard* is something that is known about without necessarily being known by the many sons and daughters born and raised in England. Opportunities to travel to where the elders – the 'big people' – grew up were often limited.

Yet in 1987 an album by a group called the Jazz Warriors made an emphatic statement on the lifeblood of history and heritage, and the way it shaped new visions. The record in question was *Out of Many, One People*. Those five weighty words told an essential story.

Although the collage of wooden masks, woodwinds and string instruments on the sleeve may have put both Africa and America in the mind of most observers, the title, reflecting precise cultural knowledge, was actually the national motto of Jamaica. London-born saxophonists Courtney Pine, Steve Williamson, Ray Carless, double bassist Gary Crosby, vocalist Cleveland Watkiss and vibraphonist Orphy Robinson were among several in the twenty-piece orchestra who would have probably known the saying, given their parentage. Yet they were joined by the descendants of other parts of the West Indies, Africa and Asia, who may have taken the adage as a call for solidarity between ex-British colonies. Drummer Mark Mondesir had roots in Saint Lucia, flautist Rowland Sutherland Saint Vincent, trumpeter Claude Deppa South Africa and trombonist Fayyaz Virji India. The Jazz Warriors were perceived as a Black big band but they really embodied a multicultural Britain that, to quote Duke Ellington, a vital touchstone, was 'Black, brown and beige' – a recognition of diversity *within* a population bearing the mark of second-class citizenship.

More precisely, the Warriors were twenty-somethings who had cut their teeth on sound systems and in reggae and funk bands, the populist electric end of African-Caribbean and American music, but they were now playing the 'serious' acoustic music that had been created by legends such as John Coltrane, Sonny Rollins and Wayne Shorter. The UK tour of Art Blakey and the Jazz Messengers, indefatigable hard bop heroes, created a loose synergy with the emergence of the Warriors. And TV documentaries, magazine covers, double-breasted suits and kipper ties triggered what was widely termed 'the British jazz revival'.

Courtney Pine, who founded the Abibi Jazz Arts organisation that incubated the Warriors, became a figurehead for both the band and young improvising musicians more generally, but of all the players who appeared on *Out of Many, One People*, Harry Beckett was arguably the most important. At 52 years of age he stood as the wise elder, the seasoned pioneer.

The Barbadian trumpeter had been in Britain since the mid-1950s, playing anything from bebop to avant-garde, fusion to prog rock, calypso and reggae to highlife and South African jazz. There were many invaluable lessons to be learned from 'father Beckett'.

Together Beckett, Pine and the other Warriors thus created a continuum. The band had *generations* rather a single generation, and that sense of a history being upheld and developed runs through the post-Warriors period of the mid-1990s. Above all, Gary Crosby, in partnership with photographer-producer Janine Irons, founded Tomorrow's Warriors exactly in order to nurture the successors of his own cohort. Workshops held in Birmingham and London bore fruit and the first significant ensemble that could be called TW graduates, J-Life, had epochal talent: Jason Yarde, Robert Mitchell, Julie Dexter, Vidal Montgomery and Gary's son Daniel. Thereafter came Denys Baptiste, Tom Skinner, Andrew McCormack, Soweto Kinch and Neil Charles to name a few – all participating in a Black music tradition open to everybody, Black or white.

In the mid-2000s the arrival of saxophonist-composer Shabaka Hutchings was significant, not just because he became a Tomorrow's Warrior after studying at the Guildhall School of Music. On one hand he strengthened the status of Birmingham as fertile soil for British jazz as he played there with Kinch. On the other, Hutchings, of Barbadian parentage, would prove a worthy heir to Harry Beckett.

Like Beckett, Hutchings placed no restrictions on his interests. With the bands Zed-U, Sons of Kemet, the Comet Is Coming, and Shabaka and the Ancestors he put his own spin on free-form improvisation, West Indian folk, New Orleans marching bands, Jamaican dub and South African jazz. The range of his output is everything one would hope for from a musician who realises the best way to uphold what might be called jazz is to eschew any rigid definitions thereof and to take a stylistic road less travelled while being mindful of the pathways opened up by innovators, be they Sun Ra or Albert Ayler.

A few years ago Hutchings founded his own label, Native Rebel Recordings, and signed the likes of Manchester-born, London-based saxophonist Chelsea Carmichael, the latest in a substantial wave of internet-age female players that makes the point that the gender balance is greater now than when Gail Thompson (and Cheryl Alleyne) were the sole women in the Warriors. Today Nubya Garcia, Cassie Kinoshi (see page 54), Camilla George, Shirley Tetteh, Cherise Adams-Burnett, Sheila Maurice-Grey, Sarah Tandy and Rosie Turton have all made a breakthrough internationally and nationally. As alumni of Tomorrow's Warriors they underline the ongoing importance of the Crosby-Irons mentoring scheme and by extension the spirit of the Jazz Warriors. It is hardly surprising that other young scions such as Femi Koleoso and Joe Armon-Jones have gone on to enjoy substantial success both as soloists and as members of the highly popular group Ezra Collective, who in 2023 became the first jazz act to win the prestigious Mercury Prize.

At a glance it is clear that the seeds planted by the Jazz Warriors some forty years ago have borne substantial fruit. The large audiences bear testimony to the impact made by Pine, Crosby, Williamson and co., and their determination to ensure that the baton they picked up in their formative years is handed down to others. Legacy has become an emblematic word in the last decade, often quite cynically used by chancer politicians, but it is entirely appropriate when assessing this essential period in the recent history of Black music in Britain. The idealism of *Out of Many, One People* is appropriate in an age of social fragmentation and division, even pre-Brexit, but if that saying still has great currency then the commitment of post-Warriors to the education and nurturing of new voices also calls to mind another form of deeply rooted Jamaican folk wisdom that has lost none of its meaning: *Each one teach one.*

JAZZ IS THE TEACHER,
FUNK IS THE PREACHER

A selection of classic albums
that build on the legacy of the
Jazz Warriors' seminal *Out of Many,
One People*. Five decades of Black
British jazz: 1974–2024.

ORPHY ROBINSON + ONNAVAS
WHEN TOMORROW COMES

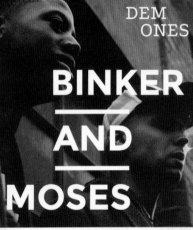

DEM ONES

BINKER AND MOSES

BYRON WALLEN'S SOUND ADVICE

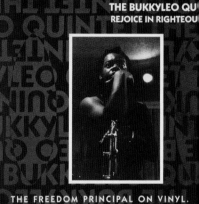

THE BUKKYLEO QU
REJOICE IN RIGHTEOU

THE FREEDOM PRINCIPLE ON VINYL.

COURTNEY PINE *"Journey To The Urge Within"*

Black Classical Music

YUSSEF KAMAAL   BLACK

SOWETO KINCH
THE BLACK PERIL

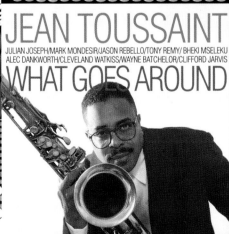

JEAN TOUSSAINT

JULIAN JOSEPH/MARK MONDESIR/JASON REBELLO/TONY REMY/ BHEKI MSELEKU
ALEC DANKWORTH/CLEVELAND WATKISS/WAYNE BATCHELOR/CLIFFORD JARVIS

WHAT GOES AROUND

DEN
BAPTIS
STEVE WIL
GAR
N
NEIL
RON

THE LATE TRANE

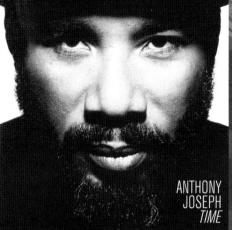

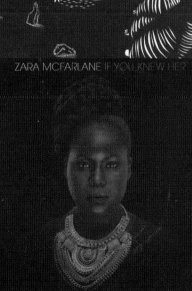

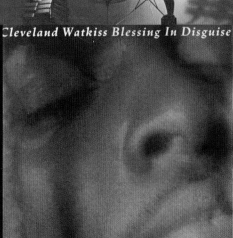

Manchester: UK Street Soul. Messages of Love from Britain's Forgotten Inner Cities

ANDY THOMAS

During the height of acid house in Manchester in the late 1980s and early 1990s, across town from the Haçienda at packed-out clubs like the Gallery and Precinct 13, it was the sounds of the city's Black urban soul music that got the biggest dance floor reaction.

As Mark Rae, DJ at Precinct 13 and future label head at 1990s Manchester soul-rooted hip-hop label Grand Central Records, explains, there was something of a divide in the clubs across the city: 'Soul music ranging from an 80 bpm two-step up to a 105 bpm bounce mixed with hip-hop didn't fit in with a predominantly white crowd on ecstasy.'

Rae moved to Manchester from the north-east of England in 1987 at a pivotal time for UK soul. 'I had fallen in love with an album by Loose Ends called *Zagora*,' he recalls. 'This 808 drum machine soul, led in part by Nick Martinelli, was very fresh sonically. More importantly, they weren't American-sounding songs. The writing style had its own British feel, which was a continuation of the ground won in the jazz funk and Brit funk scene that came before it.'

He immersed himself in the scene, becoming a regular at some of Manchester's prominent Black music clubs that had followed in the wake of the legendary Reno, where DJ Persian became the godfather of Manchester soul. 'The biggest club at the time for this was run by Soul Control at a place called the Gallery,' says Rae. 'They would take their own sound system into the club, and it would be like a reggae sound: huge bass, and MCs and DJs at the controls. This is essentially what UK street soul is: the mixing of Jamaican dynamics with the American soul hits, and then the UK interpretation of this via our own productions. In essence, it's an emotional expression of the UK inner-city experience.'

Rae would soon be spinning this music alongside the hip-hop tracks that were played at the Man Alive Club and at Precinct 13, where UK street soul became the dominant music. 'It was a place that had attracted a crowd that expected the street soul that was being pushed on pirate radio at that time,' says Rae. 'It was the best atmosphere I have ever DJd in, because it was electric – these songs really belonged to the people.'

The connection was solidified when Manchester started to produce its own street soul. 'I remember the chill running down my spine when half the club in Precinct 13 stood on the tables and banged their bottles on the ceiling when we used to drop "Just a Little More" by [Manchester group] Fifth of Heaven,' says Rae.

Bô'vel Records

33rpm

BOV 001
Ⓟ & Ⓒ 1995

This Side.
1. Life Changes You
2. i Can't Get By

Other Side.
1. Beautiful day
2. Coming Back
3. Funky Baby

Singer Songwriter by Bô'vel
Mixed & Produced by Kev Waddington
Recorded at HQ Studios MANCHESTER

INFO
0860 1888862
0370 442190

With the beautiful vocals of Manchester singer Denise Johnson – who also sang with Primal Scream and A Certain Ratio and who sadly passed away in July 2020 – Fifth of Heaven's 'Just a Little More' was the perfect UK street soul record. 'The track is 88 bpm in a minor key – which is a super sweet melancholy – and you have a club going crazy to it,' says Rae. 'It's the *opposite* of rave, it's music as an *emotional* drug, based on the need for human closeness. Denise is the heart of this story, in spirit and soul.'

Another female Manchester singer whose sweet voice was tailor-made for the 1980s production of UK street soul was Diane Charlemagne, who also passed away recently. She is best known for her vocals for Factory Records' 52nd Street, but her street soul records with Cool Down Zone are classics of the genre.

Over time Stu Allan's show *Bus Diss* on Piccadilly Radio and *Leaky Fresh* on Sunset FM became important platforms for UK street soul; but spiritually the music always remained closely linked to the pirate radio stations that were transmitted from tower blocks across the city. 'The pirates were incredibly dominant and important for UK street soul,' says Rae. 'You had [shows like] *Soul Nation*, *Front Line*, *Unity* and *Sting* – this all fit with the DIY style of the music, where you'd put your own 12-inch together and get distributed with no interference from record-label A&R.'

And even while street-soul-inspired acts like Soul II Soul and Omar made waves in the mainstream, pioneering UK street soul artists never quite caught the same above-ground success. 'These stories are sometimes forgotten, or ignored,' says Mark Rae. 'Street soul is a message of love from the often-forgotten inner cities of Britain.'

OPPOSITE Mancunian street soul classic by Bo'vel.
ABOVE 52nd Street, featuring Denise Johnson, Manchester, 1983. Photograph by Kevin Cummins.

Cybernetic Networks: The Mechanics of UK Garage

MONIQUE CHARLES

The rise and fall of UK garage in the 1990s takes us on a wild ride, from modest beginnings in the margins of London's superclubs to the high-end bling of clubs like Twice as Nice and the raves of Ayia Napa to the MOBOs, Mercury awards and the chart-topping hits of So Solid Crew, Ms Dynamite, Kele Le Roc, Mis-Teeq and Craig David.

While the roots of UK garage (UKG) might be traceable to a venue called Sterns, in Hastings in 1991 (frequented by pioneering DJs such as Dreem Team's Mikee B and Ministry of Sound DJs Harvey and Justin Berkmann), it was the notorious Sunday morning sessions – Happy Days – at the Elephant & Castle pub in 1993 that introduced the music into the clubbing mainstream. Its notoriety was due to the lack of venues playing UK garage in central London, making Happy Days *the* place to be for those

hardcore clubbers who'd just rolled out of venues like the Ministry and weren't done raving.

Taking soulful, gospel-tinged US garage and Chicago deep house as the foundation, a fresh, innovative UKG aesthetic was in the making. British DJs and partygoers preferred heavier basslines, brighter and sharper highs and faster tempos than their American counterparts. Initially London DJs would take US garage instrumental B-sides and speed up the tempo (130–132 bpm) to keep up with the energy levels of ravers who loved to dance, high, for hours on end. It was only a matter of time before a wave of self-produced music (using Akai samplers, 909 drumkits and MPC 2000s), like Bump N Flex's mix of the 'R U Sleeping' hit, took over the dance floor.

The initial lack of venue options also meant that pirate radio stations such as Heat, Deja vu, Delight, Freek and Flex FM were crucial to the growth of UKG. Listeners tuned in and recorded sessions on cassette tapes. Others did the same at live club sessions (tape packs). This was pre-internet and UKG was disseminated through 'living' networks, spread by ravers, tape packs and cassette tapes across the country.

The underground vibe of UKG added to the sense of exclusivity. This corresponded with the scene's edgy, aspirational lifestyle and outlook. A multicultural scene, it attracted a diverse range

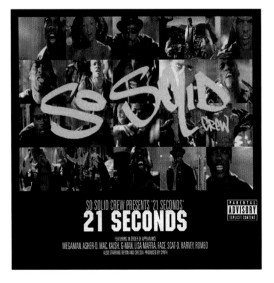

LEFT So Solid Crew's classic '21 Seconds'.
OPPOSITE Garage Nation Ayia Napa, Cyprus, 2000.
Photograph by Ewen Spencer.

of people from all walks of life, from celebrities such as Posh and Becks and Jay-Z to people from the criminal underground and every clubber in between. UKG attracted women who loved dressing up, clubbing, singing and dancing. Men followed the 'sexy ladies' into the scene. Both UKG's sound and dress code were influential. The number of ravers coming from all over the country to experience UKG gained momentum, and venue numbers and capacities increased from the mid-1990s onwards. In its heyday, garage epitomised the champagne lifestyle: Moët as standard; brandy and Coke; the sharp style of dress pioneered by the likes of the Dreem

Team, who became synonymous with suits, shirts and ties. Flamboyant and bright designer gear/garms (clothing) such as Moschino, Versace, Iceberg jeans, Gucci. Tight-fitting clothes to show the physique. Loafers for men, heels and thongs for women were the order of the day.

UKG nights were high-end and branded. The Scala, Colosseum, Twice as Nice, Garage Nation, Ministry of Sound, Sun City, Gass Club, Hanover Grand, Samantha's, La Cosa Nostra and the SW1 Club attracted thousands of regulars on a weekly basis. UKG was a culture and a lifestyle. The luxury element extended further afield, with clubbing getaways to Ayia Napa, Cyprus, for fun, drinks (Sambuca), sex (casual), to make friends

The mainstream record companies sought to jump on the trend by signing numerous UKG artists, but established DJs and producers kicked back.

and, of course, clubbing at Pzazz and Insomnia. At its peak, Ayia Napa brought together ravers from all over the UK.

Alongside the clubs and pirate radio, record shops were hubs that supported the UKG phenomenon. Producers created their own labels – for example Ice Cream Records, Nice 'N' Ripe, Unda-Vybe, i! Records – and distributed their vinyl via a network of independent record shops which were frequented by DJs and MCs such as McK, Creed, DJ Luck & MC Neat, MC DT, EZ, Pied Piper, PSG, Sticky, Zed Bias, Wookie, Dreem Team, Tuff Jam, El-B and Noodles, and many more. In addition, record shops were important multifunctional hubs that allowed for the sale of music and tickets for garage nights, but also the sale of associated tape packs (recordings of garage events themselves).

Garage *was* cybernetic: a human internet rooted in the dance floor and tapes, across

airwaves, record shops and computers. UKG peaked over a five-to-six-year period spanning the late 1990s and early 2000s, with three main iterations: speed, two-step and dark/grimy. From 1998 onwards the sound changed, evolving from speed garage into two-step (Architects ft. Nay Nay – 'Body Groove'; Genius Cru – 'Boom Selection'; DJ Luck & MC Neat – 'A Little bit of Luck'; Brasstooth – 'Pleasure'). It included skippy kicks, syncopation/offbeatness, heavy basslines and broken beats. Producers began to include elements of hip-hop, rap, soul, reggae, reggae dancehall, jungle, calypso, soca, and drum and bass, shifting the rhythmic pattern. MCs added bars (lyrics/raps) with slow phrases and clear diction in club settings and later on records. The scene introduced/included homegrown singers alongside sampled vocals: Shola Ama – 'Imagine'; Lonyo – 'Summer of Love'; Monster Boy ft. Denzie – 'Sorry (I Didn't Know)'. The sound continued onto its third iteration, dark/grimy garage, becoming darker, with more bass, less melodic, less vocals/singing styles: Wookie ft. Sia – 'Little Man (Exemen Remix)'; DJ Sticky – 'Triplets'; So Solid Crew – '21 Seconds'; K2 Family – 'Bouncing Flow'. It reverted to instrumentals for the spoken word, rapping and storytelling and short vocal phrases. Collectives, groups and artists emerged in two-step and grimy/dark garage (So Solid Crew, Heartless Crew, Kele Le Roc, Craig David, Kano, Mis-Teeq and Ms Dynamite) with varying success.

LEFT AND OPPOSITE Two archetypal records that dominated the dance floors of the garage nation: Kele Le Roc's 'My Love (10º Below Vocal Mix) and 'Booo!' by Sticky featuring MC Dynamite.

Of those achieving mainstream success, So Solid Crew pioneered the shift in UKG's sound during the gap between UKG and grime. The collective won a BRIT award (2002) and two MOBO Awards (2001), and reached UK number one with the single '21 Seconds' (2001). They had a total of five top forty hits, four of them top tens including 'They Don't Know', 'Haters' and 'Ride Wid Us'. Their garage album *They Don't Know* reached number six. Kele Le Roc won two MOBO Awards (1999) and had two top ten (RnB) singles in the late 1990s. She achieved great underground success with garage track 'Things We Do for Love', produced by DJ Sticky, and the '10° Below Vocal Mix' remix of her song 'My Love'. Niomi McLean-Daley, aka Ms Dynamite MBE, won the Mercury Prize (2002), three MOBO Awards (2003), a Garage Award (2002) and two BRIT awards (2003). Her first feature, on track 'Booo!' (produced by DJ Sticky), was an underground success, eventually reaching number twelve (2001). She had a top-ten album: *A Little Deeper*. She has a total of eleven top forty hits, six of those in the top ten. Craig David MBE achieved twenty-five top forty hits, with sixteen in the top ten and two number ones. His first (UKG) album, *Born to Do It*, reached number one. His top ten hits include 'Re-Rewind (The Crowd Say Bo Selecta)' with Artful Dodger, 'Fill Me In' and 'Woman Trouble' with Artful Dodger. David won a total of five MOBO Awards (2000, 2001) as well as three Ivor Novello Awards and a plethora of MTV awards and Grammy nominations. Girl group Mis-Teeq received a Garage Award (2001) and a MOBO Award (2002). Their RnB and garage-infused first album *Lickin' on Both Sides* peaked at number three. They

had a total of eight top forty hits, seven in the top ten. Songs included 'Why?', 'All I Want', 'One Night Stand' and 'B With Me'.

Success has its positive and negative dimensions. The mainstream record companies sought to jump on the trend by signing numerous UKG artists, but established DJs and producers kicked back. They did not like the direction the industry or the younger generation was taking the sound in, and set up a committee to preserve/gatekeep the genre as well as create the Garage Awards. However, as the clubbing side of UKG proliferated, the racialised, dog-whistle publicity around crime, drugs and violence made the whole scene vulnerable to police and government intervention. Shutting down or heavily policing UKG events simultaneously stifled business opportunities for promoters, artists and PAs, venue owners, DJs and record shops selling tape packs and event tickets, etc. Despite selling thousands of records each week, the authorities placed a stranglehold on the scene and inevitably, UKG parties eventually retreated back underground where they originally belonged.

NTS Meets Touching Bass

CHRISTIAN ADOFO

Both Femi Adeyemi and Errol Anderson have musical roots in the legendary club Plastic People and share a symbiotic vision that has led to the creation of the hugely influential 24/7 digital radio station NTS and a South London-based musical movement/curatorial platform, monthly dance/concert series, record label and bi-weekly radio show.

London has often been a welcome finishing school for subcultures of the underground, from recording studio to the pirate airwaves to the dance: a feedback loop where a buffet of Black British sounds is shared and spread with migrant communities, particularly those of the African and Caribbean diaspora who are arguably connected more than ever in real time across the digital platforms. Two important figures who embody this DIY spirit in facilitating the broadcast of sound with an open policy from the Big Smoke to the world are Femi Adeyemi and Errol Anderson.

Femi has Naija (Nigerian) roots and is the founder of NTS Radio, which started out as a DIY radio station project in 2011 and has evolved to become an influential global movement with studios in London, Manchester, Los Angeles and Shanghai. The station features over eight hundred resident hosts on heavy rotation, with three million monthly listeners tuning into an eclectic range of programming, and has built brand partnerships in the high fashion space while hosting free block parties from its OG Gillett Square location in Dalston, East London.

Errol, on the other hand, is of Jamaican and Grenadian heritage and is a musical curator, DJ and co-founder of Touching Bass. Formerly an online music interview series, the musical movement has grown into a certified club night for the steppers and a burgeoning record label championing artists and instrumentalists with soul and substance alongside a monthly show on NTS.

Both NTS and Touching Bass provide a safe space for regular online and IRL interaction. Christian Adofo spoke with Errol and Femi about growing up in the city, the influence of their heritage on their creativity, broadcasting beyond the dance and the importance of building musical communities with an old-school approach.

What's your earliest musical memory?

Femi: I lived in Lagos for a while and as a kid my uncle used to take me to Fela Kuti's shrine. My mum didn't want him to take me but he'd take me there. I don't remember much from it. I remember going back to Nigeria in 2008. I hadn't been back for twenty years and the shrine was still a very vibrant space, with a lot of colours and a lot of shit going on in there. My uncle was one of Fela's dancers.

Errol: My most profound earliest memories of music centre around family gatherings. Being at house parties I was way too young to be at, but just being enamoured by the energy within the space. You know, more often than not small, East London flats. A solitary red light. One deck. Reggae. Dub. Soca. Rice and peas. Most

importantly, it was very multi-generational, so you had young ones like myself. The combination of all of those elements is the grounding force for everything that I now do.

Are there any particular tunes from that time which you remember?

Errol: There's an artist called Sandra Cross and she put out a record called 'Country Living' which is produced by Mad Professor. That record was on repeat in my dad's car. Her voice is so special. Last August we were able to book her for a pre-Carnival dance with Touching Bass, which felt like a really full circle moment.

When it comes to those early times when you were going out. Those clubbing experiences. Can you paint a picture from Friday to Saturday night?

Femi: My musical interests were broad but going to school in inner-city London, especially in the 1990s, you'd tend to be listening to grime. White boys and some Black boys were into Oasis and Blur but most Black boys would listen to UK garage, jungle and rap too. There were very clear lines of taste at the time, mainly defined by race. I had an interest in everything, so I was listening to Oasis and Blur and I was going to parties like Twice as Nice, Metalheadz or Tongue Fu which was this hip-hop night that was big in the late 1990s/early 2000s.

So, E3 born and raised in Bow. Talk to me about how life was like growing up those times.

Errol: Growing up in Bow in the 1990s into the 2000s, it was such an innovative time, but when you're living through those moments you don't necessarily see it as such. You just see it as the everyday. Grime was the first music, beyond my parents' collection, that I could actually call my own. It naturally became the culture. When I reflect on that time, I think about Tinchy Stryder, Wiley and the Ruff Sqwads of this world. They were like superheroes to me. When I'd be in the ends I'd see (Prince) Rapid and Fuda Guy playing football a lot. I was a football guy, so I would end up kicking a ball with them, as one of the young guns or whatever. So, there was a proximity to greatness that I never felt before. That was so inspiring to someone who was just finding their own way as a music lover. It was a reminder that these man are doing it so if I wanna try a ting, then I can.

How did you make the transition into DJing as Mr Wonderful and curating your own nights?

Femi: DJing for me has never been a serious endeavour. I'm really into Chinese martial arts movies and I have a DVD called *The Magnificent Wonderman*. At my first DJ gig, my friend who booked me said, 'What do you wanna call yourself?' I said 'Magnificent Wonderman'. They changed it to Mr Wonderful on the flyer. By that time I was getting booked quite a lot so I couldn't really change it. I was mainly playing psychedelic rock, emo at the time. The name kinda suited the music I was playing.

From that point on, you were promoting and putting on nights?

Femi: In 2007, I started writing this blog called Nuts to Soup, which was a precursor to NTS. It was mainly collecting mixes and getting friends to write about music. People were booking me to DJ from that point on. I enjoyed doing it for a small group of friends but not really a big club setting. I started this blog and then, through its semi-popularity, I threw a party.

Digging into the legacy of Soul II Soul and reading Sounds Like London, I feel like what you've been building with Alex Rita is a continuum and by-product of that legacy. How did Touching Bass develop from a content series, platforming people across the world, into a physical experience with your club nights?

TOUCHING BASS

in the dance with **Ruby Savage, Alex Rita Errol & Theo Parrish**

We Out Here
Saturday 17 August 2019
20:00 - 05:00

Errol: Casting our minds back to the start of Touching Bass, I was a journalist by trade. My football career had been dashed. Hang tight my left knee! Journalism became a vehicle through which I could express myself in ways I never thought I could. I was working as a staff writer at VICE/Noisey and I just wanted a space to call my own. So Touching Bass became this portal for me to translate all the music I was digging and finding on blogs, SoundCloud and various other platforms while utilising the weight of VICE/Noisey. I didn't even realise people were picking up on it from different parts of the world. It's also the way Touching Bass moved from being this interview series into being a gathering. I also have to give a shout out to Plastic People as I managed to catch the end of that. Going to mostly FWD>> nights completely shook my world, and my thoughts, on the way people gather and party. I miss that club, man. The first Touching Bass party was myself – trying to work out how to DJ for the first time on the fly... terrible! – Wu-Lu, Maxwell Owin and my homie Sean... Born Cheating, aka Poison Zcora. I will never forget there was a moment where Wu-Lu played D'Angelo's 'Spanish Joint' at like 2am and

I was like, 'Yep, this is what I wanna do.' Up until that point I hadn't really experienced a place where people were open to whatever goes and were able to trust the DJs and trust the space. That was the start of it.

How did your association with Plastic People grow?

Femi: I went to Plastic for years. When you're growing up as a DJ with a wide, varied taste, it was a whole new place... the Mecca. It was also the place... if you got behind the decks at Plastic, it was what we all dreamed of. I met a couple of guys, Ben and Judah, at this bar called the Vortex. Ben (Benji B) used to do a night called Nonsense and he was starting to get more popular on BBC and at Deviation, he was doing his own thing. They saw me and said, 'Do you wanna join?' They booked me for a one-off night at Plastic. They loved it and added me to the set as the third part of Nonsense. Eventually I became one of the regular DJs there. It was the only period of my life where I thoroughly enjoyed

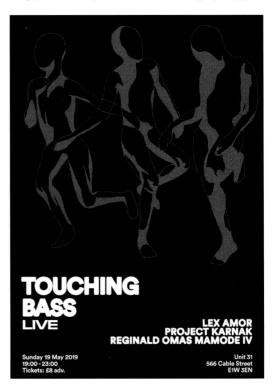

TOUCHING BASS LIVE

**LEX AMOR
PROJECT KARNAK
REGINALD OMAS MAMODE IV**

Sunday 19 May 2019
19:00 - 23:00
Tickets: £8 adv.

Unit 31
566 Cable Street
E1W 3EN

TOUCHING BASS, CALM ROOTS & OJAS PRESENT

AN AFTERNOON OF INTROSPECTIVE SONGS & SELECTED WORKS

DEVON TURNBULL: HIFI LISTENING ROOM DREAM NO. 1
LISSON GALLERY

AUGUST 23 2023
4–6PM

OJAS   LISSON

DJing. I was gassed to go there once a month and have this release. You knew you had another two hundred people there who were fucking with every single thing you were playing. It was an incredible three years and I met some incredible people who I'm still friends with to this day.

In 2011 you started the station. Can you paint a picture about getting it off the ground?

Femi: It was probably the most focused I have ever been on anything in my life. It was a life-or-death type thing. I didn't have a job and this idea had been floating in my head for a while. I knew I loved radio due to the programming of American college radio. I thought, I've got nothing to lose. I'm not a very tech-savvy person and I always thought it would involve a lot of coding but I taught myself how to do it. I got three grand from the Prince's Trust. It was all the money I had. I didn't have any savings. It was a fun challenge to try and get it off the ground. We put some posters around London. I was expecting to get twenty people on the station and ended up getting sixty people responding.

Who were the stalwarts from the start of NTS?

Femi: People like Judah, who's on the station now, Alex Nut. Martelo. Ruby Savage. I've known these people from the club for years.

For me, the policy reflects the world in one city we have here, and your slogan is 'Don't Assume'. What was that born out of?

Femi: It was born from what we were trying to create and that this isn't like your traditional set-up. It's that freestyle, freeform approach to radio, knowing you can listen to someone playing house music one minute and the next is some classical music. I didn't feel like anyone was trying to do that. Everyone else on radio was doing things that were very genre specific. I wanted to break that mould and try something different.

From the interview series to the first night at Touching Bass, what was the time frame?

Errol: The first ever Touching Bass night was in December 2014 and then the official start was in 2016.

You talked about old-school parties with that one red light. What elements of that have you taken into your own dances? The merch shirts which say Come Dance Nuh, the no-phone policy on the floor, and the text line service, which I do enjoy.

Errol: At its root, it's trying to create a space for people to be themselves and be present. At those pre-internet family house parties there were no phones on the dance floor. To have no phones on the dance floor now feels very natural. It's about being present in the space and feeling comfortable, to be able to move and dance however you want to dance. We like to see it as a bit of a sanctuary. When I'm behind the decks and I see people moving however they wanna move, it's the most happy thing. I liken that to my grandmother having the most amazing time at house parties back in the day, singing at the top of her lungs, with a paper plate in her hands.

At a Christmas dance I went to, it was one of the first times I was at a Black-owned space/ night where everyone looked like they were having fun. I remember, somehow, bonding with Wu-Lu. I love that energy of knowing you can make a friend in that way. How important is it for you to have that element of building friendship on the floor?

Errol: Yeah, it's so important. I guess if you can create an environment whereby people will feel comfortable enough to just talk with strangers then that kinda stuff can happen. That's probably one of the things I am most proud of. Being of Caribbean heritage, MCs are part of the culture and me getting on the mic and reminding people to drink enough water or to not have phones on the dance floor or just to say hello to someone next to them creates the environment to just be loose and gooey.

With Soup to Nuts, that's starter to main to dessert. When it comes to flow and curation, how does that tie with your programming across the station?

Femi: My favourite types of DJ are those who take you on a journey. I'm not really one for these overextended DJ sets anymore, where people play for seven hours. On a two-hour set you can still go on a journey with someone. That's what we'd do at Nonsense. You start with a warm-up and go to the middle and push it to the red zone and then you bring it down at the end. That's what we try and do with our programming at NTS. That's the ethos of the station and we have people who are heavily engaged with that ethos throughout the day, every day.

How have you found curating in that space NTS offers another outlet for Touching Bass?

Errol: Our methods of sharing the party via text and a little card have allowed things to ripple out from the nucleus. Projecting it on NTS Radio, where they have so many music lovers, and not just from our immediate friendship groups, has allowed the message to spread even further. The music we play is very similar to the music we play on the night, so the immediate interaction you get on the dance floor is mimicked by NTS's chatroom. You start to have regulars, people who tune in for our ting, which then feels like an expansion of what we already do. One time I was in Italy and I was having a conversation with someone, we were working on a project about the Venice Biennale with Tate Modern, and this random guy came up to me and was like, 'Are you Errol?, and I was like, 'Yeah'. He goes, 'This is super weird but I know your voice as I've been into NTS for some time.' That was the most trippy thing but also a reminder like, Wow... us lot being in a small cabin in Dalston, playing tunes... sometimes you forget how much it reverberates in different spaces.

The first real home for Touching Bass was a Senegalese restaurant called Xperience African based in Loughborough Junction. It was probably 80–100 capacity. Sweaty.

You're quite nomadic in terms of the physical spaces and unconventional with how the dances are programmed. What's behind this versatile mindset?

Errol: Well, at first it was the bane of our lives. When I look back into the history of a few of my favourite club nights they've always had a HQ or a spot, week in week out, where they can go and do their thing. Entering into the 2010s in London, having a space to call home was becoming so difficult. Gentrification was on the rise and clubs were getting more guarded. Also, a lot of our crowd, especially at the beginning, weren't really big drinkers. It became a thing where we started to occupy non-traditional venues. So, the first real home for Touching Bass was a Senegalese restaurant called Xperience African based in Loughborough Junction. It was probably 80–100 capacity. Sweaty. The uncles always jamming at the back, dancing as well. The sound wasn't great but it felt like a house party. It was so beautiful. All our friends could come into this one space and jam. Over the years we've had places like that... the Peckham Caribbean shop, at night, turns into a club where they are serving patties and ting on the floor. So, what started off as a real obstacle we've actually turned around into a positive. The party is about the people in the room as opposed to the four walls. With that in mind we can actually go anywhere and make our home feel like a home.

Do you have any favourite shows on NTS which embody that spirit?

Femi: There is a show by a Japanese DJ called Chee Shimizu and it's called Organic Music Tokyo. It's based off of Don Cherry's Organic Music series and he's my prodigy. Again it creates a mood and that's what I love. There is so much good stuff on there and I am always searching for stuff.

So, I guess you have LA, Manny and more... How do you embody this LDN to the world philosophy across the board?

Femi: I think over the years, while we see NTS as this global platform, it's still uniquely London and I don't think it could have started in any other city apart from London.

Touching Bass now works with the Barbican, sharing music from our communities. These man have their lights on all night but we've never been able to get in there and take over these art institutions. How have you found that journey of marrying sound in these spaces?

Errol: It takes time and a lot of communication. Working with the Barbican so far has been amazing. We've only done one event so far, at what I must add is one of mine and Alex's favourite venues in the UK. To have the opportunity to do things there feels quite dreamy. Marrying that with an opportunity to host some of our favourite artists, high and low, from everywhere. I definitely have some dreams of bringing it back to where I'm from.

London, Lagos, Accra...
The Transatlantic Tide
of Afrobeats

CHRISTIAN ADOFO

At universities across the UK, African-Caribbean Society raves have played a vital role in incubating the sound of UK funky and merging it with the rise of Afrobeats. Christian Adofo looks into a pivotal time for African club music in the diaspora.

In Paul Gilroy's classic exploration of UK race relations *There Ain't No Black in the Union Jack* he writes:

The town halls and municipal buildings of the inner-city in which dances are sometimes held are transformed by the power of these musics to disperse and suspend the temporal and spatial order of the dominant culture. As the sound system wires are strung up and the lights go down, dancers could be transported anywhere in the diaspora without altering the qualities of their pleasures.[1]

Gilroy's words give voice to the transcendental power music has had for the first and second generations of Caribbean heritage in the UK. Having arrived in the UK from former British colonies on the promise of plentiful work and a warm welcome, the deal for migrants in the Windrush generation was not all they had been led to believe, but these carefully and considerately curated spaces to dance offered them respite and restoration on the weekends in a place where they were no longer invisible.

A sense of this transportive reverie was felt in Steve McQueen's 2020 anthology series *Small Axe*. In the *Lovers Rock* episode, set in 1980, the saccharine, singalong chimes of Janet Kay's iconic 'Silly Games' evaporate into the damp, high ceilings of the living room. The soft opening signals of Channel 1 dub 'Kunta Kinte Dub' by the Revolutionaries unfold to attentive eardrums and, once the supportive slaps of approval hit the wallpaper, the guiding bass lifts the suspense in the room. The response through dance embodies the relief of the tension of the everyday. It is, like alchemy, turning struggle into strength in Babylon, with the smell of fresh curry goat and rice and peas adding to the sense of home from home in taste as with sound.

In the last twenty years in the UK music has continued to serve a similar function, facilitating greater prominence for children of West African heritage – particularly those from Ghana and Nigeria – and reinforcing a sense of community and pride. Through regular attendance at Independence Day events celebrating their respective motherlands from the early 1990s to the present day, a connection between Africa and the wider diaspora was being reinforced. In London and the south-east at venues like the Bel Air, Stratford Rex and the Dominion Theatre, a subconscious change was taking place at hall parties, via hiplife and Naija pop. Crucially for a UK-born younger population navigating dual cultures and identities, this was happening without a parental push.

In *The African Diaspora Population in Britain* Aspinall and Chinoya note that the Black African population in England and Wales was almost a million larger than Black Caribbean and other Black groups combined. They also noted high levels of education in this demographic, with only Chinese and Indian populations having higher proportions of degree-level qualifications. This growing population, and their route into higher education, would soon plant the seeds for an influential rave scene emerging from the African-Caribbean Societies at key universities around the M25 including Brunel and Kingston and in the East Midlands with Nottingham Trent and De Montfort.

The soundtrack to these ACS club nights encompassed the polyrhythmic productions of UK funky and the grime energy of MC-led tracks, where patois and pidgin English fused with syncopated London slang. This heralded a plethora of popular skanks, opening the door to the dance-led azonto movement, Afrobeats and the Afro-affiliated subgenres which have crossed over globally in the last few years.

'It was mainly RnB, bashment. There wasn't really much Afrobeats being played at all. We had a few songs that people knew, like "Sweet Mother" by Prince Nico Mbarga and Mzbel's "16 Years", because I am Ghanaian,' says Philip Owusu – perhaps better known as Mikael Silva – reflecting on the rare riddims that made an explicit link back to Africa in the early 2000s. Mikael was an early promoter in the university rave era who noticed a gap in the events space for young students of African heritage across the UK.

'People didn't realise that on Ghanaian or Nigerian Independence Day in the early 1990s they used to have over five or six thousand people at these events at Stratford Rex, so we knew the numbers were there,' Owusu says. 'But we also knew as a collective the Ghanaians and Nigerians, especially people from West Africa, were very focused on going to university. In 2003 and 2004 we looked at Leicester De Montfort and Birmingham University and realised there is actually a market for this.'

Becoming President of the ACS at De Montfort University served as the catalyst for Owusu to begin his journey into curating events for the Black student population in the East Midlands, many of whom were originally from London but were missing out on the regular Black events the UK capital had on offer. He started his first foray into events for this demographic via coachparty.com and built an accompanying website to cater for all the universities in one place long before the advent of social media platforms. Bringing together student populations from around the country, these linkup raves would be held every three months during term time and grew from four hundred to two thousand people within two years. As the market started to open up, with fellow promoters focusing on undergraduates in middle England, Owusu shifted his focus back to London and launched his alter ego Mikael Silva, taking inspiration from successful, Latin-influenced, contemporary house producers. The stage name was racially ambiguous enough to put on flyers and allow him to book venues in the capital, despite not technically being a DJ.

ABOVE Mista Silva on set in Brixton for the video for the song 'Woso', 2020.
OPPOSITE Mista Silva's 'Full Vim' EP.

The mid-2000s also coincided with the rise of UK funky. Heavily influenced by the tribal, deep, soulful and bassline house subgenres, it was regularly blended with Afrobeat, broken beat, minimal, electro and garage, uniting the Black Atlantic on the dance floor around a fresh, feelgood sound. During this time a younger cousin of Owusu's was starting out as a grime MC but would soon adapt his elder relative's entrepreneurial event ventures as a platform for his own influential music career, based around UK funky.

'When I went to Ghana my mind was opened to another perspective on life,' says Papa Kwame Amponsa, better known as Mista Silva. 'It started to influence how I thought about my route in music, and everything else in my life.' Hailing from Brockley, Amponsa was one of the pioneers from the uni rave scene, and he joined the first wave of UK Afrobeats artists with cult releases 'Boom Boom Tah' and 'Bo Wonsem Ma Me'. After getting into trouble in his local area, a relocation to the coastal cities of Takoradi and Tema for a brief period during his late teens allowed him to immerse himself in the nascent hiplife genre, and introduced him to artists like Samini, Bradez and the late Castro. On his return to the UK, Silva's pride for his Ghanaian roots soared further, and he began to notice sonic similarities between Afrobeats and UK funky.

'Funky house had a similar energy to some of the hiplife songs that were out there,' he explains. 'At that time I was 18, going to raves or African parties like Manjaro in Holloway Road and Ghana Independence. I was going to uni

as well and at the time there was a growing Ghanaian community coming up. We started to do raves as well and decided to put the name Silva behind ours.'

The raves joined the dots between transatlantic house pioneers like Masters at Work, Karizma and Quentin Harris and homegrown producers like Apple, Lil Silva and Fuzzy Logik, as well as DJs like Supa D, Pioneer and Neptizzle. The Silva family's nights included Silver Bunnies, Silver Mistletoes and If You're on This Let Me Know – an early precursor to events being named after funky MC's favourite reload bars. They had an open music policy, which Amponsa believes was key in developing the Afro sound of today and uniting Africans and Caribbeans subconsciously. It was the antithesis of the abundant genre battle nights (see Afrobeats vs dancehall) which projected competition instead of camaraderie.

'Look at the environment of the uni scene and it was every kind of sound being played in the rave,' says Amponsa. 'At the start you're gonna hear RnB, and then as you get to 12 am, peak times, you'll be playing funky and playing your Afro. After that you're playing your slow jams and party classics. Basically, all the sounds were getting mashed in one place anyway, so all the influences were able to form what was coming.'

At around the same time in the late 2000s another young graduate from South London was emerging as a tastemaker, learning from senior students he first encountered at an ACS event as a fresher at Surrey University. 'One thing I started doing was integrating Afrobeats music in there,' says DJ and producer Larizzle. 'Knowing how much more pro-African the ACS had started becoming, I thought it would be cool to start showcasing our sounds in these raves as well.' Hospitable, informative and a winner of multiple awards, Larizzle has been one of the leading tastemakers in Afrobeats and Afrohouse over the last decade, helping to introduce the sounds to the Ayia Napa club scene.

The shift from dancehall and bashment, he said, gave way to increasing appreciation for African hall party classics such as Magic System's Ivorian sheller '1er Gaou' and Ice Prince's Naija pop singalong 'Oleku'. He passed early DIY mix CDs to close friends on campus, which soon spread among others intrigued to hear his blend of homegrown instrumentals and vocal-led funky riddims. He would soon use the internet to further facilitate his mixes.

'I was using a file transfer site called 4Shared, and Mediafire as well,' says Larizzle, 'and the first social media platforms I used were Myspace and Hi5. I would share it on there and over time it just got a bigger listenership. I think it was one of the main driving forces which helped my career as a DJ.'

The genre's versatile ability to defrost the iciest of resting screw faces and lead a call-and-response along the same tempo created a positive atmosphere, as Larizzle recalls. 'The ladies would sing along to songs by Egypt, Princess Nyah and Kyla, but I remember those really hard-hitting instrumentals would get people gassed, and when the MCs would host and spit their known bars, that would take it up to another level.' As Mista Silva, Amponsa and Ramzee – a fellow MC of Ghanaian heritage – would regularly reaffirm African pride and Black unity across the diaspora on the floor through onomatopoeic, Twi-style ad libs.

Amponsa explained the context behind his own signature shoutout. '"Kah-de-boom-ah-go-down low" – that was more in funky where I grabbed [the mic] and said, "Yo, I can just buss my ting." It's a language, what can you say? Stop being discriminatory toward our culture – that's how I felt – and when I started doing the Afrobeats I said, "I am going full blast!"'

One of MC Ramzee's most famous bars included the lines 'You can call me Rambolo / SuperMalt is all I swallow / I'm from Ghana / Not from Congo / Mash up the beat like Deezyman Bongo'. Upcycling a cult film figure, referencing a soft drink synonymous with hall parties and a popular live musician on the uni rave circuit are all inviting assists for the crowd to raise the decibel level in the dance. Ramzee was himself affiliated with Storm Parties (formerly Storm Riders), a prominent group of South London-based promoters including Delaney, Supa and Cyrille, who emerged from playing UK garage, bashment and grime in youth clubs in the early 2000s on the uni circuit.

OPPOSITE Online flyers for various Afrobeats parties around the UK.

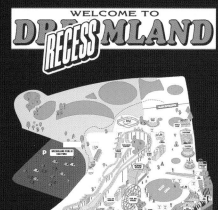

ARE YOU READY?

DJ Supa gives his thoughts on the transition from funky to grime. 'That season of funky was the UK garage for those kids at that time, before it turned into grime, if that makes sense. UK funky was this fresh breath of air.' He adds, 'There was your "Olly Olly Olly" MCs as opposed to people barring, so it was fun like a house party, and it was easy music and it blew up around the country.'

Cyrille, the main photographer of the group, agrees university was a catalyst for the sound. 'Think about that time at uni, you're just happy bruv. You've got your freedom. You've got a little bit of money. You can go to the clubs. So, mash that together with this happy sound, it connected and it just ballooned.'

The themes of positivity are now heard and seen in Afrobeats, Supa says. 'It's dance floor music. It's not the song a DJ plays when someone has ordered one hundred bottles. It's a song which kickstarts or unites the dance floor, and I think that's where the similar traits come from.'

'I think the music played a big part as Fuse ODG and the skippy Afrobeats became popular,' adds Cyrille. 'That music instilled a level of pride, to say, "This person is from my country."'

Donae'o's productions, including the healing anthem 'African Warrior' and Ghanaian stalwart Sarkodie's remix of 'Move to Da Gyal Dem' were, like 'Sway' on KG's 'Feeling Funky', influential in championing African artists from the continent on instrumentals made in the diaspora. The late Charmz's 'Buy Out Da Bar', atop Lil Silva's bouncy 'Pulse vs Flex', was a riddim synonymous with early term-time philanthropy, fuelled by the Student Loans Company and neon-coloured shots at the bar.

Another crossover track that Larizzle says marked the transition from funky to Afrobeats was Fr3e's tribal-influenced banger, 'Calm Down'. The song's producer was London-born P2J, of Nigerian heritage, now one of the key beatsmiths within the Afrobeats scene with credits for Burna Boy, Wizkid and even Beyoncé's recent *The Lion King: The Gift* album. For 'Tribal Skank', P2J described his attempt to connect both sounds. 'I dived into it trying to make it sound as African and funky as I could. That's the reason why there is some Yoruba in that song. That was the first song which gave me the bridge into the Afrobeats world.'

Outside of term time, the spaces in which to enjoy the sounds moved from UK venues to more favourable European settings. This development reflected the cool factor Afrobeats had started to accumulate, with artists like Fuse ODG and the Kanye-backed D'Banj achieving chart success. The Fresh 2 Def/Silva cohort would soon host the first Afrobeats event in Ibiza in 2012, which evolved into an annual affair called Ibiza Loves Afrobeats, which ran until the mid-2010s. A precursor to AfroNation, their line-ups included Afro B and DJ P Montana, who have had outright success since emerging from the UK funky and deep house uni rave circuit. DJ P Montana, along with DJ Funkz (aka Kofi Kyei) and Oyinboy (Ian McQuaid), were among the first to push subgenres like Afrobashment and Afroswing, supporting the likes of J Hus, Yxng Bane and Naira Marley at the start of their careers.

OPPOSITE Dank Holiday at the Cause, East London, 2023.
Below left: Ladies Love Dankie at Boxpark Wembley, London, 2023.
Below right: Dankie Sounds: DJ SKAYY at Studio 338, Greenwich, London. Photographs by Pass the lens.

… these are a holistic and joyous affirmation of sound that pushes you to do more, find power in the past and have pride in who you are.

The evolution of this welcoming and open music policy has manifested a desire for niche genre subsections of the wider African diaspora, with education and enjoyment both unified to link the past to the present through sonic storytelling.

From the dance floor to the open-air festival field, a heady liberation has seen sustained homegrown growth from the UK to the world via an entrepreneurial strain of promoters on social media who have built a loyal and increasingly international mobile cohort/base of polished ravers and hedonistic misbehavers. They make the summertime pilgrimage to the Iberian Peninsula and annually end their year on the equator, in Accra.

Nights such as Recess, DLT (Days Like This) and Dankie Sounds play integral roles in offering positive and regular touchpoints at scale in a historically hostile UK nightlife space. The former recently celebrated a century of parties, taking over Margate's Dreamland on the Kent coast with more than seven thousand people in attendance, and the growth of the subculture further solidified in the train operator extending operating times back to London to accommodate the valued exodus.

Increasingly the revival of live brass elements has started to seep into the club environment with saxophonists such as Solaariss adding an unpredictable element of improvised departures to DJ sets.

James A. Snead affirms this sonic continuity as he says, 'Whenever we encounter repetition in cultural forms, we indeed are not viewing the same thing, but its transformation.'[2] This resuscitation has come full circle within the jazz-inspired Afrobeat continuum in recent audio blessings of Kokoroko's *Could We Be More*, Yussef Dayes' *Black Classical Music* and Ezra Collective's Mercury Prize-winning album *Where I'm Meant To Be*.

Fearless, engaging and relevant commentators are deploying a cosmopolitanism which reimagines the narrative for Black British youngers simultaneously rooted in local and global contexts through African and Caribbean heritage. Whether in the haze of nocturnal transit or the empty stillness of the early morning, these are a holistic and joyous affirmation of sound that pushes you to do more, find power in the past and have pride in who you are.

In the more than thirty years since the first publication of Gilroy's book the internet has become a vital archive of the nuances and intricacies of restoring identity across the Black Atlantic. Switching between English and the mother tongue via patois and pidgin in everyday speech and song reflects the greater cultural influence of the West African migrant community in the UK and the diaspora. For a new generation proud to display their multiple identities through emoji flags on their social media bios, the music and MCs originating from the uni rave era provided the unapologetic and joyful bedrock for organic and transportive experiences in dance, the impact of which will continue to be felt for decades to come.

Tech, Language and Riddim: From Jungle to UK Drill

JULIA TOPPIN

We are living in a time where we, the children of post-war Caribbean immigrants, have now experienced at least five distinct Black British music genres: lovers' rock, jungle, garage, grime and drill.

Each of these genres was born as a result of a specific set of circumstances which make their formations necessary and uniquely British at the same time. However, while it is always pertinent to examine popular culture by looking through a prism of social and historical context, few have explored how economics and technological determinism profoundly affected the sonics of these genres.

Now that many erased histories are being uncovered it has become apparent that Black people have innovated and invented their way through various eras of oppression and structural marginalisation. Black people have sought to fully utilise any technology that they could get their hands on. Music is no different, and its technology has been an important factor in the formation of many Black British music genres where technology, language and 'riddim' have come together with powerful effect.

Let us begin.

The story of the sound system, like the story of any human life, is full of unique circumstances that accumulate into a group of people with a specific skill set that together can make magic. If Hedley Jones didn't join the Royal Air Force in 1943, train as a radar engineer and get sent off to war in Europe, would he have opened a radio repair business on his return to his homeland? Would he have gone on to build the first sound system amplifier in Jamaica, designed to present the records that he had begun selling in his shop with the best possible sound? He was designing circuitry that allowed him to individualise, enhance and remix the low, middle and high frequencies of the tracks.

If the Chinese had not emigrated to Jamaica to build the railroads there would be no Tom 'the Great Sebastian' Wong – a music hardware store owner who was known for taking his equipment to parties. Tom, on hearing the quality of sound from Hedley's amplifier as he walked past his store one day, commissioned Hedley to make a version of his invention: the Hedley Jones High Fidelity Amplifier. Tom Wong became the first person to own a sound system (which he named), in the 1950s – a system capable of playing over 30,000 watts.

Sound system dances were the primary source of entertainment in downtown Kingston in the 1950s and the primary choice of music was American rhythm & blues, with a touch of merengue and calypso. As the decade evolved, more sound systems like Duke Reid: The Trojan and Sir Coxsone Downbeat entered the arena. With the aid of local jazz musicians, these 'sound men' took to the studio to create 'specials' to play on the sound. The result was a unique, homegrown form of music that complemented Jamaica's move towards independence from Britain: that music was ska.

Music is an antidote to oppression and its descendant: stress. It builds communities. It enhances calm. It evokes powerful feelings: love; peace; bliss; righteousness.

Both Vincent Forbes, aka Duke Vin, and Wilbert Augustus Campbell, aka Count Suckle, worked for Tom the Great Sebastian before they stowed away on a ship bound for England in 1954. As 'sound men' they emerged as the foundation for a network of sound systems that took root in the Black communities of all the major urban conurbations: London, Birmingham, Bristol, Manchester, Liverpool, Leicester, Leeds and Sheffield.

Black people were not welcome in the majority of English leisure spaces when they arrived in the late 1950s to support a nation ravaged by the effects of the Second World War. The open racism and hostility made them insular. They created their own cultural institutions: the blues and the shebeen. Carpets would be rolld up. Furniture was piled high and moved to the bedroom. Kitchens would become makeshift bars. Then multiple speakers the size of wardrobes would be set up with a turntable, an amplifier and a microphone. The blues would evolve from basement sessions into community halls, youth clubs, town halls and private clubs. Though they became the target of racist policing strategies, the impact of sound systems could not be contained or curtailed. They have provided a critical strand of cultural DNA, not just within Black British music, but within British music as a whole.

Black people are natural born innovators. We use whatever tools are at our disposal to refute those attempting to suppress us, whether that is Nanny of the Maroons using leaves to repel the British soldiers or King Tubby using that

infamous echo technique to release tension. Music is an antidote to oppression and its descendant: stress. It builds communities. It enhances calm. It evokes powerful feelings: love; peace; bliss; righteousness. Music is an essential part of the DNA of Black British and Black diasporic culture.

When the uniquely Black British multicultural sonic fusion of jungle finally solidified its name in the early 1990s, it used technology to develop a new music ecosystem that was exciting as the genre was an exhilarating one that could function outside of major label interests and influence. Three technologies of production and promotion were critical to this evolution: samplers, personal computers and transistors.

The Akai S1000 16-bit stereo digital sampler coupled with an Atari or Amiga computer became the bedroom-studio main instrument for those who previously could not afford a professional studio set-up and the music scene was revolutionised. Varied and all-encompassing jungle snatched bites from young Black Britain's sonic palette of genres: reggae, hip-hop, pop, house, techno, soul, RnB, rare groove, punk, jazz, folk and classical. Add to this your innovator pushing the sampler to the limits of its capability, creating effects like 'timestretching' (which stretches the sound out over a longer period of time than the original) and 'pitch shifting' (where the pitch of the sample is raised or lowered). This created a sound that was not only unique, but *belonged* to Britain's youth. It took over the streets of London, spread into the south-east

METALHEADZ Sunday night at the Blue Note in Hoxton, London, *circa* 1995. Photograph by Eddie Otchere.

and then the rest of the nation via a proliferation of makeshift community radio stations designed to cater to the tastes of those ignored by the mainstream. The unlicensed radio stations were dubbed 'pirate radio' as they would initially broadcast from ships in international waters.

In terms of Black British music and technology, jungle pirate radio was part of a shift from craft and apprenticeship valve technology to DIY technology fuelled by a dazzling array of new electronic consumer products. It is important to note, however, that these stations still utilised peer-to-peer knowledge acquisition through apprenticeships. Young people – with some help from their knowledgeable elders – created microwave emitters, receivers and aerials using transistors, car batteries, soldering irons, cables. In addition to broadcasting the latest sounds and upcoming events, like the DJ from the original sound system, now known as the MC, a pirate radio station would inform its listenership about things that were happening in their community.

Like the acid house and rave versions that preceded then ran alongside them, pirate radio made jungle the pulsating rapid heartbeat of the London streets in the mid-1990s. Stations like Kool, Rinse and Flex fed a diet of jungle to

ravers who were getting hyped up to go out or had just returned on a hype and needed to chill and decompress before they could go to sleep. It reached out to those who were too young or too impoverished to go to the raves. It drew in those who were too far away to pick up the signal and so had to drive into the M25 London ring road to record hours of transmission to take back to their home city.

There was an ephemerality to it. The omnipresent fear that reception would be lost at any moment due to the efforts of the government's Department of Trade and Industry (DTI, and later the Office for Communications [Ofcom]). The chance exclusivity of a dub plate that you might never hear again. The hyper local shout-outs which also served to test the efficacy of the signal.

At this point mainstream media attention, genre fragmentation and police oppression reached a peak which resulted in a rebrand to the name of 'drum and bass', accompanied by a less racialised sound. This new genre was abandoned by the majority of women, Black and Asian ravers in the scene. They had found a new sound to rave to. One that also needed the technology of the turntable.

As the jungle scene was just cresting its peak in the mid-1990s, DJs in South London who needed an extended comedown from raving to house music at the Ministry of Sound, set up their decks in the Elephant and Castle pub. The event, called Happy Days, played house tracks

LEFT The Metalheadz crew: Kemistry, Goldie and Storm, 1996, Bass Clef club. Photograph by Beezer.
OPPOSITE Goldie's *Timeless* LP, 1995.

with the tempo controller pulled all the way down, speeding up the music to create chipmunk vocals and skippy rhythms. These faster rhythms and deeper basslines were designed to keep the spent Sunday morning ravers alert and awake.

The sound created an (almost religious) Sunday scene at venues like Under the Arches, the Gass Club and the legendary Colosseum. It was named after a New York style of house that focussed on gospel, disco, soul and RnB with infectious basslines. Thus, UK garage (UKG, also known as speed garage) was born.

Back across the pond, producer and DJ Todd Edwards was remixing and experimenting with house records on Pioneer CDJs, creating his own high-energy sound. Edwards utilised the Ensoniq EPS sampling keyboard, taking advantage of its 16-triplet quantising feature. UK producers would take instrumental dubs from house producers such as Edwards and Masters at Work and add a rib-shaking sound system bassline to make them their own. One Sunday a young man picked up a mic by the decks and started to spontaneously MC over the tracks (jungle and sound system style) to a rapturous response from the crowd. Many of the techniques and technologies associated with jungle, like samplers, MCs and sound clashes, were utilised in the production and presentation of the UK garage sound.

As with jungle, the DIY technology of pirate radio stations like Flex FM and Freek FM carried the sound around via aerials mounted on top of high-rise council estate blocks. As with jungle, these unlicensed radio stations played a game of cat and mouse with Ofcom and the police. Only this time the stakes (in the form of jail sentences and fines) were much higher.

Still relegated to Sundays, UKG raves also started to appear as a second-room feature on

many jungle nights. Ravers flocked to the scene, seduced by its opulent champagne and designer fashion (think Gucci, Moschino, Versace) *mise en scène*. Eventually the virality of UK garage penetrated the mainstream. It burst onto the Friday and Saturday club scene, overwhelmed Cyprus tourist resort Ayia Napa and dominated the national UK charts.

As the genre matured, a new generation came onto the scene. The luxurious feel-good opulence of the UKG scene was overshadowed by a new, grittier focus. The MC once again became the community narrator. MCs and their crews began to describe their day-to-day existence on the mean streets of London and the music took a turn to the dark side. This factor, alongside mainstream sales, also led to a rise in negative attention from the media as sound system-inspired clashes of this new iteration of UK garage brought a violent tension onto the scene. Eventually, like jungle, UKG was banned from central London clubs and other venues.

The scene went underground and became even grittier, evolving into the most successful Black British music genre of all: grime. The MCs still had pirate radio technology to distribute their sound, but it was another type of technology, the digital audio workstation or DAW,

CREATIVITY IN THE CITY Clockwise from top left: Listening session in the Ends; Bedroom studio; Writing bars; Pirate radio. All London, *circa* 1995. Photographs by Simon Wheatley.

that was instrumental in shaping the sonics.

Launched at the turn of the millennium, DAWs such as Fruity Loops and Reason allowed for more affordable home studio set-ups. Grime producers used this to craft their distinctive harsh, syncopated beats that perfectly complemented the aggressive, rapid-fire vocal delivery of the MCs. The music production technology empowered a new generation of artists to produce a mode of expression that did not require prohibitively expensive studio time, though some producers still used traditional methods of samplers and synthesisers to expand the sonics.

Reaching audiences with this music proved challenging. Shunned by venues, young Black British entrepreneurs recorded grime MC clashes with home video cameras and created

DVDs of their recordings using moving image technology like Adobe Premiere Pro on personal computers. This was further developed by branding these events and selling merchandise like T-shirts and baseball caps alongside CDs and DVDs.

In terms of online video streaming and social media platforms, the internet was truly radical for Black British music. Platforms like Myspace (2003), YouTube (2005) and SoundCloud (2007) revolutionised the ability to share your music and performances. Anybody could now broadcast and distribute their music globally. Furthermore, if you couldn't afford a video camera or a PC, your mobile phone (such as a Sony Ericsson W810) could record your music (and your music video) then upload it to YouTube. Artists would develop an international fanbase without leaving their London postcode area. This use of technology gave grime a trademark treble and mid-heavy, pixelated sound.

ABOVE Contemporary commentary on surveillance. London, *circa* 1995. Photograph by Simon Wheatley.

276

In terms of online video streaming and social media platforms, the internet was truly radical for Black British music.

The meteoric rise of grime was fuelled by these dedicated online platforms. The music thrived, despite an inability to successfully put on live events due to oppressive practices. The controversial Form 696, which requested extensive details of every performer prior to granting an entertainment licence (which was then often denied), is a prime example. However, in 2017 the legislation requiring the form was scrapped, allowing grime to go mainstream with major label signings and promoters like Live Nation putting artists in stadiums and on festival stages.

Technological advancements produced even more affordable DAWs such as Logic and Ableton. High internet speeds elevated sound quality levels and ushered in a return to the speaker-rupturing bassline. As with all Black British music genres, while one is cresting its peak, another is beginning its journey. In 2012, fuelled by the whirring sound of Chicago drill, and the rapid-fire energy of grime vocal delivery, young Black Londoners once again developed a sound that they could call their own: UK drill.

With an existence carved from decades of vicious cuts to civil society, UK drill lyrics made grime bars sound like extended fairy tales. The music streaming technology of digital service providers Spotify and Apple Music meant that incomes could be generated and careers developed in defiance of the inability to perform the music live.

And despite various tactics – for example Form 696 – employed by certain authorities, oppressive and counterproductive injunctions have not prevented UK drill from going mainstream and even acquiring a number one in the national charts.

In 2020 internet radio helped Black British online station No Signal to become a global sensation during the COVID-19 pandemic by utilising technology to create community around Black music. No Signal's 10v10 live show, inspired by sound system culture, involved a sound clash where tracks from two artists were pitted against each other. Hosted live, the show sparked intense reactions on social media site Twitter (now X), with tens of thousands of listeners voting on each track-clash within a tight ten-minute window. Its most famous episode – Vybz Kartel vs WizKid – drew in over one million live listeners.

From the craftsmanship of amplifying the perfect bassline to utilisation of the mobile phone as recording studio and video camera, Black British creatives have utilised the transformative power of technology to overcome barriers to producing and disseminating their music. Artists are presently leveraging artificial intelligence technology to produce arresting visuals to accompany their music. It will only be a matter of time before AI is used to create a genre that sounds new and exciting. Given the history of Black British music over the last sixty years, coupled with young people's ability to innovate with these advancing technologies to produce music and reach global audiences, it will most definitely come from the inner-city streets.

Inspired by Jamaica's DJs/MCs and multi-dimensional US rap, generations of UK Black youth and their peers have put pen to paper and crafted the bars they could carry into the dance, into a clash, onto pirate radio or into the studio. The albums here are a glimpse into the evolution of twenty-first century grime and UK rap. Here are some of the outstanding lyricists whose witty, turbulent, confrontational, poetic, linguistically versatile work gives an insight into daily life in the Ends.

Roots Manuva
Run Come Save Me

WILD WEST

CENTRAL CEE

LANDLORD

REVENGE IS SWEET

KREPT X KONAN

L

QUEEN'S SPEEC

RODNEY P
THE FUTURE

Shut Up and Dance

Dance Before The Police Come!

IT DREA
INNA INGLA

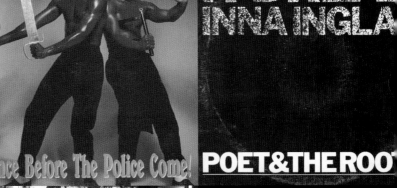

POET & THE ROOT

Queen of the South

wiley__

GHETTO

FREEDOM
OF
SPEEC

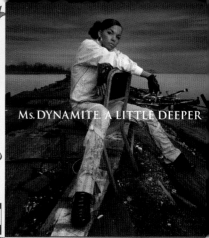

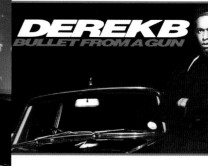

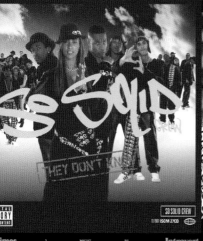

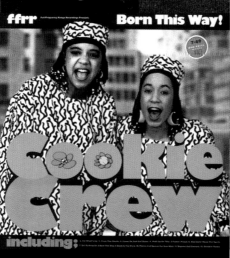

LITTLE SIMZ North London based Simbiatu 'Simbi' Abisola Abiola Ajikawo, aka Little Simz, has emerged as one the brightest stars of a generation. Following a Mercury Prize nomination for 2019's *Grey Area*, in 2021 she delivered *Sometimes I Might Be Introvert*. It was produced by Inflo (SAULT) and rocketed her from cult status to international, award-winning superstar. Commodore Ballroom, Vancouver, September 2023. Photograph by Karolina Wielocha.

Contributors

Tej Adeleye is a writer, audio producer and arts programmer. She is a radio producer for BBC Radio 3's *Freeness*, and has produced a range of cultural and current affairs programmes and features for BBC Radio 1xtra, Radio 3, Radio 4, and more. She curates cultural events, writes about music, politics and health; and is a Trustee at the George Padmore Institute archive.

Christian Adofo is an established writer, cultural curator and author based in North-East London. His writing looks at the intersection of heritage and identity in music and culture across the cultural landscape. He is a regular contributor to publications including *The Financial Times*, *Billboard* magazine and *The Guardian*, interviewing popular cultural figures across the creative spectrum within the African diaspora and beyond. His debut book *A Quick Ting on Afrobeats* (2022) is part of the first ever non-fiction series celebrating Black British culture.

Ishmahil Blagrove, Jr. has over thirty years of print media experience and is the creative director of Rice N Peas, an independent production company he founded in 1999. He has worked as a freelance producer for various international media outlets, including the BBC and Channel 4. He has a reputation for evocative, thought-provoking documentary, exhibitions and still photography works, and an authoritative reputation as well as several awards for producing hard-hitting social documentaries. He is the author of *Carnival: A Photographic and Testimonial History of Notting Hill Carnival* (2014) and *The Frontline: A Story of Struggle, Resistance and Black Identity in Notting Hill* (2022).

Stephen Bourne is the author of *Black Poppies: Britain's Black Community and the Great War* (2014), *Under Fire: Black Britain in Wartime 1939–45* (2020) and *Deep Are the Roots: Trailblazers Who Changed Black British Theatre* (2021). He is also the author of several LGBT+ history books including *Fighting Proud: The Untold Story of the Gay Men Who Served in Two World Wars* (2017). In 2006 he received a MPhil from De Montfort University. He is an honorary fellow of London South Bank University. In 1991, he became a founder member of the Black and Asian Studies Association. For further info: www.stephenbourne.co.uk.

Paul Bradshaw has been a music journalist since the mid-1970s. He contributed to the *NME* and various other publications worldwide. After launching the jazz based, club-oriented, 'designer fanzine' *Straight No Chaser* in 1988 he built a global network of musicians, DJs, writers, photographers and Illustrators. He has curated international music projects and exhibitions and hosted a monthly radio show on Worldwide FM, SNC: Interplanetary Sounds – Ancient to Future. As an editor he worked on the Mo' Wax book *Urban Archaeology* and post-COVID, Gilles Peterson's 600-page hardback *Lockdown FM: Broadcasting in a Pandemic*.

Garth Cartwright is a New Zealand-born, London-based journalist, critic and author of six non-fiction books. These include *Princes amongst Men: Journeys with Gypsy Musicians* (2005), *More Miles Than Money: Journeys through American Music* (2008), *Sweet As: Journeys in a New Zealand Summer* (2011), *Miles Davis: The Complete Illustrated History* (2012), *Going for a Song: A Chronicle of the UK Record Shop* (2018) and *London Record Shops* (2021). He regularly contributes to *The Guardian*, *The Financial Times*, *The New European*, *The Independent*, *Vive Le Rock* and *Jazzwise* and he posts in-depth features on his Substack. He has also worked as an events promoter and DJ.

Dr Monique Charles is an assistant professor of sociology at Chapman University; a cultural sociologist, theorist and methodologist. She developed the Musicological Discourse Analysis research method and a theory on Black music and spirituality in live performance/clubbing spaces (AmunRave theory). She is the creator, curator and editor of *Black Music in Britain in the 21st Century* (2023). She is on the editorial board of the *Global Hip Hop Studies Journal*. She is a sound healer.

Dalia Al-Dujaili is an Iraqi-British freelance writer, editor and producer. She tells stories on emerging creativity from the South West Asian and North African region and diaspora, on migrant narratives and communities from the margins, with bylines in *The Guardian*, WePresent, Huck, *The New Arab*, It's Nice That and more. Dalia is the digital editor of AZEEMA. Her clients include Nike, Ugg, Converse, Tate Galleries, the BFI, the Barbican and others. She founded *The Road to Nowhere* magazine. Collaborations include the Photographer's Gallery, Refuge Worldwide and the National Maritime Museum. Dalia co-produced Refugee Week 2023, and has worked with charities such as Paper Airplanes, Restless Beings, Counterpoints, Gaza Library, the IRC and the Migrant Rights Network.

Tracy Durrant was raised in Bristol with Jamaican heritage. Her musical journey began at Bristol's Malcolm X Centre, where she participated in music activities. Tracy's professional path led her to study music performance and sound engineering. She honed her skills as a songwriter, working with notable brands, and as a vocal coach she nurtured emerging talents. Tracy founded Everyone's a Singer, an arts organisation that develops workshops, events and research on the wellbeing benefits of music and storytelling, with a focus on Jamaican and Caribbean music history. Her company has become a thriving network for intergenerational music creators, offering learning and networking opportunities with industry experts.

Juliet Fletcher is a pioneer of the British gospel scene. She is the principal founder of the Gospel Music Industry Alliance (GMIA), championing its connections to the music industry along with promoting its histories and legacies and its professional, educational, and community practices. Juliet started as a gospel singer and progressed as a promoter and manager of key events and gospel groups. She was employed by the BBC (Religion & Ethics) as its sole specialist gospel and soul music researcher and became a producer. After the BBC she established GreenTree Productions. Juliet writes regularly for *Keep the Faith* magazine.

Vivien Goldman is an award-winning writer, broadcaster, educator and musician. Born in London, she resides between Jamaica and New York, where she is a long-serving adjunct professor at New York University's Clive Davis Institute of Recorded Music. Two of her seven books are on Bob Marley, including *The Book of Exodus: The Making and Meaning of Bob Marley and the Wailers' Album of the Century* (2006). Her *Revenge of the She-Punks* (2019) has been translated into several languages. Goldman's early 1980s music, including work with the Flying Lizards, is compiled on the *Resolutionary* LP; a remix version of her *Next Is Now* album, produced by Youth, was released in 2021. Her music has been employed by HBO's *The Deuce* and the BBC's *Murder in Paradise*. Fales Library at NYU houses the Vivien Goldman Punk and Reggae Collection. An anthology of her journalism is being published in 2024.

Julian Grant is the composer of twenty operas, which have been performed by English National Opera, the Royal Opera Covent Garden and Boston Lyric Opera, among others. Born in London, he moved to the US in 2010. He has been nominated for an Olivier Award and an International Opera Award, and has worked as a

broadcaster, a teacher and a music journalist, contributing regularly to *Opera* magazine. He is committed to music education for all, and has done projects with the major opera companies, Buskaid in Soweto, Capital Harmony Works in Trenton, NJ, and the Princeton Symphony Orchestra.
Further Information: www.juliangrant.net. YouTube: Julian Grant composer. http://soundcloud.com/julian-grant

Dr Aleema Gray is a Jamaican-born curator and public historian based in London. She was awarded the Yesu Persaud Scholarship for her PhD *Bun Babylon: A History of Rastafari in Britain*. Aleema's work documents Black history through the perspective of lived experiences. Her practice is driven by a concern for more historically contingent ways of understanding the present, especially in relation to notions of belonging, memory, and contested heritage. She is the lead curator for *Beyond the Bassline: 500 years of Black British Music* and the Founder of House of Dread, an anti-disciplinary heritage studio.

Dr Anthony Joseph FRSL is an award-winning Trinidad-born poet, novelist, academic and musician. He is the author of five poetry collections and three novels including *Kitch: A Fictional Biography of a Calypso Icon* (2018), shortlisted for the Republic of Consciousness Prize, the Royal Society of Literature's Encore Award and the OCM Bocas Prize for Caribbean Fiction. His most recent fiction publication is *The Frequency of Magic* (2018). In 2019 he was awarded a Jerwood Compton Poetry Fellowship. As a musician, he has released eight acclaimed albums, and in 2020 received a Paul Hamlyn Foundation Composers Award. He is a Fellow of the Royal Society of Literature and a lecturer in creative writing at King's College, London. His collection *Sonnets for Albert* (2022) won the T. S. Eliot Prize for Poetry 2022 and the OCM BOCAS Prize for Caribbean Poetry.

Julian Joseph OBE is a pianist, composer, broadcaster, educator and author. One of the finest jazz musicians to emerge this side of the Atlantic, Julian was the first Black British jazz musician to host a series at London's Wigmore Hall and headline a late-night concert at the BBC Proms. Julian has written for the symphony orchestra, big band and chamber ensemble, and received major commissions from the BBC, the City of London Festival and the London Jazz Festival. His operas and dance works include *Bridgetower* (2007), *Shadowball* (2010), *The Brown Bomber* (2012) and *Tristan and Isolde* (2018). The *Trench Brothers* project (2014–18) gave children a rare opportunity to perform and discover both classical and jazz music. His works have brought key moments in Black history into sharp focus. He was awarded a Gold Badge by BASCA (2010). Julian was elected the Ivors Academy 21st Fellow in 2020 and a Fellow of Trinity Laban Conservatory in 2023.

Cassie Kinoshi is a Mercury Prize-nominated (2019) and Ivors Academy Award-winning (2018) Berlin and London-based composer, arranger and alto-saxophonist with a focus on creating multi-disciplinarily and genre-blending performance work in various audio-visual contexts. As a bandleader, she writes for and performs with her ten-piece ensemble **seed.** which features many top London-based improvising musicians. She is a composition graduate of the Trinity Laban Conservatoire of Music and Dance, where she studied with Andrew Poppy and Stephen Montague.

Kevin Le Gendre is a journalist and broadcaster with a special interest in Black music, literature and culture. Since the late 1990s he has written about soul, funk, jazz and hip-hop, as well as African and Caribbean authors for *Echoes*, *Jazzwise*, *The Guardian*, *The Independent*, Qwest TV (France) and *The Times Literary Supplement* Online and more. He contributes to BBC Radio 4's *Front Row* and presents Radio 3's *J To Z*. He wrote *Don't Stop the Carnival: Black Music in Britain Vol.1* (2018) and *Hear My Train a Comin': The Songs of Jimi Hendrix* (2020).

Charis McGowan is a music and cultural writer with a focus on South America and the Caribbean. She is the former music editor at *gal-dem* magazine and her writing has appeared in *The Guardian*, *Mixmag*, BBC.com and more. Her work reflects a profound understanding of the subject matter and a dedication to amplifying under-represented voices in cultural sectors. Born to a British-Caribbean family, she grew up immersed in the sounds of Carnival. Her passion for music is a personal connection and a professional pursuit.
https://charismcgowan.com/ tweet @charis_mcgowan

Rasheda Ashanti Malcolm is a writer, a playwright and the founder of the *Candace Magazine*, aimed at women of colour. Her initiatives have been rewarded by many prizes, including the Black Business Woman of the Year, the National Black Women Achievement Award and, more recently, the Pandora Award for Publishing. Rasheda's first novel was a runner-up in the Saga Literary Prize. She initiated the Candace Black Women Achievement Award, and WILDE International Network. She currently teaches creative writing in London.

Tony Montague is an arts journalist who chanced on a compelling image of Billy Waters in Dublin five years ago, leading him to explore all facets of this extraordinary pioneer of African-American music and dance. An article on Waters' life appeared in *The Guardian* in March 2023 on the bicentenary of his death, and a book is in progress. Raised in Notting Hill, London, Tony divides his time between the UK and Canada. He gained a Masters degree in creative writing in 1981, and has worked as a schoolteacher, storyteller, musician and writer – chiefly for Vancouver weekly *The Georgia Straight* and *fRoots* magazine in the UK. He's dedicated to seeing Billy Waters widely recognised. An Early Day Motion in Parliament [EDM 856], drafted for Streatham MP Bell Ribeiro-Addy, hails Waters' unique contribution to popular culture in Britain.

Malik Al Nasir is an author, poet and academic from Liverpool. His memoir *Letters to Gil* (2022) is a compelling account of his childhood experiences in a brutal UK local authority care system, which left him traumatised, semi-literate, homeless and destitute. A chance meeting with Gil Scott-Heron was to prove life-changing, setting him on a path to success. Malik is currently reading for a PhD in history at the University of Cambridge on a full ESRC scholarship, and he's recently been awarded the prestigious Sydney Smith Memorial Prize for outstanding achievement at St Catharine's College, Cambridge as well as the Vice-Chancellor's Award for Global Impact.

Sharon O'Brien is a British/Jamaican writer, journalist, lecturer and broadcaster. She has been a nurse, politician, charity boss and nun. She served as an advisor to a MEP in Brussels and Strasbourg. As an elected politician she was chair of arts and a member of the ALA. Sharon edited *Caribbean Times*, wrote for numerous publications and has published *Classic Caribbean Cookery*, and contributed to many books on the Caribbean. For radio she wrote and presented a programme on Joe Harriott and for the stage a show, *Kinda Dukeish* (a celebration in words, music, and dance of Duke Ellington). She has lectured on many subjects for various establishments around the world.

Michael I. Ohajuru FRSA: Fellow of the Royal Society of Arts (2022), Senior Fellow of the Institute of Commonwealth Studies (2017), honours degrees in physics (1974) and art history (2008). Blogs, writes and speaks regularly on the Black presence in Renaissance Europe. He has spoken at the Metropolitan Museum of Art, New York and in London at the National Gallery, Tate Britain, the British Library, the National Archives and the Victoria and Albert Museum. Founder of Image of the Black in London Galleries, a series of gallery tours, the project director and chief evangelist of the John Blanke Project: an art and archive project. He is co-convenor of the Institute of Commonwealth Studies What's Happening in Black British History series of workshops and founder member of the Black Presence in British Portraiture network.
https://about.me/michaelohajuru/ @Michael1952

Lisa Amanda Palmer is an associate professor and interim director of the Stephen Lawrence Research Centre (SLRC) at De Montfort University. Her research focuses on Black feminism, Black cultural politics and the intersection of race, racism, gender and sexuality. Her writing covers a broad spectrum including the gendered politics of lovers' rock music, Black and racialised community archives and knowledge production, the reframing of Black life in green urban spaces, and the misogynoir faced by Black women in British public life. She works closely in partnership with local educators on the strategic delivery of the SLRC's Teaching to Transform and Introduction to Racial Literacy Programmes that are shaping education policies across secondary schools in Leicester. Lisa has contributed to documentaries on BBC radio and ITV.

Amar Patel is a writer and editor who has worked with *Straight No Chaser*, The Quietus, GUAP, Factory International, Broccoli Productions, Lexus, Vodafone and Clear Channel. He moves between journalism, copywriting, creative writing, scripting and broadcasting, and is devoted to arts and culture, particularly music. Past interviewees include Karriem Riggins, Georgia Anne Muldrow, Donna Thompson, Amadou & Mariam, Peven Everett and Pastor T. L. Barrett. Amar also mentors at the Ministry of Stories and with Arts Emergency. imakesense.org.

Mykaell Riley, founder member of Steel Pulse, has profoundly impacted British music. Currently a curator on the Black British Music exhibition, he's also on the and Leeds Arts' and Museum of London's academic boards. His achievements include forming the Reggae Philharmonic Orchestra and earning three UK number ones as a writer/producer. He founded the Black Music Research Unit at the University of Westminster, leading the influential Bass Culture project, which impacted London's Metropolitan policing. His efforts contributed to CREAM and the School of Arts' top Impact ranking in the UK by THES.

Ade Egun Crispin Robinson is a percussionist and educator with a special interest in Black identity and music of the African diaspora. He holds a Masters degree in Ethnomusicology from SOAS and has taught music at the University of London and University of Essex. A specialist in Afrocuban Orisha arts he is an omo Alaña, Olorisha and babalawo. He was sworn to the drums in 2004 and has played in hundreds of religious ceremonies all over Havana. He was crowned Obatala in 2010 and made Ifa in 2012. He is the custodian of Oke bi Aña, the only set of consecrated fundamento batá drums in the UK, born from the hands of Oba Oriate Angel Bolaños. He is a member of Afrojazz group Balimaya Project, plays music with various UK jazz artists and directs religious activities for Orisha devotees in London.

Angus Taylor is a writer, selector, broadcaster and panel host, specialising in Jamaican music and its influences. Angus has conducted more than five hundred interviews with reggae artists, producers and musicians. His byline has appeared in *Riddim*, *Reggaeville*, *United Reggae* and *World a Reggae*. He has written reggae album reviews for the BBC and reggae film reviews for *Sight and Sound* magazine. Angus has chaired panel discussions with artists at Overjam festival in Slovenia and Moogfest in the USA. He has spun records at numerous high-profile festivals and clubs in the UK and Jamaica. He has written liner notes for various record labels: Strut, Iroko, Nubian and Fruits. He hosts Rebel Hop at www.vdubradio.com + Sounds of Freedom, a weekly, all-vinyl show at www.realrootsradio.net. www.angustaylorwriter.com

Chardine Taylor-Stone is an award-winning activist, cultural producer, musician and writer. Alongside several years of community work, public speaking, curation and activism she formerly played drums in all-Black women band Big Joanie, who were nominated for a MOBO Award in the new Best Alternative Act category. She works as a multidisciplinary artist and burgeoning music producer. www.chardinetaylorstone.com

IG: https://www.instagram.com/chardinetaylorstone/
Twitter: https://twitter.com/ChardineTaylor

Andy Thomas is a writer who has contributed regularly to *Straight No Chaser*, *Wax Poetics*, *We Jazz*, *Red Bull Music Academy*, *Bandcamp Daily* and *Everything Jazz*. He has written liner notes for Strut, Counterpoint, Soul Jazz and Brownswood Recordings and storyboards for short films at Red Bull Music Academy.

Julia Toppin is lecturer in music enterprise and entrepreneurship at the University of Westminster and manages the music department's live showcase events. She primarily writes about the history of jungle and women in jungle and drum and bass, and sits on the editorial board of the *International Journal of Music Business Research*. Julia has been a guest speaker at Oxford and London Metropolitan universities and a panellist for Guardian Live, Doc and Roll Film Festival, Velocity Press and Picador. She co-owns drum and bass label Digital 101 Recordings with DJ Grimeminister, has contributed to several books and written for *DJ Mag*, *Disco Pogo*, *Nostalgia 99*, *The Quietus*, *The Conversation* and *Beatportal*. Julia tweets and toks @Miss_Toppin. She contributes to New Nationwide Project on Repeater Radio and hosts Conscious Lyrics. She is writing her memoir, *Miles To Go*, for Repeater Books.

Ayanna van der Maten McCalman is a recent graduate from King's College London's critical theory MA program. She is also a steel pan musician and fiction writer. Ayanna was recently shortlisted for #Merky Books New Writers' Prize 23/24.

Richard Williams has written about music since the 1960s, for *The Times*, *The Guardian*, *The Independent*, *Uncut* and more. He was in an R&B band before joining his local Nottingham paper, where his first reviews – such acts as Jimi Hendrix, Cream and Ike & Tina Turner – were published. In the 1970s he edited *Melody Maker* and *Time Out*, and was head of A&R at Island Records. He was artistic director of the Berlin Jazz Festival. He has written books about Miles Davis, Bob Dylan and Phil Spector. He writes for his own music blog: thebluemoment.com.

Val Wilmer is a journalist and independent historian. Her first articles on Black British musicians were written for a Black readership: a profile of saxophonist Joe Harriott for *Tropic* (1960), and the series Musicians of the Caribbean for *Flamingo* (1963–64). She has lectured, broadcast and written over three hundred articles on Black British musicians and entrepreneurs, including entries in the *Oxford Dictionary of National Biography*. She contributed seventeen oral histories of Caribbean, African and British-born Black musicians to the National Sound Archive of the British Library, including the surviving members of the Ken 'Snakehips' Johnson Orchestra and Ray Ellington Quartet.

Anthony Wright was born in Cardiff to a Jamaican father and Welsh mother. He spent most of the Thatcher era unemployed, but formed a reggae/soul band and emerged as a well-known local songwriter. He graduated, writing a dissertation on Welsh-based reggae sound systems. During these studies he discovered that he was dyslexic. He then embarked on a career as a playwright, writing and producing plays based on the Welsh Black experience. He recently obtained an MA in Scriptwriting and is setting up a writing/production company – Barddgriot-Productions – and working on a play about his late father, a Black coal miner in Wales, for the National Museum of Wales. anthonywright40@hotmail.com. https://www.barddgriot-productions.com/

Bibliography

Abdurraqib, Hanif, *A Little Devil in America: Notes in Praise of Black Performance* (New York: Random House, 2021).

Abulafia, David, *The Boundless Sea: A Human History of the Ocean* (London: Allen Lane, 2019).

Allen, William F., McKim Garrison, Lucy and Ware, Charles P., *Slave Songs of the United States* (New York: A. Simpson & Co., 1867).

Anglo, Sydney, 'The Court Festivals of Henry VII: A Study Based upon the Account Books of John Heron, Treasurer of the Chamber', *Bulletin of John Rylands Library Volume 43(1)* pp. 12–45 (1960).

Anglo, Sydney, *The Great Tournament Roll of Westminster* (Oxford: Clarendon Press, 1968).

Aspinall, Peter J. and Chinouya, Martha J. *The African Diaspora Population in Britain* (London: Palgrave Macmillan, 2016).

Bennett-Coverley, Louise, 'Colonization in Reverse', from *Jamaica Labrish: Jamaica Dialect Poems* (Kingston: Sangster's Book Stores, 1966).

Blackwell, Chris, *The Islander: My Life in Music and Beyond* (London: Nine Eight Books, 2022).

Bourne, Stephen, *Black in the British Frame: The Black Experience in British Film and Television* (London and New York: Continuum, 2001).

Bourne, Stephen, *Elisabeth Welch: Soft Lights and Sweet Music* (Lanham, MD: Scarecrow Press, 2005).

Bourne, Stephen, *Fighting Proud: The Untold Story of the Gay Men Who Served in Two World Wars* (London: Bloomsbury, 2017).

Breese, Charlotte, *Hutch* (London: Bloomsbury, 1999).

Costello, Ray, *Black Salt: Seafarers of African Descent on British Ships* (Liverpool: Liverpool University Press, 2012).

DJ Target, *Grime Kids: The Inside Story of the Global Grime Takeover* (London: Trapeze, 2018).

Douglass, Frederick, *The Narrative of the Life of Frederick Douglass, an American Slave* (Boston: Anti-Slavery Office, 1845).

Du Bois, W. E. B., 'Of the Sorrow Songs', *The Souls of Black Folk: Essays and Sketches* (Chicago: A. C. McClurg & Company, 1903).

Egan, Pierce, *Life in London* (London: Sherwood, Neely & Jones, 1821).

Epstein, Dena J., *Sinful Tunes and Spirituals: Black Folk Music to the Civil War* (Urbana: University of Illinois Press, 1977).

Equiano, Olaudah, *The Interesting Narrative of the Life of Olaudah Equiano* (London, 1789).

Eshun, Kodwo, *More Brilliant Than the Sun: Adventures in Sonic Fiction* (London: Quartet Books, 1998).

Francis, Roy N., *How to Make Gospel Music Work for You* (London: Filament Publishing, 2019).

Francis, Roy N., *A Personal Story: Windrush and the Black Pentecostal Church in Britain* (London: Filament Publishing, 2020).

Gilroy, Paul, *There Ain't No Black in the Union Jack* (London: Hutchinson, 1987).

Goto, John, *Lovers' Rock* (Manchester: Cornerhouse Publications, 2013).

Hartman, Saidiya, *Wayward Lives, Beautiful Experiments: Intimate Histories of Social Upheaval* (New York: W. W. Norton & Company, 2019).

Henry, Lenny, *Rising to the Surface* (London: Faber & Faber, 2022).

Hindley, Charles, *The True History of Tom and Jerry* (London: Charles Hindley, 1888).

Jerrold, Douglas, *The Ballad-Singer* (London, 1840).

Joseph, Anthony, *Kitch: A Fictional Biography of a Calypso Icon* (Leeds: Peepal Tree Press, 2018).

Kaufmann, Miranda, *Black Tudors: The Untold Story* (London: Oneworld, 2017).

Keep the Faith magazine, https://issuu.com/keepthefaith.

Ohajuru, Michael I., 'Before and after the Eighteenth Century: The John Blanke Project', in Grezina, Gretchen H. (ed.), *Britain's Black Past,* pp. 7–25 (Liverpool: Liverpool University Press, 2020).

Ohajuru, Michael I., 'Insights into John Blanke's Image from the John Blanke Project', in Bolland, Charlotte (ed.) *The Tudors: Passion, Power and Politics*, pp. 28–30 (London: National Portrait Gallery Publications, 2022).

Selvon, Samuel, *The Lonely Londoners* (London: Allan Wingate, 1956).

Simons, Andrew, notes compiled for the CD release *Black British Swing* (Topic Records, 2001).

Snead, James A., 'On Repetition in Black Culture', *Black American Literature Forum Volume 15(4)* (1981).

Southern, Eileen, *The Music of Black Americans: A History* (New York and London: Newton, 1983).

Thompson, Leslie with Green, Jeffrey, *Leslie Thompson: An Autobiography* (Crawley: Rabbit Press, 1985).

Ward, Andrew, *Midnight When I Rise: The Story of the Jubilee Singers Who Introduced the World to the Music of Black America* (New York: Farrar, Straus, and Giroux, 2000).

White, Shane, 'We Dwell in Safety and Pursue Our Honest Callings: Free Blacks in New York City, 1783–1810', *Journal of American History Volume 75(2)* pp. 445–470 (1988).

White, Shane, 'The Death of James Johnson', *American Quarterly Volume 51(4)* (1999).

White, Shane, *Stories of Freedom in Black New York* (Cambridge, MA and London: Harvard University Press, 2007).

Notes

Preface
1 Speech at the founding rally of the Organisation of Afro-American Unity (28 June 1964) .

Tides, Trade and Tribulation
1 David Abulafia, *The Boundless Sea*, 2019.
2 DJ Target, *Grime Kids*, 2018.
3 Illegal Migration Act 2023.

Journey of the Drum
1 Kodwo Eshun, *More Brilliant Than the Sun*, 1998.

John Blanke
1 Sydney Anglo, 'The Court Festivals of Henry VII: A Study Based upon the Account Books of John Heron, Treasurer of the Chamber', 1960.
2 John Blanke's Petition to Henry VIII.
3 The John Blanke Project: https://www.johnblanke.com.

The Life, Times and Music of Billy Waters
1 *New Times* (London), 6 September 1822.
2 Jane Palm-Gold, *Camden New Journal*, 24 March 2023.
3 Shane White, *Stories of Freedom in Black New York*, 2002.
4 https://www.youtube.com/watch?v=mOYgOcih-_M
   https://www.youtube.com/watch?v=85WTwG1Df-A
   https://www.youtube.com/watch?v=cTjA1a1CjQs

https://www.folkstreams.net/films/life-and-times-of-joe-thompson.

Tones Loud, Long and Deep
1 Frederick Douglass, *The Narrative of the Life of Frederick Douglass, an American Slave*, 1845.
2 William F. Allen, Lucy McKim Garrison and Charles P. Ware, *Slave Songs of the United States*, 1867.
3 *New York Herald*, 21 May 1893.
4 Letter to Tom Hood, Mark Twain, 1873, Mark Twain Project: https://www.marktwainproject.org/.
5 *Daily Telegraph & Courier*, 8 May 1873.
6 *The Times*, 1873.
7 William Du Bois, 'Of the Sorrow Songs,' in *The Souls of Black Folk: Essays and Sketches*, 1903.
8 Andrew Ward, *Midnight When I Rise: The Story of the Jubilee Singers Who Introduced the World to the Music of Black America*, 2000.
9 https://www.loc.gov/item/jukebox-128141/.

Ken 'Snakehips' Johnson
1 Joe Deniz, interview with Stephen Bourne, London, 10 August 1993.
2 Leslie Thompson with Jeffrey Green, *Leslie Thompson: An Autobiography*, 1985.
3 Stephen Bourne, *Fighting Proud: The Untold Story of the Gay Men Who Served in Two World Wars*, 2017.

Hutch

1 Hanif Abdurraqib, *A Little Devil in America: Notes in Praise of Black Performance*, 2021.
2 Charlotte Breese, *Hutch*, 1999.
3 *Evening Times*, Glasgow, 1932.
4 *In Search of Hutch*, BBC Radio 4, 2001.
5 https://content.time.com/time/subscriber/article/0,33009,753381-1,00.html.
6 https://edition.cnn.com/style/article/leslie-hutchinson-black-history-month-gbr-intl/index.html.
7 Charlotte Breese, *Hutch*, 1999..
8 *Radio Times*, March 1935.

Sophisticated Ladies

1 Lenny Henry, *Rising to the Surface*, 2022.
2 Stephen Bourne, *Black in the British Frame: Black People in British Film and Television 1896–1996*, 1998.
3 Stephen Bourne, *Elisabeth Welch: Soft Lights and Sweet Music*, 2005.

Ambrose Adeyoka Campbell

1, 2, 3 Interview with the author.
4 A slightly different version of this article appeared in *Mojo* (London).

Kitch!

1 Anthony Joseph, *Kitch: A Fictional Biography of a Calypso Icon*, 2018.
2 Louise Bennett-Coverley, 'Colonization in Reverse', 1966.
3–6 Anthony Joseph, *Kitch: A Fictional Biography of a Calypso Icon*, 2018.

Rockin' With Ray

1 Interview with the author.
2 A slightly different version of this article appeared in *Mojo* (London).

50 Carnaby Street

1 The Sunset – Bebop Nights Where The Buddleia Bloomed, Val Wilmer (*Jazzwise* #276, August 2022).

Woodbine's Boys

1, 2 Interview with the author.

Sonny Roberts

1 Chris Blackwell, *The Islander*, 2022.

Sir Coxsone Outernational

1 Interviews with Lloydie Coxsone by Mykaell Riley/Bass Culture – Westminster Research/University of Westminster and Paul Bradshaw/*Straight No Chaser* archive.

Jah Shaka

1 This story first appeared in *NME* as 'The Big Big Sound System Splashdown', 2 February 1981.

Bristol: Sound of the City

1 A law that allowed police officers to stop and search anybody (a 'suspected person'), with a low threshold for evidence. Heavy abuse of the law contributed to race riots in many British cities.

The Bamboo Club

1 Thanks to Yvonne Mills, Sonia Burgess, Basil Russell, Larry Stabbins and Locksley Gichie – their conversations have helped me paint a picture of this iconic club.

The Reno

1 https://www.visitmanchester.com/ideas-and-inspiration/blog/read/2019/07/meet-the-artist-whose-project-to-uncover-underground-moss-side-club-the-reno-has-connection-to-personal-histories-peterloo-and-more-b910#:~:text=-%22But%20the%20first%20night%20I,really%20hard%20NOT%20to%20dance.
2 Lisa Ayegun interview: https://mancunion.com/2023/12/12/phil-magbotiwan-honouring-the-face-behind-the-reno/.

Black Music, Black Vinyl...

1 https://www.britishrecordshoparchive.org/.

The Art of Buying Reggae Music

1 All the record shops between Dalston and Tottenham have since vanished. Dub Vendor still flies the flag via an online shop.

British Gospel Music

1 For me this is 'the Kingdom of Heaven. Not just meat and drink, but righteousness, peace and joy in the Holy Spirit': Romans 14: 17–23.

Lovers' Rock

1 *The Story of Lover's Rock*, 2011: https://menelikshabazz.co.uk/project/the-story-of-lovers-rock/.

Devotional

1 Saidiya Hartman, *Wayward Lives, Beautiful Experiments: Intimate Histories of Social Upheaval*, 2019.

London, Lagos, Accra...

1 Paul Gilroy, *There Ain't No Black in the Union Jack*, 1987.
2 James A. Snead, 'On Repetition in Black Culture', 1981.

Picture Credits

a = above, b = below, l = left, r = right

2–3 © David Hoffman. 10–13 *Straight No Chaser* Archive. 15 Courtesy Tayo Rapoport and Rohan Ayinde; and Touching Bass. 19 Courtesy Gerard Hanson. 20 © Chris Steele-Perkins/Magnum Photos. 21 Courtesy Mykaell Riley. 27 The Menil Collection, Houston. © Frank Bowling. All Rights Reserved, DACS 2024. 28 New York Public Library. 29 British Library, T.1140.(3.). 31 Contraband Collection/Alamy Stock Photo. 32 Tim Ring/Alamy Stock Photo. 35 Courtesy Errol Lloyd. 36 British Museum, Am,SLMisc.1368. © The Trustees of the British Museum. 38–39, 40 © David Corio. 41 © Simon Wheatley. 43 College of Arms MS Westminster Tournament Roll, 1511, membrane 28. Reproduced by permission of the Kings, Heralds and Pursuivants of Arms. 44 Artist Stephen B. Whatley. Private collection, UK. 47 British Library, 7742.e.19 (2). 48a Wellcome Collection. 48b British Library, 838.i.2. 49 British Library, 12331.h.25. 51 British Museum, 1876,0708.2379. © The Trustees of the British Museum. 52al, 52ar, 52b Production Shots © 2024 James Joseph Music Management. 55 Royal College of Music/ArenaPAL. 56 Stephen Bourne Collection. 57a Production photos from 'Recognition' co-created by Amanda Wilkin and Rachael Nanyonjo. Photo Gifty Dzenyo, Courtesy Talawa Theatre Company. 57b Production photos from 'Recognition' co-created by Amanda Wilkin and Rachael Nanyonjo. Photo Gifty Dzenyo, Courtesy Talawa Theatre Company. 58 British Library, 1607/1717. 59 Photo grahamdelacy.com. 61 Look and Learn/Peter Jackson Collection/Bridgeman Images. 62 NPG Smithsonian. 64 Topical Press Agency/Hulton Archive/Getty Images. 65 George Konig/Keystone Features/Hulton Archive/Getty Images. 67 New York Public Library. 68, 69 Courtesy Brighton Dome. 73a, 73b BBC Photo. 74 Stephen Bourne Collection. 75 Reg Speller/Fox Photos/Getty Images. 77, 78 Stephen Bourne Collection. 79 Private collection. 80 Stephen Bourne Collection. 82 BBC Photo. 83 Stephen Bourne Collection. 85 BBC Photo. 86 Hulton-Deutsch Collection/Corbis via Getty Images. 87 Stephen Bourne Collection. 89 Reg Speller/Fox Photos/Hulton Archive/Getty Images. 90 Photo Dezo Hoffman © Val Wilmer Collection. 95 Photo TopFoto. 97 BBC Photo. 98–99 © Val Wilmer Collection. 103 Popperfoto/Getty Images. 104 © Val Wilmer Collection. 106–107 RB/Redferns/Getty Images. 109 Keystone Features/Getty Images. 110–111 Max Scheler - K&K/Redferns/Getty Images. 112 John Pratt/Keystone Features/Getty Images. 115 *TV Times* via Getty Images. 116 Private collection. 117 David Redfern/Redferns/Getty Images. 122, 123 *Evening Standard*/Hulton Archive/Getty Images. 124–125 Courtesy Horace Ové Archives. 127 Courtesy Capitan/RiceNpeas Archive. 128 Keystone/Hulton Archive/Getty Images. 131 Keystone-France/Gamma-Keystone via Getty Images. 132 Reach Plc/Mirrorpix. 135 Steve Eason/Hulton Archive/Getty Images. 136 Museum of London/Heritage Images/Getty Images. 139 British Library, Mike Braybrook Archive, Deposit MS 10962. 140 Courtesy Horace Ové Archives. 141 Monty Fresco/Mirrorpix/Getty Images. 142a © Adrian Boot/urbanimage.tv. 142b Courtesy Horace Ové Archives. 143a © Tony Davis. 143bl, 143br © Adrian Boot/urbanimage.tv. 144, 145, 146–147 © @beezerphotos. 149 © David Corio. 151 BBC Photo. 152 Private collection. 154, 157, 158, 159, 161 © Jean-Bernard Sohiez. 156, 160 *Straight No Chaser* Archive. 163, 164, 165a, 165b © @beezerphotos. 166 © Jean-Bernard Sohiez. 168, 169a, 169b © @beezerphotos. 170 David Corio/Redferns/Getty Images. 173 Pete Williams. 175 British Library, LD.31.b.1797. © The Estate of David King. 176a © David Corio. 176b © Syd Shelton. 177 *Straight No Chaser* Archive. 178a © Nubian Records. 178b © Adrian Boot, All Rights Reserved. 179a © Adrian Boot/urbanimage.tv. 179b Virginia Turbett/Redferns/Getty Images. 180–181 © John Sturrock/reportdigital.co.uk. 183 Ebet Roberts/Getty Images. 184 Ebet Roberts/Redferns/Getty Images. 185 Virginia Turbett/Redferns/Getty Images. 186 Chalkie Davies/Getty Images. 187 *Straight No Chaser* Archive. 189 © Adrian Boot/urbanimage.tv. 190 *Bristol Post*/Mirrorpix via Getty Images. 191 Donovan Jackson collection. 192 Courtesy https://thereno.live. 197 © Richard Saunders/urbanimages.tv. 198 Courtesy the owner. 199 Bob Baker/Redferns/Getty Images. 200 Photo Chris Lane, courtesy Noel Hawks. 201a Duncan Baxter/*Evening Standard*/Hulton Archive/Getty Images. 201b © David Corio. 203 © Alan Denney. 204 *Straight No Chaser* Archive. 205 © Jean-Bernard Sohiez . 207 © Martin Mayer/reportdigital.co.uk. 208 *Straight No Chaser* Archive. 211, 212–213 © Vanley Burke. All rights reserved, DACS 2024. 216 Peter Simon Collection, Robert S. Cox Special Collections and University Archives Research Center, UMass Amherst Libraries. Photo © Peter Simon. 218 Photo 12/Alamy Stock Photo. 219a *Straight No Chaser* Archive. 219b © Chris Steele-Perkins/Magnum Photos. 221 British Library, 1SE0110506. 222 © Richard Saunders/urbanimage.tv. 223 © Jean-Bernard Sohiez. 225 British Library, 1LP0258130. 229 Photo Rachel Deakin Middlesbrough Collection at MIMA. Presented by the Contemporary Art Society through the Rapid Response Fund with support from MIMA, 2020. © Sonia Boyce. All Rights Reserved, DACS 2024. 233 Al Levine/NBCU Photo Bank/NBCUniversal via Getty Images. 234–235 Catherine McGann/Getty Images. 240, 241 *Straight No Chaser* Archive. 242–243 Photo Suki Dhanda, courtesy Tomorrow's Warriors. 244 *Straight No Chaser* Archive. 245 Kevin Cummins/Getty Images. 246 *Straight No Chaser* Archive. 247 © Ewen Spencer. 248, 249 Private collection. 251, 252, 254, 255 Courtesy Touching Bass. 253 Courtesy NTS. 260, 261 Photo courtesy Mista Silva. 263 Private collection. 264 Pass the lens. 267 © Thomas Duffield. 270–271 © Eddie Otchere. 272 © @beezerphotos. 273 Private collection. 274, 275, 276 © Simon Wheatley. 280–281 Private collection. 282 Adrian Dennis/AFP via Getty Images. 283a Dave J Hogan/Getty Images. 283b Samir Hussein/WireImage/Getty Images. 284–285 © Karolina Wielocha.